TRANSFORMING FAITH

Recent Titles in
Contributions to the Study of Religion

Exorcising the Trouble Makers: Magic, Science, and Culture
Francis L. K. Hsu

The Cross, The Flag, and The Bomb: American Catholics Debate War and Peace,
1960–1983
William A. Au

Religious Conflict in Social Context: The Resurgence of Orthodox Judaism in
Frankfurt Am Main, 1838–1877
Robert Liberles

Triumph over Silence: Women in Protestant History
Richard L. Greaves, editor

Neighbors, Friends, or Madmen: The Puritan Adjustment to Quakerism in
Seventeenth-Century Massachusetts Bay
Jonathan M. Chu

Cities of Gods: Faith, Politics and Pluralism in Judaism, Christianity and Islam
Nigel Biggar, Jamie S. Scott, William Schweiker, editors

Theodicies in Conflict: A Dilemma in Puritan Ethics and Nineteenth-Century American
Literature
Richard Forrer

Gilbert Tennent, Son of Thunder: A Case Study of Continental Pietism's Impact on
the First Great Awakening in the Middle Colonies
Milton J Coalter, Jr.

Lighten Their Darkness: The Evangelical Mission to Working-Class London, 1828–
1860
Donald M. Lewis

The United Synod of the South: The Southern New School Presbyterian Church
Harold M. Parker, Jr.

Covenant and Community in Modern Judaism
S. Daniel Breslauer

The Religious Press in Britain, 1760–1900
Josef L. Altholz

TRANSFORMING FAITH

The Sacred and Secular in Modern American History

EDITED BY

M. L. BRADBURY
& JAMES B. GILBERT

CONTRIBUTIONS TO THE STUDY OF RELIGION, NUMBER 23

Jon L. Wakelyn, *Adviser*

GREENWOOD PRESS
New York • Westport, Connecticut • London

Library of Congress Cataloging-in-Publication Data

Transforming faith : the sacred and secular in modern American history
/ edited by M. L. Bradbury and James B. Gilbert.
    p.   cm. — (Contributions to the study of religion, ISSN
0196–7053 ; no. 23)
   Includes index.
   ISBN 0–313–25707–8 (lib. bdg. : alk. paper)
   1. United States—Religion—1960– —Congresses. 2. Secularism—
United States—History—20th century—Congresses. I. Bradbury, M. L.
II. Gilbert, James Burkhart. III. Series.
BL2525.T7   1989
291′.0973—dc 20   89–7478

British Library Cataloguing in Publication Data is available.

Library of Congress Catalog Card Number: 89–7478
ISBN: 0–313–25707–8
ISSN: 0196–7053

First published in 1989

Greenwood Press, Inc.
88 Post Road West, Westport, Connecticut 06881

Printed in the United States of America

CONTENTS

Preface

This book results from a conference on religion and modern American society held at the University of Maryland at College Park in May 1987. The purpose of the conference was to examine the question of the persistence of religious belief in an America that in many respects has become increasingly secular. It did not focus, except incidentally, on theoretical aspects of the question. Speakers were asked to address specific aspects of the interaction between the sacred and secular in modern American history. It was thought that detailed analysis of this kind would produce a better sense of the complex patterns of accommodation between the two, in the course of which each has, in a sense, transformed the other. Speakers were given complete freedom to interpret their subject matter as they wished, within the context of the conference theme. They used this freedom inventively, in ways for which we were not always prepared. For example, it resulted in some matters being slighted, despite our initial intention to include them. We think there is ample compensation for these omissions in the originality with which the speakers interpreted the subjects they did discuss. The revised conference papers compose the essays in this volume. Except for making the usual efforts to impose some sort of editorial unity on the whole, we have let each paper speak for itself. Each has something unique to say about the relationship between religion and society in modern America.

The efforts of many people contributed to the holding of the conference and the appearance of this book. By their useful comments the following improved the intellectual clarity of these essays: John Farina of the Paulist Press and the Paulist Office of History and Archives, Michael J. Lacey of the Woodrow Wilson International Center for Scholars of the Smithsonian Institution, Donald M. Scott of the New School for Social Research, and Charles H. Whittier of the Congressional Research Service of the Library of Congress.

We acknowledge the assistance in matters large and small of colleagues at the University of Maryland at College Park, whose willingness to help extended far beyond the usual boundaries of collegiality: Mark P. Leone (Anthropology); Joseph P. Ansell and James G. Thorpe (Design); Claire G. Moses (Women's Studies); and, from the History Department, Richard T. Farrell, Robert Friedel, David Goodblatt (now at the University of California, San Diego), Gay L. Gullickson, Alfred Moss, Fred Nicklason, B. Marie Perinbam, and Marsha L. Rozenblit.

The conference received financial support from the Maryland Humanities Council, Inc., and the National Endowment for the Humanities. Wofford K. Smith, then Episcopal chaplain at College Park, persuaded Mark Harris, then Coordinator for the Ministry in Higher Education of the Episcopal Church, to earmark part of his already small budget for our project. Emory G. Evans and Richard G. Price, the former and current chairmen of the History Department, provided needed funding, as did Richard D. Brecht, then Acting Dean of the College of Arts and Humanities. Esther Mackintosh of the National Federation of State Humanities Councils contributed to the success of the gathering, as did the co-operating chaplains at College Park—in particular, Robert O. Burdette (United Campus Ministry), Peter W. Peters (Episcopal), and Elizabeth Platz (Lutheran). E. Susan Barber, our graduate teaching assistant for one semester, undertook much of the work of organization and by her competence and conscientious attention to detail made our task much easier.

We are convinced that the secretarial staff of the History Department is without peer in the intelligent support it gives to the work of department members. Thanks to the efforts of Margaret V. Burkett, June Charney, Pat A. Honey, Susan Oetken, and Abid Qureshi, the conference was more fun to organize, and the resulting book finished more quickly than would otherwise have been the case. Without Darlene King these essays quite literally would never have appeared in print.

INTRODUCTION

To place religious expression in the midst of modern American culture is a complex and difficult task. Obviously it has been and remains a vital part of American society, unlikely to fade permanently, or to become an artifact of an outmoded and useless past. Yet, the sources of its vitality and renewal remain elusive in many ways, particularly if one tries to be alert to the expressions of the sacred that are outside the religious mainstream.

Part of the difficulty lies in the persistence of vocabularies of historical explanation that remain rooted in the conceptions of the Enlightenment. The residues of the Enlightenment in the modern language of social change are essentially anti-religious, and their survival is related to the ongoing vitality of one of the fundamental axioms of Western social thought. This axiom embodies the anti-establishment vocabulary of the Enlightenment by positing a historic opposition between the sacred and secular and holding that progress—the inexorable appearance of the modern, in whatever guise, in social institutions, culture, and technology—undercuts and diminishes the hold of religious ideas and institutions. From this point of view the evolution of society tends inevitably in a secular direction. Religion at best can hope to survive only as some sort of attenuated cultural ethos, without vitality or transformative power. Although it has been challenged in any number of ways, this view of religion still has explanatory power for many, particularly for those who want to explain the otherwise unintelligible survival of fundamentalism in modern American society. If the beliefs of traditional religion are naive, uninformed, and possibly superstitious, as they must inevitably be in this formulation, then it follows they can be vital and alive only among those caught in some sort of time warp, or marginalization. Thus, or so the argument has sometimes been made, the religious groups that are resurgent in the twentieth century are evangelical sects, or groups or churches, whether Christian or not, that are essentially fundamentalist in orientation. Although troubling in some respects, their persistence does not challenge the basic equation that progress equals secularization. Indeed, it seems to confirm it. Their increase thus testifies implicitly to the rapidity with which America has become a secular, technological society.

In particular, there is an American version of this Enlightenment/religious dispensation imbedded in the language of the Constitution and the practice of separation of church and state. For a variety of reasons this legal partition between the cities of God and man has come to mean conflicting things. On the one hand, it is the mainstay of cultural pluralism, the rule of first resort in deciding the political geography of civil religion, the support beneath the modern trilogy of civic religion—Protestant, Catholic, Jew. Pushed to the extreme, it is also the legal support for there being no religion at all, the legal recognition of the primacy of the secular society. But at the same time, this separation is a huge land-grant of power to private religious culture. To view the government as a small secular peninsula in a religious sea is as valid an interpretation of the civic/religious tension as any other. In fact, however, this nation-founding separation has been the source of serious confusion, for it has diverted attention to political squabbles, and away from the richer and far more complex problems inherent in American religious culture.

To replace both the Enlightenment and American Constitutional expectations about religion requires a polemically neutral effort to comprehend the cultural role and function of religion, an effort that makes no statements for or against religion but recognizes that religion wherever it appears historically is located in a particular culture. Or, to paraphrase Erik H. Erikson, all institutions, just as all people, are located historically in particular times and places, no matter what their ultimate longevity. To recognize this fact—from a historical point of view—says nothing for or against whatever claims specific religious groups may make about transcendence or about those who reject such claims.

If one grants this argument, then one of the most significant aspects of the role of religion in modern American life is its cultural parallelism, its efforts to embody in some degree the institutions and aspirations of the secular society—its participation, in other words, in secular life at every point. Such parallelism can have complex consequences. Institutions initially founded as part of such cultural parallelism—religious-educational institutions, television and radio stations, and social service agencies—can over time develop a dynamic of their own that divorces them from the religious intent of their founders or that forces change upon the religious bodies with which they were initially affiliated.

But such cultural parallelism can work in other ways as well. To some extent it validates participation in the secular culture for religious individuals; to a degree, it can work to distance them as well, to shield them from the perceived intrusions of secularization without the need to abandon the larger society. At the same time it forces secular cultural expressions to accommodate themselves to religious attitudes and beliefs in ways that they would not otherwise have to.

"Accommodation," of course, may not do justice to the complexities of the relationship. "Challenge" might be an equally valid term to describe this confrontation. A world in which religious groups withdrew into a cultural ghetto might be a less taxing one from the point of view of many secular institutions, but it might be a more sterile one even from a strictly secular point of view. Finally, cultural parallelism contributes to the rich and complex range of responses of American society to perceived threats to social stability and the need for social change. American society can, for example, discuss the meaning of political freedom in any number of venues. From a historical point of view, *where* in the society these discussions take place is equally as important as *when* they take place.

The purpose of the essays that follow is to develop, in some tentative measure, a new sort of vocabulary to discuss the complex relations in America between the religious perspective and other formats for the interpretation of culture. They range widely from the discussion of religion and popular culture, ethnicity and race, religion and women, religion and medicine, to the persistence of evangelical traditions, and at the same time attempt to place American religion in a larger, historical framework. If anything is to be singled out as a lesson from this effort, it is that the formulation "religion and . . . " is inadequate to describe an American culture that is so suffused with religious ideas and traces that to force a separation of terms, except for the sake of discussion, is misleading.

TRANSFORMING FAITH

1

THE SACRED AND SECULAR IN AMERICAN HISTORY

Martin E. Marty

A generation ago the scholarly world turned its attention to the concept of the secular. At the last possible moment it was foreseen as the dominating character of unfolding civilizations. Today the concept of the sacred receives similar attention. In *The Closing of the American Mind* (1987) Allan Bloom has called attention to the way in which "the respect for the Sacred—the latest fad—has soared." He goes on: "In our earlier free-thinking enthusiasm, we tended to neglect it." With a final swoop he scores: "These sociologists who talk so facilely about the sacred are like a man who keeps a toothless old circus lion around the house in order to experience the thrills of the jungle."[1]

Contributors to this book could be accused of riding two fadwagons, one a creaky, twenty-year-old vehicle and the other a smart new model just ready to display signs of planned obsolescence. Yet this topic should transcend interests of the moment or the decade. It helps people reflect on the character of American culture and society. A brief background survey through American history is in place.

MODELS FOR HISTORICAL INQUIRY

History, it is often said, is the account of what one age finds remarkable in another. The historian who would effectively tell a story, however brief it must be, does well to let hearers or readers know what she or he is seeking in order to help the "remarkables" stand out. The storyteller is a sort of guide through the past leading into the present. Again, a guide who would build confidence may take a preliminary moment to describe the landmarks along the trail, to anticipate its inclines, terrain, and turns—in short, to offer a number of models of "remarkability." For the sake of convenience, they will match up with a number of academic disciplines or modes of pursuing knowledge.

First, an *anthropological* model, the religio-secular. Whatever the syntactical force of the hyphen, and whatever else it may do, it suggests some sort of tension and also some sort of fusion between two categories that were long posed against each other. The one sees the human as essentially, ontologically, and in historical emergences, "religious" by nature. The other sees the human as developing into an essentially, and eventually permanently, "secular" being.

Mircea Eliade has led the historians of religion who posit and find remarkable the persistence of homo religiosus. This being may have "fallen" into modernity, which seeks to disenchant the world, and chooses to live in a desacralized cosmos, but something of its religious character survives. Such a being lives amid myths and symbols, at the edge of transcendence, finding meaning in an apparently random and plotless world. Critics of this view claim that its holders do not do justice to a new human phenotype, first called secular *man* to match the masculine of the Latin *homo*.[2]

Secular man was to have been post-religious. He or she was to be unmoved by myths and symbols, living in a world that had rendered opaque the transcendent orders of being, content to live without a full-scale effort to find meaning by reference to them. A modern classic statement of this secular presence came from the late John Courtney Murray, S. J.: "The problem of God has, as its obverse, the problem of the godless man, the *atheos*." The religious tradition of the West had also suggested that the presence of God "is integral to the very structure, as it were, of man's historical existence. . . . Therefore the man who does not fear God somehow does not exist, and his nature is somehow not human. On the other hand, there he is. That is the problem."[3] True, godly-godless does not exactly match up with religious-secular, but to underscore and note the emergence of a surprising being, they can appear at least analogous.

Against the notions of the human as religious or secular one might pose the religio-secular being, however inelegant and provisional that term must be. Somehow to make sense of history and the presence in stories about humans in their individual or collective existence, it is important to note how indeterminate, volatile, complex, "unfinished" the human is in respect to the most profound responses—and how uncertain one must remain about future phenotypes or emergences. Surprises have taken place in the past and present, and may well in the future.

Second, a *psychological* model: This one fuses the operative and the passional sides of personal and social existence. Because they are thus fused, confusion of stories will result if one sees Americans, or anyone else for that matter, as people who are content with one side of life alone. The notion of a secular society derives chiefly from observations of the individual or the group operative in practical life. Operative means "characterized by operating or working; active in producing, or having the power to produce, effects."[4] It is possible to associate it with most of the adjectives in the string Herman Kahn used in his famed depiction of "the basic, long-term multifold trend" of an "increasingly sensate" culture. "Empirical, This-Worldly, Secular, Humanistic, Pragmatic, Utilitarian, Contractual, Epicurean or Hedonistic, and the Like."[5]

Some looked at this "increasingly sensate" culture and foresaw a day when alternatives to it would disappear in individual or group psychological understandings. Yet Kahn also reported on what Pitirim Sorokin (the inventor of the label sensate) and most other philosophers of history of the nineteenth and twentieth centuries saw: namely, that a new kind of religious stage would follow the sensate culture. This religious phase might refer to a spiritual-intellectual one or be "properly religious," including elements of Christianity, religions of East and West, including science, or whatever. Macrohistorians, Kahn said, foresaw a "more or less painful rebirth following a time of chaos, anarchy, nihilism, and irrationality."[6]

Whether viewed so negatively or more positively, this historical unfolding is characterized by the passional dimension of human existence. But why see the sensate and the religious as more or less mutually exclusive on the historical scene, with one succeeding the other? Why not refer to both as profound and perhaps permanent elements of life? When viewed operatively, the human does not patently respond to signals of transcendence. One gets the work done. Yet that same human must cope with finitude and contingency and reaches for meaning, usually with instruments one associates with the sacred. Call this the operative-passional connection.

Third is a *sociological* corollary, the sacro-secular model for society. Once more the term is sufficiently inelegant to prevent its catching on and becoming the subject of a fad. Yet the compound term may do more justice to reality than the notion that would separate the elements. A generation ago people spoke of a secular society, made up of secular men who had moved beyond the sacred. Today it is argued that the sacred pervades the structures of reality for anyone who cares to look carefully, and that almost anything one does, even in the operation of machines or states, is somehow an expression of the sacred. Yet in practice, the two understandings are webbed. It is hard to disentangle them from each other. People responding to "the sacred" very often are "secular" by almost any definition of the term. People, being secular, are often best understood by reference to symbols and myths they do not know they are exemplifying or pursuing. In history, at least in American history, a secular society has not replaced a sacral one, nor is a new sacral society now in turn displacing a secular one. Almost wherever one looks in the past, one finds the two tangled, interposed, mirroring each other.

Three corollaries to these models exist in humanities disciplines and their understandings. The first, a *historical* one, has been implied throughout. One does not look for a stage-theory of development but finds that just as secular man did not arrive on schedule, in ideal type form, to acquire permanent status, so the religious human is not going to displace the secular one and reign ever more. The historian does well to pursue the fused model, whether the focus is on the individual or society.

In *literary* analysis, similarly, it seems clear that modern classics can rarely be classified in pure religious or secular terms. Ever since Matthew Arnold foresaw literature replacing religion, it has come to be the fashion for scholars to see secular aspects to religious texts—as in the historical-critical approach to the Bible—as well as religious dimensions to secular texts. Contemporary hermeneutics has driven literary critics to focus on sacred texts to see what they might disclose. This has gone so far that critics like Jonathan Culler have come to protest: Isn't the modern university supposed to be secular, rationalistic, anti-religious? Then why allow the great scholars like Northrop Frye, Frank Kermode, Robert Alter, and others in the field of literature to waste their years with biblical texts? No Cullerian ban will keep them from seeking access to those texts, whether to deconstruct or reconstruct them and their meanings.[7]

Philosophy, it seemed for a while, had taken the most decisive steps against religious, sacred, and passional understandings. At least in the Anglo-American schools where linguistic and analytic philosophies ruled out reference to the metaphysical, there seemed to be no possibility of finding religious meanings until people began to look, as Paul Van Buren did, at the "edges of language," or at odd uses, or at "the human phenomenon," and so on. There is not more of a surge among philosophers than among people in other disciplines to let their new openings become affirmations of faith. Yet there is what we might call disarray in the ranks of those who had thought that modern philosophy had closed off inquiries of a sort to which classic philosophy had been attentive.[8]

It is not necessary to pursue these observations to their philosophical ends, but only to use them as signals of what one may notice as "remarkable," as landmarks through historical inquiry in the American past. Whether or not humans have an essence, one can see with José Ortega y Gassett that they do have a history, a drama.[9] And that drama is one that leaves many traces of religio-secular, operative-passional, sacro-secular entanglements and doublesidedness.

Venturesome folk might apply these heuristic devices to world history. Might it be that the northern industrial belt of free nations, from Sweden across England and Canada through Japan, will be simply secular societies filled with new kinds of human beings, while everything south of them will continue to manifest signs of explosive religiousness, whether of Christian, Islamic, tribal, or neo- forms of expression? Is the "chaos, anarchy, nihilism, and irrationality" of some of that religious explosion but a temporary stage toward a new sensate culture?[10] American history has been filled with that peculiar mix. Some very broad-brushed portrayals, some very generalized statements, must suffice to establish that point about some turning points in the American past.

SACRO-SECULAR AMERICAN HISTORY AND THE PRESENT

Discovery and Exploration: God and Gold

The glimpses of pre-European history in this hemisphere give little chance for observers to separate the sacred and the secular. While Native Americans lived lives that must have had simple operative sides, most traces, especially when romantically enhanced in recall, found them living with nature and tribe, myth and symbol, rite and ceremony in ways that give occasion for speaking of them as sacred societies. At any rate, it is with the coming of Europeans in continuities after 1492 that historians find the traces that have led them to have to ponder the sacred-secular mixes.

America was discovered in the century when Renaissance Humanism came to characterize the intellectual, artistic, and spiritual life of some of the sending nations of Europe or of the interpreters of America who stayed behind. One could say that from the perspective of world history through European eyes, the Western Hemisphere and what became the United States within it should have been "born secular."

The first century of chiefly Iberian exploration has come down as an epic "God and Gold" venture, followed by French and English "God and Furs" or "God and Northwest Passage Search" adventures. It is possible to show whole shelves full of history books that treat this era in simply and starkly secular terms. Portugal and Spain sent out men who would take great risks to enlarge the domains of their emerging nations, who would find the coast of Asia and bring back spices, gold, personal and national riches. Succeeding centuries should have seen nothing but an extension of this spirit. Historians should have been content with stories of ships and shipping, economic policies and cartographical ventures, investments and yields, killings and survivals. American history texts now used in elementary and secondary public schools, according to all the surveys, speak thus of this moment of the emergent secular, post-medieval, post-Christendom world.

However, when one takes a second look at things, from a post-secondary text-level, a different picture emerges. Men like Columbus saw themselves and must be seen in millennial and missionary frameworks as well. Their journals and the early biographies, their reports and their interpretations, show most of them to have been classically involved with locating themselves in patterns of ultimate meaning, as agents of the expansion of religious domains. One can speak of the religiosity of the conquistadors and the more humane explorers alike as "bad" faith, but faith of some sort was certainly present. Few were agents of secular man, isolated operative existence, or simply secular society. So abundant are the evidences of openness to transcendence and explicit living out of religious mandates that one could retell the whole discovery and exploration story in passional and sacral terms. Some do. But, one might say, that was all long ago, a late-medieval phenomenon. The purely secular had not yet been born free.

Settlement and Expansion

From 1565 in St. Augustine, Florida, or 1607 in Virginia, or 1608 in New France, or 1610 in Santa Fe, or 1620 and 1630 in New England on, people from Europe made permanent settlements in the New World. To settle, says Mircea Eliade, is to "consecrate" a place, to make an investment that acquires sacral characteristics.[11] This period saw anything but a desacralization, a merely operative existence. The very names of the settlements, the importations from Europe, the steeplescaping of the villages, the declared intentions of the founders, the provisions for worship, the religious justifications for removing or exterminating or converting the Native Americans and, most of all, the mytho-symbolic casting of the stories of "pilgrims," "exiles," people who lived in cities "set upon a hill," suggest a more complicated story than those one often hears when economic, demographic, or polity concerns predominate in historians' retellings.

It is true that a close-up view of colonial life shows many countersigns. It is possible to keep on writing books of the sort the critics from left to right fault today, books that can talk of Puritans without mentioning their faith, or of religious exiles without mentioning their religion. It is certainly plausible to isolate the operative sides of life and to recognize that the people of the early seventeenth century were also in many ways "empirical, this-worldly, . . . humanistic, pragmatic, utilitarian, contractual," in some climes "epicurean or hedonistic," and even "secular."[12] Selling textbooks that do such isolating is an easier task than writing and marketing books that try to do justice to controversial theological commitments of the past in the pluralistic society of the present.

What happened to obscure the fuller story? Certainly cowardice in the face of a pluralist market cannot be all that is at stake. One must also surmise that an atrophy of the imagination had occurred. Authors of histories who thought they left behind the religious ethos and spiritual envelope of their smalltown girlhoods or ghetto boyhoods found no reason to find remarkable anything about the ancestral colonial religion than that it was progressively disappearing. Colonials who got busy with stockades, trade, and politics, had no reason to continue consorting with God or resorting to myth and symbol. The move from Puritan to Yankee was seen as simply a secularizing one—until people began to notice that Yankeedom, like the ever-practical Anglican world of the southern colonies, also was a passional world open to sacral interpretations. The Dutch at New Amsterdam putatively "loved guilders more than godliness," but soon there was an established church, and there were miniature holy wars.[13] And who is to say that Boston, the Virginia shore, or New York, a third of a millennium later, is devoid of sacral and religious contexts? The story is complex, in constant need of retelling; it will be a story of fused, not polarized existence on the religio-secular, operative-passional, sacro-secular lines. But that was long ago. Certainly the next stage changed the story line, as the post-Renaissance secular Americans, victims of cultural lag and not yet fully emergent, would be proper eighteenth-century Enlightenment secularists.

Awakenings, Enlightenment, Nation-Building

The third great chapter in the North American and especially the U.S. epic in the eighteenth century should indeed have brought about the post-sacral, post-religious, fully secular age. The Europeans who imagined the Enlightenment that America realized, as Henry Steele Commager likes to speak of the movement, fancied that at last an Empire of Reason would emerge.[14] No longer would the "infamy" of the church, "priestcraft and superstition," or anything else that was retrogressive rule. The American founders put on their seal *Novus Ordo Seclorum*, a new order of ages was to be here. They then associated that motto with ancient and arcane, partly scriptural and obviously Masonic, religious symbols of pyramids and the Seeing Eye of God.

The mix reappeared. The first half of the century looked, to the historians of the Enlightenment like Peter Gay, to be a great waste of talent, on Jonathan Edwards's scale, on metaphysical projects that were throwbacks to medieval Europe.[15] In other words, a religious Great Awakening was said to have occurred, was widely noticed. Yet, one hoped, that was a last gasp of religious fever before the American Enlightenment. Certainly, as Commager and others have shown, the Founding Fathers—is that a non-mythical term?—had their secular-operative side. They were devoted to politics, deserted clerical professions, left the pews they paid for empty, and wrote a Constitution intentionally devoid of religious claims. Theirs was a different age from that of medieval or Awakening times. But was it not passional, sacral in new ways? Most historians of the Enlightenment have joined Carl Becker in seeing the eighteenth-century philosophers as having their own "heavenly city." America did not simply turn secular, but it relocated religion, fashioned what Benjamin Franklin called "a Publick Religion," and began to associate explicit religious symbols of a new sort to the new nation.[16]

The First Amendment to the Constitution, because it drew what James Madison called a line of distinction between civil and religious authorities, or separated church and state, put a new burden on the public, state-supported historians. They felt they had to expunge most positive references to religion in order to be fair, to give equal time to religion by giving no space to it at all. Pile this on the ideology that expected mere or utter secularity, and on atrophied imaginations, and one has the writing of history that leaves out the passional side because it did not manifest the old forms for the passions—and leaves out even the new forms (New Side, New Light, New School, New Measures, New Divinity) that have come to be called "the old-time religion." After Perry Miller and most of his heirs, even including the social historians, this kind of sorting out is no longer possible. The people at the end of the eighteenth century, and through much of the nineteenth, were too obviously exemplars of religio-secular, operative-passional, sacro-secular life and society to be so sundered today. But they, of course, lived long ago. The secular was still to emerge.

Modernization, Urbanization, and the Like

Late in the nineteenth century as the Industrial Revolution, the building of industrial cities, corporate life, organized labor, and a thousand other particularities of a revolution occurred, America and its historians were ready for the final fulfillment of a purely secular society. Europe, after all, had seen the emptying of churches in the move from village to city, from farm to factory, from *shul* to university. Labor was "lost" to religion, and intellectuals "killed" God or, worse, ignored God, in most tellings. Americans were overcoming cultural lag and catching up. Wait and see.

Waiters and seers saw, however, when they cared to look, that this great societal transformation also occurred with religious resymbolization. The urbanites built new churches, and the new immigrants in many cases made these churches the centers of their passional and social existence. The classic philosophers, people like William James and Josiah Royce and John Dewey, left behind the old faiths but still pursued *Varieties of Religious Experience* (1902), explicitly Christian themes, or a *Common Faith* (1934). The social scientists and historians, whether conservatives or progressives, saw old faiths and especially their childhood faiths fade, and thought they were secular. Today one reads them to see how they re-religionized life. Labor did not turn atheistic Communist but got the blessing of the Catholic church, and the magnates in Protestantism built seminaries. There was some new sophistication in the secular interpretation, but when it dropped "the other side of the hyphen" in the religio-secular or sacro-secular combinations, it did not do justice to American life. But, after all, all that was long ago.

The Second Transformation

Still another time to find the emergence of the secular model occurred during the past twenty-five years, after the era of Will Herberg's *Protestant, Catholic, Jew* (1955) or the Eisenhower-era revivals. Now the adjectives of Herman Kahn applied at first to an optimistic and progressively secular generation in a sensate culture. European theologians taught Americans how to embrace the secular and to foresee the agencies of Judaism and Christianity as advancers of the long-overdue secular unfolding.

Whoever writes the history of these decades without doing justice to both the oppressive and liberating aspects of secularity—the sensate, empirical, this-worldly, secular, humanistic, pragmatic, utilitarian, contractual, epicurean, hedonistic side—will certainly not be recognizably dealing with modern America. Yet, concurrently, the stakes are raised also on the other side. Passional, not rationalist, forms of religion have come to prosper—not least of all in the high-tech areas of the Sunbelt. Passional, not operative, dimensions of life receive most attention at the fringes of universities, in the most sophisticated subcultures of suburbia, California, academia. The New Age outlook, anything but non-religious, accompanies the way of life of those most at home in what was supposed to have been the secular.

Could it be that Kahn's report on the macrohistorians has seen too soon a prophetic fulfillment, that a new age of religion, with all its passions, has arrived? What remains of the secular in the world of Shi'ite Islam, the Muslim Brotherhood, the racist ideology of the Dutch Reformed Church in South Africa's apartheid society, in Sikh-Hindu or Muslim-Jewish warfare, in Protestant-Catholic battles in Ireland? The passions, the symbols, the religious motivations are prominent. But that is far away.

Then one notes that even the most putatively secular aspects of American life have their passional dimensions, too. Even "organized religion" is in the thick of it all. It speaks of refugee resettlement, the sanctuary movement, or calls for divestment in South Africa, black church support of metropolitan mayoral candidates, Minister Farrakhan, synagogal support for Israel, New Right Protestant politics, Bishops' Letters, the peace movement, the ecological movement. In all this one finds that perduring presence of the passional in its sacral and religious forms. Behind these public occasions are intense private and small-group searches—not by those left behind in the culture but by those in the advance.

A CONCLUSION THAT IS TO SIGNAL A START

History, of course, proves nothing about the future. Just because Americans sustained realities "on both sides of the hyphen" for half a millennium is not to say that they will do so in another half of the millennium. A new post-religious phenotype may emerge, a post-sacral society might unfold.

If five grand historical phases have unfolded, a sixth may be really different. There are reductionist models of human behavior and deconstructive readings of texts that deprive the spiritual search of its seriousness. They may be right. They may prevail. Artificial Intelligence and Neurophilosophy are the current reducers, succeeding Sociobiology and Behaviorism and the like. The historian, or at least this one, cannot disprove them philosophically or empirically. This one at least finds something in each that helps to inspire and inform historical inquiry. The philosopher John Searle has said that he has in his adult life outlasted eight final, all-purpose, fully explanatory models of human behavior and presumes that more may be in the future.[17] So in all likelihood there will be sixth, and seventh, and eighth great stanzas in the American epic, that religio-secular, operative-passional, sacro-secular mix that has been around for so long and shows no sign of appearing disentangled, leaving realities on either side of the hyphen permanently behind.

NOTES

1. Allan Bloom, *The Closing of the American Mind* (New York, 1987), 56, 216.

2. The Eliade corpus is vast. A bibliography of works up to 1978 appears in Douglas Allen, *Structure and Creativity in Religion: Hermeneutics in Mircea Eliade's Phenomenology and New Directions* (New York and The Hague, 1978). There are extensive discussions of homo religiosus in Allen's and Eliade's works. See also, Guilford Dudley III, *Religion on Trial: Mircea Eliade and His Critics* (Philadelphia, 1977).

3. John Courtney Murray, "The Structure of the Problem of God," *Theological Studies* 23 (1962): 16–17.

4. *The Oxford English Dictionary* (Oxford, 1933), 7:145.

5. Herman Kahn and Anthony J. Wiener, *The Year 2000: A Framework for Speculation on the Next Thirty-Five Years* (New York, 1967), 38.

6. Kahn and Wiener, *Year 2000*, 48. Pitirim A. Sorokin, *Social and Cultural Dynamics* (New York, 1962), 1: chaps. 7–10, develops the concept of the sensate.

7. For Jonathan Culler's criticism of the religious preoccupation of secular literary critics, see his "A Critic Against the Christians," *Times Literary Supplement*, 23 November 1984, 1327ff. For examples of the extent of religious preoccupations by such critics, see Robert Alter and Frank Kermode, eds., *The Literary Guide to the Bible* (Cambridge, Mass., 1987).

8. See Paul M. Van Buren, *The Edges of Language: An Essay on the Logic of Religion* (New York, 1972).

9. Ortega's concept of human life as a drama is constant in his untranslated works; a good discussion of these appears in Karl J. Weintraub, *Visions of Culture* (Chicago, 1966), 247–288.

10. On "chaos, anarchy, nihilism, and irrationality" between periods of history, see Kahn and Wiener, *Year 2000*, 48.

11. "To settle in a territory is . . . equivalent to consecrating it." Mircea Eliade discusses this concept in *The Sacred and the Profane: The Nature of Religion* (New York, 1961), 31–34.

12. Kahn and Wiener, *Year 2000*, 39.

13. George L. Smith, *Religion and Trade in New Netherland: Dutch Origins and American Development* (Ithaca, N.Y., 1973), 1.

14. Henry Steele Commager, *The Empire of Reason: How Europe Imagined and America Realized the Enlightenment* (Garden City, N.Y., 1977).

15. Peter Gay, *A Loss of Mastery* (Berkeley, Calif., 1966).

16. On the Founding Fathers, see Commager, *Empire of Reason*; Carl Becker, *The Heavenly City of the Eighteenth-Century Philosophers* (New Haven, 1932); Chester E. Jorgenson and Frank Luther Mott, eds., *Benjamin Franklin: Representative Selections, with Introduction, Bibliography, and Notes* (New York, 1962), 203; Henry F. May, *The Enlightenment in America* (New York, 1976).

17. John Searle, "The Myth of the Computer," *N.Y. Review of Books*, 29 April 1982, 3.

2

From Covenant to Constitution: The Americanization of Judaism

Hasia Diner

The history of Judaism and Jewish life in America has often been portrayed as a dramatic story of change. A people derived largely from traditional Jewish communities in eastern Europe quickly Americanized, experienced rapid social mobility, overcame anti-Semitism, and won acceptance of its religion as one of America's three great faiths, with the numerically insignificant Judaism joining Catholicism and Protestantism in the mainstream of American civil religion.[1]

Although historians and sociologists have described this process in detail, they have failed to recognize one central aspect of the Jewish adaptation to America. In its style, structure, and rhetoric, Judaism grafted onto itself elements of the American political structure. As Jews created new institutions and tinkered with old ones, they often looked to American models and symbols for inspiration. They searched the American lexicon for idioms and concepts to justify innovations and at the same time claimed that by stressing voluntarism, pluralism, and democracy they operated in a Jewish framework. American Jews, both consciously and unconsciously, sought to mold their institutions to fit those of American life. They wanted to project an image consistent with the American creed of democracy, as embodied in the Declaration of Independence and the Constitution, one that stressed voluntarism, equalitarianism, and majority rule. Furthermore, the Jewish community came to be characterized by an internal separation between its "religious" and its "secular" components that paralleled the separation of church and state in American life. While these values were not totally alien to traditional Judaism, they came to play a far greater role in American Judaism.

This process of Americanization is primarily a phenomenon of the mid-nineteenth and twentieth centuries. The creation of a Jewish society and culture patterned along American lines coincided, not surprisingly, with the period of the great waves of migration from central and eastern Europe, and the subsequent absorption of the newcomers and their children into America. While the process of creating an American Judaism clearly had roots in earlier decades, and glints of it can be seen even at the beginning of the nineteenth century, Jews did not represent a critical mass in America until after the Civil War. Previously, Jews had been too small a group and produced too little in the way of a culture—as measured by institution building, creation of an indigenous leadership, development of a popular culture, and production of texts—to consider the possibility of fitting in. American society also changed, and these changes made possible, indeed imperative, the Jewish accommodation. Before the 1830s and 1840s some American states still had religious qualifications for voting and office-holding. Pre-Jacksonian nineteenth-century America still bore some resemblance to the hierarchical world of Europe. Yet, by the time the masses of Jews began to emigrate to the United States, it had become a society fiercely devoted to voluntarism, individualism, pluralism, and unfettered freedom, with obvious, important limitations.[2]

Certainly the issue of Americanization has been extensively discussed in the literature of American Jewish history where references to it abound. Yet, very little is known about how it occurred, what it meant, and what was implied by the reformulation of Judaism along specifically American lines. Few scholars have made any attempt to go beyond merely describing changes and assuming that these changes involved the process called Americanization. They have tended to consider any modifications in the ways Jews organized their communities in the United States, or alterations in the patterns of their religious lives, as being part and parcel of this adjustment. Most historians have held up such measures of adaptation as the increased use of English or the greater degree of decorum in religious ritual as evidence of Americanization. They have assumed that the rise of the Reform movement in the mid-nineteenth century was a prime example of Americanization. Undoubtedly, these examples did indeed indicate some basic adjustments to America, but these scholars have not extended their analysis to explore exactly how these changes spelled out Americanization.

Perhaps scholars have tended to glide over Americanization because so many have stressed the parallels and the consistency between Americanism and Judaism. Frequent references in the historic sources to the Puritans' self-identification with the Israelites of the Bible and the Old Testament roots of the American commonwealth have led many historians to assume that American political values and Jewish political values dovetailed neatly with one another. Typical, for example, were the words of Rabbi Abraham A. Neuman of Philadelphia's Mikveh Israel Congregation in honor of the 150th anniversary of the U.S. Constitution. He linked the framers of the Constitution with classical and rabbinic Judaism. Not only did he see the Constitution as the direct heir of New England Puritanism, but that New England tradition, he believed, was ''in essence, the rebirth of the Hebrew spirit in the Christian conscience. It was the Hebrew religious genius come to life to wage battle for God.'' According to

Neuman, one could easily discern a "striking parallel between the reforms introduced by the Puritans in the Church and town government of the New England settlements and the community organizations of the Jewish Kahal in the Middle Ages." The spirit of this line of reasoning has flowed directly into the work of scholars like Milton Konvitz and Daniel Elazar, who have asserted that the Jewish concept of the covenant fits nicely with American political values. Clearly, by looking for parallels one does not see the process of adaptation.[3]

In probing this process of Americanization and in trying to understand how American forms came to be adapted to Jewish life, one must begin with a few conceptual points. First, Americanization involved more than modernization. The Jewish confrontation with modernity occurred in many different national political settings. Judaism was also coming to terms with other modern societies in the same early decades of the twentieth century. In Great Britain, Canada, Latin America, France, and Germany, Jewish life also made a set of specific adjustments to the realities of these cultures and their politics. In each of these settings the Judaism that emerged conformed to the political structure of the host society and, as such, differed from the American variant at the same time it also represented a departure from "traditional" Jewish life.

The contrast between the United States and Britain is a particularly rewarding one to pursue. The two societies appear to be equally "modern" and, certainly since the mid-nineteenth century, roughly equal in level of democracy and similar in degree of economic development. Yet, they have produced different forms of Judaism and different types of Jewish life. Most obviously, England has a Chief Rabbi, appointed by the Crown, who serves in a capacity for the Jews equivalent to that of the Archbishop of Canterbury for Anglicans. This has led to a much slower rate of religious differentiation among Jews. They have experienced less in the way of internal denominationalism, and British Jewish institutions have developed less clearly along religious-secular lines than in the United States. Clearly, American Jews and British (which includes Commonwealth) Jews adapted to different political realities. How else does one explain that the system of the *Bet Din*, or religious court, has taken much greater root in England and the Commonwealth nations than in America? According to the political scientists Daniel Elazar and Stephen Goldstein,

because of the individualistic nature of the American Jewish community, standing rabbinical courts do not have the same regularized status in dispute resolution as do, for example, rabbinical courts in the British Commonwealth. In contrast to the situation in the United States, in the British Commonwealth Orthodoxy has remained the dominant form of Jewish communal expression despite declining levels of personal observance. . . . As a result the voluntary adherents to the Jewish community in the Commonwealth accept the authority of Orthodox rabbinical courts, which therefore have a much more prominent place in the life of the total Jewish community.

Elazar and Goldstein proceed to note that in Sydney, Australia, the Jewish community center has a special courtroom set aside for the *Bet Din*, which in its physical appearance resembles a secular Australian courtroom. In contrast, when the community center movement spread out across Jewish America in the early twentieth century, it was avowedly nonsectarian, that is, it was for all Jews regardless of their religious practices. Religious functions of all kinds—let alone legal ones—were scrupulously excluded. Some centers indeed did not maintain Kosher eating facilities, nor did they close down swimming pools and gymnasia for the Sabbath.[4]

A contrast could also be drawn between the United States and other modern Jewish societies. Judith Laikin Elkin has drawn a very stark comparison between Jewish life in the United States and in contemporary Latin America by focusing sharply on the differences between the political and social cultures of the two host societies. She notes, for example, "in Latin America, more than in other sectors of the Diaspora, it appears that a choice must be made between being in or out of the Jewish community. As in national life, there seems to be little room for compromise."[5]

Thus, the process of coming to terms with the host culture was hardly unique or idiosyncratic to the United States. But the ways in which Jews adapted to America demonstrate that the modern rabbis and other Americanizers were correct when they boasted that "America was different." The process of Americanization differed qualitatively from the process of Germanization or Frenchification—if one can be permitted the use of such terms—in a number of profound ways. American Jews did not live in a political culture that had chosen grudgingly to grant them rights. They never needed to appeal to allies to enfranchise them nor to endow them piecemeal with civil equality. The status of the Jews in the United States was never a subject of intense public debate, and the halls of Congress and the state legislatures did not echo with arguments about the worthiness, or lack thereof, of the Jews to America. From the beginning, American Jews had, with some slight local exceptions, legal rights, whereas French Jews or German Jews had to become emancipated. The Jews of Paris or Berlin or London stayed put physically, but their civil status went through a number of alterations over the course of the eighteenth, nineteenth, and twentieth centuries. For the Jews of the United States, migration had involved not just a change of scenery, but a fundamental shift in civil status.

Furthermore, only American Jews lived in a society that was politically and culturally dedicated to a separation of church and state. While courts and legislatures may still not have resolved exactly what this means vis-à-vis school prayer, Sunday blue laws, public Christmas pageants, and the like, it is clear that as far as the American political system is concerned, religions exist purely as voluntary institutions, supported only by those individuals who choose to affiliate with them. Religious authorities are recognized only as a matter of private choice, and religious-ethnic bodies can organize however they feel inclined. Not so in the other modern societies with which Jews were coming to terms. Scholars like Salo Baron and Jacob Katz have not only stressed the varying Jewish accommodations to diverse political and social circumstances, but they have examined the internal Jewish implications of differing levels of state involvement in religious matters. Thus, both Baron and Katz studied the ways in which the political structure of Germany affected the communal struggle between Orthodox and Reform elements. Both sides sought to use the state to advance their quests for hegemony, and the state had to make decisions that affected the outcome of what in America would be viewed as purely voluntary matter, of no concern to the larger, non-Jewish society.[6]

This reality not only shaped the historic uniqueness of America but had a tremendous impact on the process of Americanization. One of the most distinctive characteristics to evolve within American Judaism was an internal separation of church and state. Just as Americans regarded their religious and political lives as separate and resented the interference of the state in matters of religion, and religious institutions in public affairs, so American Jews erected a wall between the two halves of their Jewishness, with each one sovereign in its own sphere. An internal separation of "church and state" became one of the most distinctive characteristics of American Judaism.

Other immigrant religions seem also to have gone through this process of internal Americanization and democratization. Will Herberg's classic, *Protestant, Catholic, Jew* (1955), as well as John Murray Cuddihy's *No Offense* (1978), point out clearly that all imported historic religions both have had to, and have chosen to, reformulate themselves in order to synchronize with America. The process seems to have operated on both a conscious and an unconscious level. Given the level of interaction between individual members of the ethnic group and the larger society, in the marketplace, in schools, trade unions, and the army, it may have been inevitable that American forms would rub off onto the behavior patterns and ideologies of the newcomers. The impact of American popular culture undoubtedly played an important role in teaching immigrants and their children what America expected of them.[7]

But it was not a totally automatic development. Group leaders—clergy, educators, writers, intellectuals, philanthropists—were keenly aware of their minority status and strove to change group behavior and ideology to lessen the chasm between themselves and the dominant society. In searching for models they selectively turned to American patterns of action and thought. At the same time communal leaders sought to find ways to sustain group solidarity and foster continued loyalty, particularly among the young, American-born generations, who, they feared, would be lured away by the attractions of American life. Appeals to tradition were augmented with claims that ethnic group values dovetailed neatly with American values. Young Catholics and Jews need not feel conflict between their two cultures because they harmonized so well, one with the other. Thus, internal Americanization served the double, and perhaps contradictory, purpose of both winning acceptance for the minority culture in the larger society and solidifying communal bonds within the traditional one.

Although all immigrants passed through the portals of the Americanization process, the Jewish experience can be viewed at some level as sui generis. Jews were the most permanent of immigrants to the United States, with no place to return to. Therefore, they were particularly eager to come to terms with the new environment. Also, Jewishness differed from Irish or Italian ethnicity, for example. It posed different kinds of adjustment problems from Catholicism or Eastern Orthodoxy. Judaism involved more than both ethnic identity and religion. In the setting from which they were migrating, Jews had lived in varying degrees in a "state within a state." In the traditional communities of Europe, Jews had occupied a separate world where the Jewish community collected taxes, convened courts, supervised education, dispensed charity, and enforced standards of personal behavior. Jews knew that they lived by two sets of laws: those of the state and those of traditional Judaism. Both had the power of enforcement; both had to be obeyed. This system could not survive in America where voluntarism was the key to religious identification, where the state recognized no religion, and where religious institutions functioned by the consent of the governed alone. Thus by moving to America, Judaism had to strip itself of some of its most fundamental characteristics and functions.

However profound and wrenching this adjustment proved to be for Judaism, it was not the first time that Jews and Judaism had had to mold themselves to the form and substance of new settings. The history of the Jewish people since the cessation of national political sovereignty in the first century of the Common Era can be seen as a series of adjustments to a variety of host environments, each with its political culture and social patterns. The relationship between Judaism and the host society always involved a set of complex interactions, and Jews actively borrowed from the surrounding society and adapted their traditional forms to fit the environment in which they found themselves.

The works of Jewish historians like Salo Baron and Jacob Katz are replete with examples of how in highly centralized, autocratic political systems, Judaism developed highly centralized, autocratic forms. Louis Finkelstein, one of the outstanding intellectual leaders of Conservative Judaism, speculated in a 1964 essay that the fundamentally democratic impulses of the Jewish tradition had become historically dormant when Jews found themselves "surrounded by a feudal system which left little room for democratic thought and practice." Israel Friedlander, an early twentieth-century scholar of Jewish-Arab culture, painstakingly demonstrated how much Jews had borrowed and internalized from the surrounding Arab culture, particularly in Spain under the Moors, how much they had innovated with new philosophic and aesthetic forms. So universal had been the plasticity in Jewish life that Mordecai Kaplan, probably American Jewry's single most important intellectual-activist of the twentieth century, could proclaim: "The reason Judaism and Jewish people have managed to survive, despite adversities which no other civilization, country, or people has survived, is that its tradition was always reinterpreted to meet the intellectual, social, and spiritual demands of the age in which we lived."[8]

It is therefore all the more surprising and anomalous that historians of American Judaism have not attempted to demonstrate the ways in which Judaism in America came to take on many of the characteristics of American life, especially to resemble its political structure. The failure of historians to tackle this phenomenon is also striking in that contemporary observers of Jewish life in the late nineteenth and early twentieth centuries did note the adaptability of Jewish life to the hospitable—some believed overly hospitable—climate of America. The highly observant, the most Orthodox, trembled as they saw Jewish institutions come to look like American institutions, and they decried the fact that in a democratic society where institutions functioned by majority rule, and where religion derived its strength from purely voluntary loyalties, traditional rabbinic authority had eroded to the point of being merely symbolic. Orthodox rabbis in the early and mid-twentieth century, for example, issued several orders of *herem*, or excommunication, against Mordecai Kaplan, with no results whatsoever. Few Jews cared that a band of Orthodox rabbis considered his revised Americanized prayerbooks of the mid–1940s to be heretical.[9] In Europe such a ban would have cut Kaplan off from influence, but in America he continued to teach at the Jewish Theological Seminary in New York and serve as a pulpit rabbi. Other Jews bought his books and invited him to speak in their congregations. The *herem* clearly had been reduced to impotence, and, in a society where power was decentralized into a myriad of autonomous units, Orthodox rabbis recognized that traditional forms of communal control could not be sustained.

For this reason the rabbis of eastern Europe attempted to discourage Jewish migration to the United States, an impure and godless country. It may be that the most tradition-bound Jews did not in fact make the move, in part because of the grim predictions as to what awaited them on the other side of the Atlantic. According to one European rabbi, Jacob David Willonski, "America is a *treif* [unclean] land where even the stones are impure." By Willonski's reckoning the lack of piety in America was "to be blamed on the land . . . where groups with varying viewpoints and opinions came to be settled and no one recognized any authority." So widespread was the perception that America and traditional Judaism could not mix that even the young Morris Raphael Cohen at age seven wrote from Minsk to his father already in America "expressing my fear of the irreligious surroundings to which I would thus be subject and my hope that he would allow me to continue my pious studies where I was."[10]

The fears of Cohen and many others like him seem to have been quite warranted. They saw that in America Jewish law was not law. It had behind it no power of enforcement. The rabbinate had been reduced from a central position of communal legal authority to being voluntary leaders of a voluntary community, dependent on pleasing the majority. Efforts to revive the rabbinate in America and to reinvigorate the force of Jewish law were usually stillborn. In the 1880s, for example, New York Orthodox congregations actually tried to create the office of a Chief Rabbi. They secured Rabbi Jacob Joseph of Vilna to fill the seat. The experiment, which had been modeled along British lines, was declared a failure after less than a decade of scandal and dissension. Whatever personality and financial problems beset it, it was in the final analysis the nature of the American political culture that spelled its doom. Even before Jacob Joseph arrived and attempted to set up his *Bet Din*, a sympathetic magazine, the *Jewish Messenger*, warned that he would succeed only if he recognized that "with all our freedom the law of the land is supreme over rabbinical interpretations, that in marriages and divorces the courts of the State must be sought for redress, not the rabbinical court."[11]

Some seventy-five years later, in the 1950s, the Conservative movement's Rabbinical Assembly launched a Sabbath revitalization campaign, a campaign intended to stimulate greater adherence to the observance of the laws of the Sabbath. Observers from outside, and rabbis from within, Conservatism acknowledged that the effort had been basically for naught. The rank-and-file of the movement complied with Sabbath precepts no more than before. The major accomplishment of the campaign was a decision by the Rabbinical Assembly to permit driving on the Sabbath for the purpose of attendance at synagogue. What in essence the Assembly did was to give the aura of legal sanction to popular behavior, a clear indication again of the historic pattern whereby American principles of majority rule and consent of the governed crept into Jewish life, here into a movement dedicated to the preservation of *halachah* (the corpus of Jewish life).

It was not just the Orthodox who recognized the malleability of Judaism to the American political environment. While they decried this plasticity, innovators of all kinds celebrated the ways in which an oriental, medieval set of institutions could become modern and American. To many, particularly those associated with the Reform movement, the freedom of America, the voluntarism, the separation of church and state, allowed Jewish life finally to be purged of its most onerous and extraneous encumbrances. One Reform rabbi, Philip David Bookstaber, noted in a 1939 book, *Judaism and the American Mind*, that only in America could freedom of religion come to play a role in the internal life of Judaism. In Europe only orthodoxy prevailed. "However, in this age of ours, and in this country of ours, with the substratum of our foundation that gives us an American mind and attitude towards all theories and beliefs, we have a most 'decent respect' for the various 'sects' in Judaism; they are, in truth, the warp and woof of the intellectual and social climate, through which competition and struggle, we emerge with a still greater understanding." That is, one of the implications of living in the American system was that Judaism would allow ideas to compete against each other, and that in turn would "find Judaism in America more vital, more energizing and ever-wider in influence" than it could have ever been under Europe's less democratic conditions. These sentiments echoed those of the turn-of-the-twentieth-century reform leader Rabbi Kaufmann Kohler. Kohler acknowledged not only the truth that the Reform movement in the United States differed from that in Germany, in that the American variant had been launched and inspired by lay people, but that this form of innovation, he believed, represented "the religion of the future."[12]

This essay has already alluded to a number of cardinal principles of the

American political tradition, such as majority rule, separation of church and state, and separation of powers within a federal system. These came to be the basis for American Jewish institutions. Because the state in America stood aloof from religious matters, the rabbis lost the communal authority that they had enjoyed in Europe. This aloofness of the state from internal Jewish concerns was something new. From it came numerous efforts, some more successful than others, to create structures of Jewish communal life that were at the same time voluntary, formal, and authoritative. The failure of New York Orthodoxy to install a Chief Rabbi, the creation and demise of that city's *Kehillah* (community) in the early decades of the twentieth century, the creation of an American Jewish Congress after World War I, and the emergence of local Jewish community councils in the 1930s and 1940s indicate how problematic the issue of internal self-governance was in America. The hallmark of American Jewish communal organization and culture has been a fierce commitment to basic American values of individualism and voluntarism. All efforts to create unity have failed, certainly on a national level. Even on a local level the creation of the community councils, which began in the 1930s, has been predicated on the democratic and voluntary nature of the community. In the nearly fifty years of its existence, the Jewish Community Council of Washington, D.C., to offer one illustration, has expelled only one organization. Constituent groups have been free to pursue policies at odds with those set by the Council, with the minor restriction that they must submit a written statement of their intent to dissent.[13]

Thus, in America, individual Jews—laymen, innovators, those who might elsewhere have been considered deviants or heretics—could create new institutions, or take over and reshape old ones. Individual Jews, no matter what the level of their piety, wealth, or learning—the traditional criteria for communal leadership—could choose to affiliate with communal institutions on their own terms. The principle of majority rule allowed the voices of more ordinary Jews to count equally with those more pious, more learned, and more wealthy.

Democracy meant that within Jewish institutions, be they synagogues, welfare institutions, or schools, rituals and practices rose or fell according to the wishes of the majority rather than because of the authority of the rabbinate and the other elites. The indifference of the state to the internal concerns of religious communities opened the door to innovation and majority rule and left Jewish men and women free to pursue their particular forms of Jewish identification. Membership in the American Jewish community, either as a formal body or as an informal community of faith, developed along pluralistic lines. Thus, participation was opened to all regardless of ideology, wealth, learning, or piety. In his extensive writings on the nature of the American Jewish community, both as a description of what was, and as a statement of an ideal, Mordecai Kaplan postulated that membership and leadership in what he called the "organic community" must not be limited to any group or type of Jew. All opinions and orientations should be encouraged to flourish. All types of "Jewish" institutions were legitimate. Thus, in the community councils all kinds of institutions—

synagogues and workers' groups, social service agencies and culture clubs, Zionist societies and athletic associations—were brought together to formulate a Jewish consensus on the issues of the day and on the nature of the Jewish relationship to the larger society. All groups had the same vote. That of the rabbis counted for no more than that of the representative of the Workman's Circle, for example.[14]

From the national to the local level Jews erected an almost impenetrable wall separating their own church and state, with the rabbis, seminaries, and denominational bodies on one side, and social welfare, defense, and political organizations on the other. Each jealously guarded its ground, wary of any encroachment by the other. The movement of religion to one side of the wall, divorced from the secular functions of the community, can be illustrated graphically by the development of Jewish social work and social services. In the initial decades of Jewish settlement in the eighteenth century and into the mid-nineteenth century, charitable enterprises emanated from the synagogue. The rabbi played an active role in efforts to help orphans, widows, the unemployed, and the like. But from the middle of the nineteenth century, social services moved into community-wide, secular agencies that were generally devoid of any religious function and merely dispensed aid to the Jewish needy in a neutral, efficient manner, with the Jewishness of the agency deriving from the fact that recipients, donors, and social workers happened to be Jewish. They paid little or no attention, however, to traditional *halachic* precepts regarding the giving or receiving of charity, nor was there any rabbinic input or participation in these institutions. This absence of a "Jewish" content to this social work occupied a great deal of Mordecai Kaplan's attention and led to a number of efforts on his part and that of the Jewish Theological Seminary to create a school for Jewish social service that would bridge the wall between church and state.[15] Within the religious and secular spheres a wide array of institutions competed for the allegiance of the people and, as such, created a system of delicate checks and balances between the various constituency groups. This separation of powers insured that no single segment of the community could tyrannize the other.

In a similar manner American Jews asserted their right to see the law changed through new, looser amendment procedures, although the changes were often still justified by the traditional texts and precepts. They likewise espoused a passionate belief in freedom of speech and freedom of expression. No element in the community had the power of censorship, and communal bodies on the local or the national level sought ways to compromise ideological differences so that American Jews could concentrate their energies on the pressing problems of relations with the outside, non-Jewish world.

Probably no issue demonstrates this desire to Americanize better than the question of the role of women within Judaism. From the vantage point of traditional Judaism, American women in the early twentieth century enjoyed political and social equality. Various Jewish institutions in the religious and the secular spheres sought to alter the status of women within the Jewish community, to bring it into the conformity with their status in America. Most of the pronouncements articulated before the 1960s that decried the inferior position occupied by women within Jewish life came not from women but from men, like Mordecai Kaplan, Kaufmann Kohler, and others. They sharply felt the need to minimize the dissonance between America's options and expectations for women, and that of Judaism. Thus, Kaplan in 1922, two years after the passage of the Suffrage Amendment, created the ceremony of the Bat Mitzvah whereby a young Jewish woman would be accepted into the community as an adult member. In his *Sabbath Prayer Book* (1945) he excised all references to gender difference, and, most important, that phrase in the morning prayer whereby a man gave thanks to God, for "not having made me a woman." All the pre–1960s changes in womens' roles in synagogue life—for example, mixed seating, counting women in the quorum for prayer, and changes in the marriage laws—came not as a result of organized lobbying by Jewish women, but through the innovations of male communal leaders, who believed that within the Jewish community women ought not occupy a place radically at odds with their position in America.

Each step in the process of Americanization, each element adapted from the American political creed, represented a break with the past. These steps were, however, justified in terms of tradition. Reformers and innovators claimed that their tamperings fit perfectly with the fundamental principles of Judaism and that rather than deviating from fundamental principles of Judaism and its history, they were actually returning to a more authentic form. Thus, for example, as Judaism democratized internally and as rabbis, intellectuals, the writers of children's textbooks, and various community leaders embraced democracy with a passion, a new vision of the Jewish past took shape, which claimed that Judaism had always carried with it the seeds of democracy. Gone in the textbooks and sermons of the 1940s, 1950s, and 1960s was the struggle between Jewish values of corporatism and American values of individualism, of Jewish commitment to tradition and America's commitment to innovation. Instead Judaism and America were thought to fit together perfectly. Only in the 1960s, as a result of that decade's profound critique of American values and the rise of Holocaust consciousness, did Jewish writers and publicists begin to reexamine the fit.

The shapers of the democratized American Judaism believed not only that Jewish life had to be brought up to the standards of the American political system but that Judaism had to be explained to the American public in terms of the American creed. Thus, in the same years that rituals, texts, and forms of communal organization were reshaped along American lines, so, too, key concepts, in particular that of the Chosen People, were rethought and rephrased in order to harmonize with American beliefs. While few Jewish thinkers went as far as Mordecai Kaplan, who abhorred the concept of "chosenness," found it odious to his American sensibilities, and had it expurgated from every one of his Reconstructionist texts, others felt the need to justify it in American terms. The Reform movement of the nineteenth century maintained the concept of the Chosen People in its prayerbooks and in its various pronouncements and statements of principles, but rearticulated it to link up to American progressivism. All peoples were chosen, but Jews had been chosen to help, in concert with other like-minded Americans, to usher in a golden age of liberalism, an age that not surprisingly resonated along the lines of the Declaration of Independence and stressed the primacy of life, liberty, and the pursuit of happiness. The Conservative movement, consistent with its desire simultaneously to innovate and to preserve tradition, felt called upon to justify the concept in its first authoritative prayerbook, that edited by Rabbi Morris Silverman in 1946. It offered the justification, or proposition, that the historic concept does not in any way contradict modern American truths of the fundamental equality of all people. Rather it should be viewed as a historic legacy whereby Jews were chosen *only* to receive the Torah and not to be deemed better than others. In the Silverman prayerbook one profound statement of chosenness—that of the "Aleinu" prayer, a prayer of thanksgiving to God for not "having made us like the other nations of the earth, for not having placed us like the families of the earth"—is offered intact in the Hebrew, which most worshippers would not understand, but translated loosely and inoffensively in the English.[16] As Jewish men and women in positions of leadership strove to foster more positive relations with the larger society, so, too, they strove to invent an ideology that legitimized Judaism as consistent with America, worthy of inclusion in the sacred turf of American civic religion.

These reforms and innovations were the products not just of accommodation to a modern society but of specific adjustment to American culture. These changes could not have come about anyplace else. They grew out of a complex series of interactions between a Judaism that fundamentally stressed communalism and the unity of the Jewish people, and an American society that put its greatest stress on individualism and pluralism. The movement from traditional Judaism, that is from European Judaism to American, did not proceed along a straight line, nor did it encompass all elements of the community in the same way and at the same rate. But, clearly, the basic elements of the political culture of America seeped into Jewish life and created a product unlike that produced anywhere else.

NOTES

1. A few examples from the large literature are: Henry Finegold, *Zion in America: The Jewish Experience from Colonial Times to the Present* (New York, 1974) and *A Midrash on American Jewish History* (Albany, New York, 1982); Charles Silberman, *A Certain People: American Jews and Their Lives Today* (New York, 1985); and Jacob Neusner, *Stranger at Home* (Chicago, 1981).

2. Michael Kammen, *People of Paradox* (New York, 1973); Rowland Berthoff, *An Unsettled People* (New York, 1971).

3. Leon Jick, *The Americanization of the Synagogue, 1820–1870* (Hanover, N.H., 1976); Milton R. Konvitz, *Judaism and the American Ideal* (Ithaca, New York, 1978); Daniel Elazar, *Covenant as the Basis of the Jewish Political Tradition. Working Paper*

No. 1: Workshop in the Covenant Idea and the Jewish Political Tradition (Ramat Gan, Israel, 1977); and Abraham Neuman, *Relation of the Hebrew Scriptures to American Institutions* (New York, 1943).

4. Daniel Elazar and Stephen J. Goldstein, "The Legal Status of the American Jewish Community," *American Jewish Yearbook: 1972* (New York, 1972), 84.

5. Judith Laikin Elkin, "Latin American Jewry Today," *American Jewish Yearbook: 1985* (New York, 1984), 21.

6. Salo W. Baron, "Freedom and Constraint in the Jewish Community: A Historic Episode," in Israel Davidson, ed., *Essays and Studies in Memory of Linda R. Miller* (New York, 1938), 9–23; Jacob Katz, *Out of the Ghetto: The Social Background of Jewish Emancipation, 1770–1870* (New York, 1978).

7. Will Herberg, *Protestant, Catholic, Jew: An Essay in American Religious Sociology* (Garden City, N.Y., 1955); John Murray Cuddihy, *No Offense: Civil Religion and Protestant Taste* (New York, 1978).

8. Salo Baron, *The Jewish Community: Its History and Structure to the American Revolution*, 3 vols. (Philadelphia, 1942); Jacob Katz, *Tradition and Crisis: Jewish Society at the End of the Middle Ages* (Glencoe, Ill., 1961); Louis Finkelstein, "Hebrew Sources: Scriptures and Talmud," in Ernest F. Johnson, ed., *Foundations of Democracy: A Series of Addresses* (New York, 1964), 33; Israel Friedlander, *Past and Present: A Collection of Jewish Essays* (Cincinnati, 1919), 264–266; and Mordecai Kaplan and Arthur A. Cohen, *If Not Now, When: Toward a Reconstruction of the Jewish People* (New York, 1973), 98.

9. Mordecai M. Kaplan and Eugene Kohn, eds., *Sabbath Prayer Book* (New York, 1945); and Mordecai Kaplan, Eugene Kohn, and Ira Eisenstein, eds., *High Holiday Prayer Book*, 2 vols. (New York, 1948).

10. Jeffrey Gurock, "Resisters and Accommodators: Varieties of Orthodox Rabbis in America, 1886–1983," in Jacob R. Marcus and Abraham J. Peck, eds., *The American Rabbinate: A Century of Continuity and Change, 1883–1983* (Hoboken, N.J., 1985), 10–97; Morris Raphael Cohen, *A Dreamer's Journey* (Glencoe, Ill., 1949), 211.

11. Quoted in Abraham Karp, "New York Chooses a Chief Rabbi," *Publication of the American Jewish Historical Society* 44 (1955):150.

12. Philip David Bookstaber, *Judaism and the American Mind* (New York, 1939), 13, 19; Samuel S. Cahan, "Kaufmann Kohler The Reformer," in Moshe Davis, ed., *Mordecai M. Kaplan, Jubilee Volume on the Occasion of His Seventieth Birthday;* English Section (New York, 1953), 137–155.

13. Daniel J. Elazar, "The Reconstruction of Jewish Communities in the Post-War Period," *Jewish Journal of Sociology* 11 (1969): 187–226; Isaac Franck, "The Changing American Jewish Community," in Eugene Kohn, ed., *American Jewry: The Tercentenary and After* (New York, 1953), 18–45; Isaiah Minkoff, "Development of Jewish Communal Organization in America: 1900–1956," in Harry Schneiderman, ed., *Two Generations in Perspective: Notable Events and Trends, 1896–1956* (New York, 1957), 110–38; and Maurice Taylor, "Jewish Community Organization and Jewish Community Life," *YIVO Annual of Jewish Social Science* (New York, 1954), 179–204.

14. For Mordecai Kaplan's vision of the "organic community," see his *Judaism as a Civilization: Towards a Reconstruction of American-Jewish Life* (New York, 1934), 280–99.

15. Samuel Kohs, "Mordecai M. Kaplan's Contribution to Jewish Social Work," in

Ira Eisenstein and Eugene Kohn, eds., *Mordecai M. Kaplan: An Evaluation* (New York, 1952), 65–83.

16. *Sabbath and Festival Prayer Book, with a New Translation, Supplementary Readings and Notes* (New York, 1946), 158.

3

Black Theology and Historical Necessity

James Oliver Horton and Lois E. Horton

During the late 1960s Afro-American theologians attempted to reconcile the political and social aims of black power with black religious traditions and conceived their task as the construction of a black theology. Many were dissatisfied with the established black church, which they saw as failing to provide a philosophical basis for black liberation. They sought an activist theology rooted in the black experience. Joseph Washington's *Black Religion* (1964) charged that the black church, cut off from the dominant white Christian tradition, was in fact "a church without a theology," merely a "folk religion."[1]

Others disagreed with this assessment and saw black churches as a particular version of "white" Christianity. C. Eric Lincoln asked; "Isn't 'black religion' the same as 'white religion' except that the preaching is more colorful and protracted and the people more responsive?" "Isn't 'black religion' simply 'white religion' in black face?" For these critics a new black theology was needed to replace the existing theology derived from the "slaveholders' religion." Although these assessments of the essential nature of the black church differed, their aim was the same—to build a theology that suited the needs of an oppressed people.[2]

In the 1960s the task of black theologians was hindered by the relative scarcity of historical studies that illustrated the complexities of Afro-American religion within the context of 350 years of black American experience. In the years since, however, there has been an explosion of scholarly work that illuminates this history. During the 1970s historians focused their attention on the black community, both slave and free. There were efforts to understand the unique black customs and institutions that survived the devastating effects of slavery. In the light of this prolific scholarship and the new legitimacy it bestowed on black institutions, the task for students of Afro-American religion became not so much the invention of a new black theology as the rediscovery of the black theological tradition deeply rooted in the history of black America.[3] Albert J. Raboteau spoke directly to the issue of the historical black religious experience in his book, *Slave Religion* (1978). Influenced by earlier studies of slave communities, Raboteau traced the religious life of Afro-Americans from its African roots into the plantation slave quarters of the American South. The slave church, he asserted, sustained human dignity and encouraged resistance to the dehumanizing intent of bondage.[4] One belief, universally contained in the many varieties of African religion transported to America, has profoundly influenced the development of Afro-American religion. It is what Aylward Shorter described as "the vision of wholeness or integration of life—'sacred' and 'profane' are relative terms." Sterling Stuckey described this integration as an essential trait of African religion before the penetration of western Christianity. "The division between the sacred and the secular, so prominent a feature of modern western culture," he said, "did not exist in black Africa in the years of the slave trade."[5]

William B. McClain noted that black religious belief in America also formed a strong link between the present world and the heavenly world. Thus, he echoed the sentiments of a mid-nineteenth-century Virginia slave who explained that God was in the midst of his people. "He (God) wasn't way off, up in the sky: He was a-seein' everybody an' a listin' to ever' word an' a-promisin' to 'let his love come down.' " Clearly, the slave's God was of this world as well as of the next. This integration of the sacred and the secular worlds provided the slave with a powerful ally in the struggle for survival and self-respect.[6]

It was not only the heritage of African religion that bridged the gap between the spiritual and the profane for slaves. The necessities of daily life on the plantation encouraged the use of holy practices as one form of resistance. Lawrence Levine, in his book *Black Culture and Black Consciousness* (1977), analyzed slave songs and found that they were used for almost every purpose, from coordinating the routines of work, to providing a diversion from the daily suffering, to maintaining a system of internal communication within the quarters. Yet, these songs did more—they reinforced connections between slaves and with their African heritage in ways that helped to forge the links of the slave community. Whether they told of love, youth, or a veiled anger, slave songs empowered those who composed and sang them.[7]

More religious songs have survived than any others. Levine believed that these songs could be preserved more easily because they were seemingly more harmless. Masters were willing to allow slaves to seek freedom in the afterworld so long as they posed no threat to the here-and-now world of the plantation. Slaves could not display open dissent or rebellion without threatening their survival. Thus, messages unacceptable to whites were encoded in the apparently innocuous songs. Since Afro-American religious traditions included the integration of sacred and secular, the double meanings of spirituals provided a natural vehicle for otherwise prohibited communications. It was not simply a matter of using religious images to camouflage political ambitions and secular longings. Sacred songs already carried both types of messages, since both worlds were inextricably linked.

As the conversion of slaves to Christianity increased in the years before the Civil War, spirituals gained in popularity within the slave community. The words expressed traditional western-European religious values, but Afro-Americans did not simply adopt European religion and its theology. They adapted European Christianity to their situation, beliefs, and practices, and gave new meanings to those religious concepts and to the reality of enslavement. Oppression and freedom are constant themes in the religious thought of black Americans. In slave gatherings in forest clearings, in churches in northern free-black urban communities in the nineteenth century, in rural churches in the twentieth-century South, songs and sermons have identified blacks in America with the children of Israel whom Moses led out of bondage in Egypt. The river Jordan is both a heavenly metaphor and a physical boundary between North and South, slavery and freedom, oppressive segregation and political liberation.

The black adaptation of Christianity is well illustrated by the place of dance in the life of the slave community. Although many white Christian leaders considered dancing secular, even sinful, Africans built it into their religious lives. To the African, dancing during religious ceremonies was like praying. It was the outward expression of connectedness with ancestors and with God. On the solemn occasion of a burial, for example, dance that involved the total rhythmic expression of the body was an integral part of religious ceremony.[8]

The conversion of Africans to Afro-American Christians did not destroy traditional worship forms. A Virginia slave recalled one religious service in striking detail:

The way in which we worshiped is almost indescribable. The singing was accompanied by a certain ecstasy of motion, clapping of hands, tossing of heads, which could continue without cessation about half an hour; one would lead off in a kind of recitative style, others joining in the chorus. The old house partook of the ecstasy; it rang with their jubilant shouts, and shook in all its joints.[9]

Such unrestrained religious celebrations were commonly remarked upon by nineteenth-century witnesses. Charles Joyner, in his study of slave life in the low country of South Carolina, quoted contemporary observers who were struck by the "noisy demonstrations of hands and feet, and extravagant, wild, hysterical gyrations of the body." Folklorist Lydia Parrish, studying black culture in the Georgia Sea Islands almost one hundred years after emancipation, observed that religious dances like the ring shout continued to be performed. John Lomax saw shouts danced in Texas, Louisiana, and Georgia in the post–World War II years. He described a total emotional and physical involvement, "with the whole body, with hands, feet, belly, and hips." "The worship," he reported "is, basically, a dancing-singing phenomenon."[10]

To the European-trained eye such gyrations, made blasphemous by their religious context, illustrated the total debasement of the African "heathen." Masters less concerned with the spiritual life of their slaves were likely to find these "carryings on" amusing. Yet, to the African, the separation of sacred and secular seemed as artificial as the separation of physical and spiritual. From the African, and consequently the Afro-American, viewpoint no such distinction seemed reasonable—nor was it practical.

Just as Afro-American religious ceremonies could take on what appeared to whites to be secular sounds and movements, so what appeared as secular entertainment might include sacred form and content. One slave explained how an informal social gathering might slip naturally into a community celebration of life and the power of the spirit. "At night, especially in the summer time, after everybody had eaten supper, it was a common thing for us to sit outside. . . . Sometimes someone would start humming an old hymn and then the next door neighbor would pick it up." As the song spread, so did a strengthening of the resolve to resist the institution geared to strip the slave of basic humanity. Such spontaneous interludes reaffirmed human community through a spiritual convention both religious and socio-political.[11]

This combining of sacred and secular was also evident in the political organization of the slave quarters. As was true in West Africa, religious leaders often represented slaves in political matters. Planters and overseers realized the influence that the plantation exhorter had over the slaves and were often suspicious of his power. Whites watched those who ministered to the religious needs of the slaves for signs that sacred messages might carry potentially dangerous consequences. This situation encouraged the use of double messages between minister and congregation, and ultimately among members of the slave community.[12]

Religious beliefs also reflected both the African roots and the political circumstance of the slave. The Christian concept of original sin did not exist in traditional West African religion. African slaves and their Afro-American descendants refused to accept completely the notion held by their masters that human beings were inherently sinful. Planters found a justification for human bondage in the biblical story of the sins and consequent curse of Ham, but slaves rejected the belief that their bondage was justified as God's punishment inflicted on their race. "I was not very long in finding out," recalled Frederick Douglass, that "it was not color, but crime, not God, but man, that afforded the true explanation of the existence of slavery."[13]

When slaves spoke of sin, they understood it to encompass unjust human acts. Those who enslaved fellow humans committed a grave sin that a just God would not ignore. "You'll see de world on fire," went one spiritual, "see the moon a-bleedin' . . . see the forked lightning . . . see the righteous marching . . . no sun to burn you . . . no hard trails . . . no whip a-crackin' . . . no evil doers." The Africans accepted no guilt for their enslavement. Instead they celebrated life and were sure that God would collect outstanding debts on judgment day.[14]

The conception of a just God who was active in the world also held within it the basis for a theology of resistance. Compatible with a philosophy that drew few distinctions between the present world and the hereafter, this brand of theology, in the hands of a black rebel, could become a powerful tool for inspiring slave rebellion. Denmark Vesey, free craftsman and former slave, linked the right of slaves to rise against their bondage to God's plan for this world. Using the African Methodist Church as a base, Vesey planned and organized an abortive slave uprising in Charleston, South Carolina. The slave minister Nat Turner, who led the most devastating slave revolt in American history, used the Bible and religious visions as evidence of God's blessing on his strike in Virginia.[15]

In keeping with what Eugene Genovese in *Roll, Jordan, Roll* (1974) called "a necessary and intrinsic ambiguity that reflects a view of the world in which the spiritual and the material merge," the consequences of God's justice for the Afro-American were also ambiguous. The belief in a just God could counsel either uprising against oppressors, as it did for Vesey, or a forbearance in the face of the assurance of the eventual triumph of justice. Just as slave songs carried messages for the sacred and the secular worlds, both exhortations to rebellion and counsels of patience could coexist, with the emphasis shifting according to concrete circumstance.[16]

From the relative safety of the North, free blacks and fugitive slaves were at greater liberty to espouse publicly the call to action that was a part of Afro-Christian theology. David Walker in his famous 1830 *Appeal* argued that Christian duty compelled the slave to seek freedom actively, by violent means if necessary. In light of subsequent historical debates and of the aims of slaveholders, Walker's assumption that Christianity had not incapacitated slaves for active resistance is noteworthy. For blacks, Christianity simultaneously comforted in suffering, promised freedom, and urged the liberation of the oppressed.[17]

Slaves who were convinced by scriptural admonitions to obey their masters often exasperated other slaves. "I could entertain no such nonsense as this; and I almost lost my patience when I found any colored man weak enough to believe such stuff," wrote Douglass. John White was slightly more tolerant of a black preacher's call for the acceptance of white superiority and authority. "I reckon," he said, "the old preacher was worrying more about the bullwhip than the Bible." Even white ministers understood the reaction of black audiences to such messages. In 1833 one-half the southern black listeners walked out on a white evangelist's sermon that stressed fidelity and obedience. Of those who remained, he recounted, many declared "they did not care if they ever heard me preach again."[18]

Escaped slaves sometimes preached to their former masters on the sinfulness of slaveholding. In 1852 Henry Bibb penned a clear indictment to his one-time owner, Albert Silbey, and poured out his anger at the misery inflicted on his family. "Be not deceived," he wrote, "by the long practice of your church; you have an awful account to render the great Judge of the Universe, slaveholding religion is of the devil."[19]

As black theology supported the attack on slavery, it also formed the basis for active involvement in the cause of social and economic justice for free blacks. In urban areas where free blacks established communities, the church was the major social, cultural, and political institution. It provided a forum for debate and for protest organization, as well as a podium for the most controversial issues and speakers in antebellum society. When the radical white abolitionist William Lloyd Garrison needed a platform in Boston, when former slave Sojourner Truth railed against racism and sexism, when the militant black minister Henry Highland Garnet called for the participation of free blacks in slave rebellions, or when the white revolutionary John Brown recruited followers and solicited funds for his strike against slavery, the black church provided them with pulpits and enthusiastic support.[20]

While nineteenth-century white churches generally held themselves aloof from the politics of the secular world, black churches did not. Before the Civil War, Afro-Americans established many churches independent of white denominational hierarchies. One important reason for this was the freedom it provided for the participation of ministers and their congregations in political organization and protest.

Those who remained under the control of the white church often found their ministry limited. Peter Williams, Jr., the first black priest ordained in the Episcopal Church, served St. Philip's Church in New York City from 1818 to 1849. Williams's outspoken stand against the American Colonization Society and in favor of militant abolitionism embarrassed the white bishops of the Episcopal Church. They demanded the impossible—that he "confine his ministry to the gospel and stay out of political affairs." Most black ministers serving independent Afro-American congregations had no such constraints.[21]

As the abolition movement spread its message through the North, Afro-American churches contributed major organizers and theoreticians to the effort. Although some radical abolitionists criticized American churches for failing to stand against slavery, most saw the black church as an important ally. Black ministers rejected religious justifications of slavery and scripture-based support for white supremacy.

One such minister was Henry Highland Garnet, a scholar, political theoretician, and theologian.[22] Like many other black clergymen of the period, Garnet was politically active. He was a member of the antislavery Liberty Party and a regular participant in the black convention movement. He attracted national attention in 1843 at the meeting of the national black convention held that year in Buffalo, New York, where he delivered a stirring address calling for a general slave uprising. As David Walker had done a generation before, Garnet used the language of Christianity to condemn slaveholding. He also admonished slaves that "it is sinful in the extreme for you to make voluntary submission." Slaves must not wait for God to save them from bondage, for, as Garnet explained, God expected slaves to take responsibility for acquiring their own freedom. "Neither God, Nor Angels, [nor] just men, command you to suffer for a single moment. Therefore it is your solemn and imperative duty to use every means, both moral, intellectual, and physical, that promises success." Thus, not only was the destruction of slavery part of God's plan, but Garnet believed that it was part of the slaves' "Christian duty" to take an active role in the process. This is one of the most straightforward statements of the liberation perspective of black theology in the nineteenth century, and Garnet was one of the most important figures in its formulation.[23]

After the Civil War brought the abolition of slavery, the black church and hundreds of Afro-American ministers played significant roles in Reconstruction. Chaplains and missionaries supplied by the African Methodist Episcopal Church (AME) and individual independent churches ministered to the religious needs of freedmen while organizing them into effective political units. Black preachers became, in fact, the backbone of the Republican political effort in the Reconstruction South. J.T. White, a Baptist minister from Arkansas, served on the state constitutional convention and later as a member of the legislature. Despite his full political career he never relinquished his church responsibilities.[24] Before serving as United States senator, the AME minister Hiram R. Revels from Mississippi organized churches in Vicksburg and Jackson. Rev. Richard H. Cain became a formidable politician in Charleston and served on the state constitutional convention and in the state senate. He used his Emmanuel Church as his political base. Jonathan C. Gibbs, Florida's secretary of state and superintendent of education, and the Mississippi Republican James Lynch offer further examples of black preachers who were significant political leaders while not giving up their religious roles.[25]

These clergymen and their churches saw no conflict between their religious and political duties. The AME proudly announced the important political leadership its ministers were providing, and noted that "all these men remembered the 'rock whence they were hewn'—they remained strong African Methodists and are using their increased influence to spread its borders." As some of the most educated members of the community, ministers were well equipped to be political leaders, but the positive support of congregations and church hierarchies suggest additional factors. The traditional involvements and concerns of the black church, the historical position of the church in the community, and the development of black theology all supported an activist role for black ministers.[26]

As the black population began to shift toward the urban North in the early decades of the twentieth century, the growing urban ghetto became the basis for a cultural revival, symbolized by the Harlem Renaissance and the rise of what Alain Locke termed the "new Negro," a militant cultural activist. The radical politics of this era led many black intellectuals to criticize religion that pacified rather than activated the black population. Further, they wondered at a Christianity that tolerated the persecution and even murder of black Christians. How could such a religion provide a viable foundation for the black church and black progress?[27]

These criticisms notwithstanding, many large churches in the growing ghettos built on the traditional convergence of sacred and secular and espoused a theology that allowed them to become an increasingly potent political force. In such cities as Chicago, New York, and Detroit, it was common for single black churches to claim as many as 10,000 members. By 1928 there were almost 300 black churches in Chicago. The five largest boasted a seating capacity of 2,000 and memberships exceeding 10,000 each.[28]

Such concentrations of potential voters were not ignored by white or black politicians. Often political candidates made sizable contributions to a church in return for being invited to address the congregation on matters that in white churches might have been deemed inappropriately secular. The support of black ministers and their churches was important to any political campaign aimed at black voters. In 1928 Oscar DePriest was elected to represent Chicago's First Congressional District as the first Afro-American to serve in Congress since Reconstruction. Although DePriest was not a minister, he received crucial support from the city's black churches.[29]

Charles V. Hamilton, in *The Black Preacher in America* (1972), discussed the traditional role of the black preacher in ways that detailed the connection between religious leadership and political power. A large congregation provided ready-made constituents and campaign workers for a minister with political ambitions. The Sunday collection plate could yield a sizeable war chest for the campaign. A theology that called for freedom for the oppressed and stressed the interconnection between God's plan and His people's concrete responsibility impelled many ministers to political action. Nor did minister-politicians discontinue their ministerial duties once elected. "Very seldom will a preacher give up his church when he enters politics," according to Hamilton. "In a sense that would be tantamount to giving up one's political home base, which simply is not done."[30]

The importance of the church as a political springboard is amply illustrated by the career of Adam Clayton Powell, Jr., who by the mid–1960s became one of the most powerful politicians in America. Powell's father, Adam, Sr., was the pastor of Harlem's Abyssinian Baptist Church during the 1920s and early 1930s. By 1937 when Adam, Jr., succeeded his father, the church had at least 11,000 members, a permanent staff of 33, almost $500,000 in property, and an annual budget of $46,000. It owned a newspaper with a circulation of 55,000. That was an enviable base from which to launch a political move, as Powell did first with a successful run for New York City Council and next for the U.S. House of Representatives.[31]

Powell converted the Abyssinian Baptist Church into an independent political machine that freed him from the obligations other New York politicians owed Tammany Hall. With this autonomy he became a militant black leader. Although Adam Clayton Powell was more independent than most, political machines based in the church were established in other cities. As with other political machines, these black church-based ones rewarded political supporters and punished political enemies.

Even when black ministers were not running for political office, their congregations pressured them to be involved in political affairs. St. Clair Drake and Horace R. Cayton observed that to retain the allegiance of their followers [black ministers were] forced to concern themselves with a wide range of secular activities—political action, protest against discrimination, advice on securing jobs, and legal aid, and the encouragement of Negro business enterprises.[32]

There was also criticism from those who took a narrower view of the proper role of the church. Drake and Cayton, studying black Chicago in the 1940s, related criticisms of too much secular involvement that were levelled at black churches in that city. Although extremely well-attended, some claimed, "Church is a racket. . . . There's no real religion among the members. . . . Ministers don't preach against sin. . . . Church places too much emphasis upon money." Some were critical of the church, which, they said, drew large numbers of people for other than religious reasons: "[because] They 'like good singing' and 'good speaking' or because the services are 'restful and beautiful.' " These criticisms are valid only if the church is understood as solely a sacred institution divorced from active participation in the secular world. They are not so alarming if the multiple identities of the black church and the historical dictates of black theology are understood.[33]

By the middle of the twentieth century, historical circumstances had made the black church the best available institution for black political action. This, and its theological blending of sacred and secular, provided an Afro-American understanding of God upon which the civil rights movement of the 1950s and 1960s was built. Aldon Morris, Doug McAdam, and others who have recently studied the civil rights movement have emphasized the role of the black ministers and churches. The church provided the staging area for protest, the conference setting for the development of protest strategy, and the philosophy that sanctioned the civil rights movement.[34]

This view has not gone unquestioned, however. In a recent work, Adolph L. Reed, Jr., noting Martin Luther King, Jr.'s, criticism of apathetic black ministers and many southern ministers' reluctance to support confrontational strategies, argued that the black church did not universally support the civil rights movement. Basing his argument on evidence that ministers were not the majority of black leaders, that many did not support the strategies of King, and that many protest groups were not organized in the church, Reed contended that the church was not the pivotal base of the struggle for civil rights.[35] Echoing the criticisms of the early twentieth century, Reed argued that the church's political and social conservatism impeded political activism. Citing Gunnar Myrdal, E. Franklin Frazier, and John Dollard, Reed contended that the church channelled political energies to other-worldly concerns. He recognized that northern urban churches during the 1930s and 1940s did produce important political leaders, but attributed this more to the improper secularization of the church than to the imperatives of black religious organization.

Reed argued, in fact, that there is an inherent contradiction in the church's involvement in political activities, which weakens political development in black

America. Ignoring contrary historical evidence, he rigidly separated the domains of religion and politics, limited the legitimate activity of the black church solely to the religious sphere, and then defined church-based political activity as illegitimate. His central concern was "that the projection of the church as the source of leadership authenticity assigns responsibility for political legitimation to an intrinsically antipolitical agency."[36]

From this analysis Reed argued that Jesse Jackson's presidential campaign in 1984 symbolized the essential illegitimacy of the involvement of the clerical elite in democratic politics. The church, which he contended operated historically as an institution that failed to challenge oppression, had no mandate to direct sociopolitical change. The multiplicity of black interests, the contending interests of diverse groups in black society, could not be represented by someone whose standing derived from his leadership in an other-worldly institution in essential opposition to the world of politics.

Reed failed to interpret accurately the historical or contemporary role of the black church. Part of what he interpreted as history was the record of the slaves' concealment from the master of the threatening implications of black theological concepts. It is not surprising that southern black churches were less publicly supportive of civil protest in the 1930s and 1940s than their northern counterparts. There were greater risks for such support in Birmingham or even Atlanta than in Chicago or New York. The same had been true in the years before the Civil War, as Garnet and others recognized.

Reed dismissed Everett Ladd's study of black leadership in mid–1960s Winston-Salem, North Carolina, and Greenville, South Carolina, simply because it failed to show that black ministers constituted the majority of that leadership. Yet, from 22 to 28 percent of these leaders were ministers. It is significant that these percentages were far greater than the percentage of ministers in the black populations of these cities. Ministers were not the majority of the leadership, but they were disproportionately represented among the leaders.[37]

Reed criticized Aldon Morris for singling out the church as the major institutional base during the civil rights movement and pointed out that black colleges also were important institutional supporters. Of course, Morris did not argue that the church was the only institutional base of the movement, but equally important is the fact that no black college during the 1950s and 1960s was unaffected by the traditional black church. That all Afro-American churches and ministers, North and South, did not agree on the tactics and strategies of individual civil rights campaigns, or that there were many personality and philosophical differences within the religious community should not be surprising, especially not to Reed who rightly argued that blacks are not politically monolithic.

Jesse Jackson's presidential campaigns must be understood in the context of the historical relationship between political action and religious expression in black society. The continuing acceptance of their legitimate interconnection is further underscored by the careers of minister-politicians like Andrew Young,

William Gray III, and Walter Fauntroy, or the many other black politicians who draw heavily on the support of the black church. Explanations of this phenomenon must necessarily rest on an understanding of the development of Afro-American theology.

Historical studies are now available to theologians studying the evolution and function of religion in black society. Their task is an important one, for it illuminates the religious basis from which racial oppression has been confronted and from which the oppressed have worked toward liberation. Such study gives a better understanding of the dynamic nature of the Judeo-Christian tradition, which developed and continues to develop in response to historical necessity.

Studying black theology in its Afro-American historical context has much to offer the wider religious community as well. In one sense, Christianity emerged as a ''folk religion,'' with a theology grounded in the experience of an oppressed people. Black theology, then, may provide a new perspective on the historical basis of Christianity and a new appreciation for the concrete, everyday relevance of its developing theology.

NOTES

The authors express their appreciation to Rob Forbes for his insightful comments on this article.

   1. According to the black theologian James Cone,

   the origin of black theology has three contexts: (1) the civil rights movement of the 1950s and 1960s, largely associated with Martin Luther King, Jr.; (2) the publication of Joseph Washington's book, *Black Religion* (1964); and (3) the rise of the black power movement, strongly influenced by Malcolm X's philosophy of black nationalism.

James H. Cone, *For My People* (New York, 1984), 6. See also James Cone, *A Black Theology of Liberation* (2nd ed., Maryknoll, N.Y., 1986). For the Washington quotation, see Cone, *For My People*, 9.
   2. Eric Lincoln, ed., *The Black Experience in Religion* (New York, 1974), 1.
   3. See, for example, John Blassingame, *The Slave Community* (New York, 1972); Eugene Genovese, *Roll, Jordan, Roll* (New York, 1974); Lawrence W. Levine, *Black Culture and Black Consciousness* (New York, 1977); James Oliver Horton and Lois E. Horton, *Black Bostonians* (New York, 1979).
   4. Albert J. Raboteau, *Slave Religion* (New York, 1978); Monroe Fordham, *Major Themes in Northern Black Thought, 1800–1860* (Hicksville, N.Y., 1975).
   5. Aylward Shorter, quoted in James Deotis Roberts, *Black Theology Today* (Lewiston, N.Y., 1983), 8; Sterling Stuckey, *Slave Culture* (New York, 1987), 24.
   6. Stuckey, *Slave Culture*, 33.
   7. Levine, *Black Culture*, 15–18.
   8. Stuckey, *Slave Culture*.
   9. James L. Smith, *Autobiography of James L. Smith* (Norwich, Conn., 1881), 27.
   10. Charles Joyner, *Down by the Riverside* (Urbana, Ill., 1984), 160; Lydia Parrish,

Slave Songs of the Georgia Sea Islands (New York, 1942); John A. Lomax and Alan Lomax, *Folk Song U.S.A.* (New York, 1947), 335.

11. Leslie Howard Owens, *This Species of Property: Slave Life and Culture in the Old South* (New York, 1976), 159.

12. There are many historical accounts of this phenomenon. See Genovese, *Roll, Jordan, Roll*, or Charles V. Hamilton, *The Black Preacher in America* (New York, 1972). Genovese aptly observed that "the preacher walked a tightrope," caught between the requirements of the master and the needs and expectations of the slave congregation (p. 263).

13. Stuckey, *Slave Culture*, 30–31; Frederick Douglass, *My Bondage and My Freedom* (New York, 1855), 90.

14. Levine, *Black Culture*, 38.

15. Robert S. Starobin, ed., *Denmark Vesey: The Slave Conspiracy of 1822* (Englewood Cliffs, N.J., 1970); Thomas R. Gray, ed., *The Confessions of Nat Turner, the Leader of the Late Insurrection in Southampton (County) Va.* (Baltimore, 1831).

16. Genovese, *Roll, Jordan, Roll*, 248–49.

17. David Walker, *Walker's Appeal in Four Articles* (Boston, 1830).

18. Douglass, *My Bondage*, 159; John White, quoted in V. P. Franklin, *Black Self-Determination* (Westport, Conn., 1984), 57.

19. Henry Bibb, quoted in Franklin, *Black Self-Determination*, 59.

20. For the social and political importance of the church, see Horton and Horton, *Black Bostonians*; Leonard P. Curry, *The Free Black in Urban America, 1800–1850* (Chicago, 1981); Philip S. Foner, *History of Black Americans* (Westport, Conn., 1975–1983), vols. 1–3; Vincent Harding, *There Is a River* (New York, 1981).

21. Hamilton, *Black Preacher in America*, 41.

22. As a child, Garnet escaped with his family from slavery in Maryland. He lived for a time in New York City, was educated at Oneida Institute in Whitesboro, N.Y., and finally became minister of a Presbyterian church in Troy, N.Y. Henry J. Young, *Major Black Religious Leaders, 1755–1940* (Nashville, 1977), 85–97.

23. Ibid., 93. The National Negro Convention, begun in 1830, served as a forum for the discussion of antislavery, anti-colonization, and other issues of concern to Afro-Americans. Delegates were selected from many northern states. The convention met eleven times before the Civil War, and five of its first six meetings were held in Philadelphia. See Howard Holman Bell, *A Survey of the Negro Convention Movement, 1830–1861* (New York, 1969). There were also periodic state and local conventions. For information on these, see Philip S. Foner and George E. Walker, eds., *Proceedings of the Black State Conventions, 1840–1865* (Philadelphia, 1979).

24. Hamilton, *Black Preacher in America*.

25. Leon Litwack, *Been in the Storm So Long* (New York, 1979).

26. Ibid., 471.

27. Earl E. Thorpe, *The Mind of the Negro: An Intellectual History of Negro Americans* (Baton Rouge, 1961); Benjamin Mays, *The Negro's God* (Boston, 1939).

28. St. Clair Drake and Horace R. Cayton, *Black Metropolis* (New York, 1945); Allan H. Spear, *Black Chicago: The Making of a Negro Ghetto, 1890–1920* (Chicago, 1967).

29. Ibid.

30. Hamilton, *Black Preacher in America*, 111.

31. Ibid.

32. St. Clair Drake and Horace R. Cayton, "The Churches of Bronzeville," in Milton

C. Sernett, ed., *Afro-American Religious History: A Documentary Witness* (Durham, N.C., 1985), 362, 347–63.

33. Drake and Cayton, *Black Metropolis*, 419, 423.

34. Aldon D. Morris, *The Origins of the Civil Rights Movement* (New York, 1984); Doug McAdam, *Political Process and the Development of Black Insurgency, 1930–1970* (Chicago, 1982).

35. Adolph L. Reed, Jr., *The Jesse Jackson Phenomenon: The Crisis of Purpose in Afro-American Politics* (New Haven, 1986).

36. Ibid., 60.

37. See Everett Carl Ladd, Jr., *Negro Political Leadership in the South* (Ithaca, N.Y., 1966). For Reed's evaluation of Ladd, see Reed, Jr., *Jesse Jackson Phenomenon*, 50–51.

4

Southern Protestant Clergy and the Disfranchisement of Blacks

Jon L. Wakelyn

At the end of the nineteenth century, in legislatures and constitutional conventions, political leaders throughout most of the southern states devised laws to restrict or abolish black voting. These acts of disfranchisement followed years of post-Reconstruction racial prejudice and violence that had steadily eroded black rights. The white leaders blamed agrarian political unrest, voter corruption, and the need for progressive reforms in state governments as factors contributing to their acts of disfranchisement. Political reformers and reactionaries alike supported and lobbied for this action, and heralded it as in the best interests of blacks as well as whites.[1]

Many of the South's mainline Protestant ministers verbally, and sometimes actively, joined in this near unanimity of white agitation for black disfranchisement. In doing so they continued a role in public life that had begun for many during the Civil War, although it seemingly violated the historical prejudice of the clergy against social-political action or cooperation with and use of the civil authority. The efforts of these clergy to achieve disfranchisement built on their earlier activity, and reveal much of what they expected from the so-called reform state governments.[2] Analysis of their actions also tells something about the process that transformed a number of southern clergy into social-political activists. Many other southern clergy claimed to be shocked by the activities of their reform-minded brethren and charged them with abandoning the sacred beliefs of individual regeneration for Arminianism and worldly concerns.[3] The bitterness of their language betrayed the way in which clerical involvement in the secular world contradicted religious beliefs that dated back to the American Revolution, if not to the origins of Protestantism itself.[4]

Separation from the state and non-involvement in social action had made up part of the faith statement of the mainline Protestant denominations, North and

South, since the Revolutionary era. Products of evangelical religious revivals, of emerging individualistic, capitalistic values, and of distrust of state interference in church affairs, their clerical leaders had preached anti-institutionalism and self-regeneration. They had seen their duty as instructors to assist each person to understand the need for personal salvation. They had also claimed that concern for personal salvation separated them from interest in the needs of this world. Thus, the majority of early nineteenth-century mainline clergy had simply rejected the idea of any institutional activity to achieve personal salvation. This led them to repudiate state action and to oppose organized social reform activities.[5]

However, during the early nineteenth century a number of northern clergy had begun to question these beliefs. They had come to the conclusion that their abstention from secular concerns and their faith in other-worldliness actually turned them toward reform activity, which included moral condemnation of the evils of slave ownership for both slaves and slaveowners. Their theology of self-help had led them to search for signs of good deeds among their brethren. But these clerical reformers had not been able to agree on how to recognize these signs, or how to accomplish these deeds. Stanley Elkins's skilled analysis of these reform activities has discovered at their core an anti-institutional and therefore anti-governmental bias. These beliefs forced many reform clergy to organize their own extra-governmental, voluntary reform societies.[6]

In the conservative, race-obsessed, intensely self-conscious antebellum South, the majority of evangelical clergy had refused to respond to the problems of slavery. If individuals chose to own slaves, the clergy had stated, then the owners had to develop their moral criteria for the treatment of slaves. The clergy's opposition to participating in worldly issues had nullified most of them as commentators on that system of labor. Nevertheless, as Anne Loveland has shown, a few reform-minded southern Protestant clergy had railed against the evils of slavery in hopes of saving white planters' souls. The temptation to ill-treatment, to wantonness, to setting a poor example for one's neighbors, from owning slaves had led some clergy to call for moral reform, in terms of individual salvation, of course. A few mainline ministers had taken the next step and directly or indirectly lobbied state governments and courts to revise laws to protect the slaves' rights.[7]

During the Civil War and Reconstruction, a time of troubles for the region, a number of mainline southern Protestant clergy had become active in socio-political life. Many of them had openly supported secession. Others had become chaplains, medics, and even combatants in order to support the troops and to defend the homeland. A number of these young men would later rise to positions of prominence in the church and seminary life of the New South. Other preachers had remained at home to rally support for the Confederate government. These clergy, both behind and on the battle lines, had turned their theological beliefs into instruments of social and political action.[8] But because they believed their task to be merely to attend to spiritual needs, most clergy had stayed out of the fray and preached on individual self-help and the fatalistic acceptance of God's will.[9]

Whether politically active or passive in the war, many southern ministers encountered even greater public needs for their services afterwards, because of what they perceived as a leadership vacuum during the dark days of Reconstruction and the the early, more hopeful ones of the New South. Perhaps also because of the need for spiritual regeneration in a region many thought God had deserted, a number of clergy overcame their fears of secularism to propagandize from the pulpit for a new, restored southern society. Others actually attempted social action as they helped to feed and clothe the many whites left destitute from the war. Some took part in schemes to educate the white masses in order to prepare them for the new industrial age. The plight of the freedman also interested southern clergy who had turned to social action. Their motives might have mixed humanitarian concerns with a desire to proselytize or to control the newly freed man, but they did assist blacks to participate in the economic and social life of the New South. To aid their people, some of those reform-minded clergy were willing to work with hated northern churches and private organizations, and even to support federal government activities.[10]

But the historical religious values that had so long been a source of clerical resistance to social action continued to influence the activities of many southern clergy. In 1898 the Baptist minister, social reformer, and former Confederate congressman, Jabez L. M. Curry, spoke for many a worried minister when he attacked northern governmental interference in southern life. Curry called for an end to all clerical cooperation with governmental agencies. Perhaps because of resentment among their white flocks, other reform-minded clergy refused assistance to former slaves. Paul Gaston, probably the most sensitive critic of the language of post-Reconstruction southern economic reform, has noted that in the 1880s, with the South's failure to achieve economic and social reforms, many of the clergy retreated from activism into individual spiritual healing.[11]

Despite their disappointments and the resentment towards them of many, a number of clerical reformers continued to support social activities throughout the last decade of the century. Reforms in education became their preeminent interest and the issue to which they turned with the most fervor. These reformers believed that the poorer whites had to be made literate in order for them to participate in both the spiritual and the material life of the New South. Even the wary reformer Jabez L. M. Curry supported southern attempts to gain financial aid from northern voluntary charitable organizations in order to upgrade the South's public school system. Clerical leaders in higher education asked for state aid to private denominational colleges. After all, antebellum southern church schools had long been in the habit of lobbying for some kind of state support. This experience came in handy as New South church leaders made an all out effort to gain state funds to upgrade and reform college and seminary curricula in hopes of meeting the religious needs of a changing society. Most notable in this endeavor were the actions of the Methodist minister-educators, such as Atticus Greene Haygood and Warren Aiken Candler of Emory University, and John C. Kilgo of Duke. Beginning in 1894, Candler lobbied the Georgia legislature to relieve the Emory endowment from taxation and to endow a chair in political economy. Haygood and Kilgo lectured their alumni, wrote in their school papers, and edited college religious journals, all in the name of upgrading the level of education for a responsible clergy and laity.[12]

Education for blacks also interested the reform-minded clergy. They believed that the New South needed educated blacks, who would then be knowledgeable participants in politics and support the interests of a white-imposed social order. (None seemed to grasp that an educated black people might produce the opposite effect.) Bishop Haygood gave up a clerical post in 1883 to become director of the Slater Fund for black education, and he personally raised funds for black schools. Haygood's protégé, Warren Aiken Candler, also called for the states as well as the churches to invest in higher education for black students. During the 1890s Candler served on the board of trustees of Paine College, a black institution. At first he sought to link black education with black attendance at white churches. But by the 1890s Candler supported separate black education and churches.[13]

The Episcopal bishop of Kentucky, Thomas Underwood Dudley, spoke for many clerical reformers when he declared that the church and the southern people had a God-given responsibility to care for black people. Dudley helped to develop food programs for blacks, and he also participated in the formation of home mission societies. Edgar Gardner Murphy, an Episcopal minister from Montgomery, Alabama, promoted separate business and education for the black community, acts that he believed would someday aid all southern society. A symposium on society and religion that Murphy held at Montgomery in January 1901, had as its main theme the scientific study of race relations. He lobbied for funds for a proposed magazine, *Race Relations*, but was unable to raise adequate funding. Murphy resigned his pulpit in 1901 to direct the Southern Education Board, a fundraising and lobbying organization devoted to many reform causes, including the quality of black life. In his 1904 book, *The Problem of the Present South*, Murphy announced what became a most important reform activity of the southern clergy. He accepted segregation of the races, but vowed to support the movement for equal governmental expenditures for blacks.[14]

Other reform activities of the New South clergy in the 1890s included efforts to pass child labor laws, anti-gambling laws, and laws to prohibit alcohol consumption. In the Charlotte-based *Presbyterian Standard*, the Presbyterian minister Alexander McKelway spoke out against the exploitation of children in the work force. McKelway and his friend Edgar Gardner Murphy demanded that state governments perform like churches and show compassion for poor youths. Murphy urged his fellow clergy to analyze societal needs so that they could support the southern social order. Because the southern family served as a bulwark of the social order, child care in the work force became his special concern. Bishop Candler hoped that the South would take care of its work-place problems without outside interference. He supported state child labor laws, and during the early years of the new century he assisted his friend, the political leader Hoke Smith, to write such laws for Georgia. Other clerical reformers claimed that state gambling laws and alcohol consumption contributed to moral evil and political corruption. In 1908 Edgar Young Mullins, president of the Baptist Theological Seminary, called for reform of gambling and alcohol consumption throughout the South. But Mullins made it clear that his use of the state was to legislate on personal morality only.[15]

These late-nineteenth-century clerical reform leaders had entered the public arena vigorously. A number of them attempted to analyze and explain their actions because they sensed resistance from other church leaders. Their new religious beliefs required a revised theology, and they needed a strategy for their new social-political activities. Those clergy who wrote about their activities attempted to repudiate charges of worldliness, fought among themselves about how to explain their new theology, and tried to describe how their new social action worked. In doing so, they revealed some of the reasons that eventually led them to deny black people the right to vote.

But most clerical reformers never really attempted to explain their activities. This seeming silence and inattention to the relationship between their actions and their beliefs has led historians such as Samuel Hill to ignore the writings of reform clergy and to insist that most mainline Protestant reformers separated their social from their spiritual mission, and thus weakened their will to participate in social movements.[16] This charge against those reformers resonates throughout the history of the modern South, for it describes the dilemma between the felt need for social-political action and the means to achieve it that continues in the southern churches to the present. But, of course, they did participate in social reform, even if some of their actions appeared to nullify the very reforms they sought.

Some clerical reformers offered arguments against reform, and thus appeared to repudiate their own actions. Edgar Young Mullins was the Mississippi-born son of a wealthy slave-owning planter, a Baptist minister, and president of the prestigious Southern Baptist Theological Seminary from 1899 to 1928. In his most important work, *The Axioms of Religion* (1908), he struggled with his response to the social gospel. He wrote, "We need, therefore, a clearer grasp of the nature and limits of the social duties of the church." Although personally a social activist, Mullins maintained an anti-institutional stance and condemned his Episcopal and Methodist brothers for operating collectively within the jurisdiction of the state. He expected individuals to decide on reform activities for themselves and rejected "mere sociological Christianity" with the evangelical warning that "inequalities in human personality will always create inequalities of condition." That meant reformers gained the freedom to determine their own actions, but there was little they could hope to accomplish. Moreover, Mullins warned, graft and corruption in government kept religious reformers from use of the state as the instrument of their actions.[17] Organized social action, then, seemed both religiously unacceptable and politically impossible.

Other social-political reformers among the clergy also used the Bible to justify, explain, and guide them, but they drew opposite conclusions from Mullins. One writer in the *Baptist Review and Expositor*, edited at Mullins's Southern Baptist Theological Seminary, declared in 1904 that Christianity is "essentially a political principle and a political power." He claimed that Christian stewardship justified social action. Wilbur Fisk Tillett wrote that "as long as improvement of worldly conditions" had roots in Christian salvation, men should "use the power of this world for beneficial ends in the present." In short, social-reform clergy found "something sacred in the secular and much that is divine in what is most human."[18]

These arguments from the southern clergy necessarily pointed to a view of man's nature that attempted to revise the historic Protestant theory of human behavior. They had modified traditional Christian doctrine to comply "with the age's spirit of affirmation of the capacity of human beings to bring about moral and material progress." St. Paul thus defeated Calvin in this struggle to humanize Christ, an action that led to an image of salvation-through-deeds that insisted that human nature could evolve for the better. The call to action rooted salvation in the improvement of worldly conditions.[19] Thus, the reform-minded minister Dean William Porcher DuBose of the Protestant Episcopal Seminary at Sewanee, Tennessee, had learned about social responsibility as a soldier in the Confederacy. He admonished his students to follow Christ; they understood what he meant when he proclaimed that "no man lives unto himself."[20]

In order to break down the "artificial barriers between the sacred and the secular," to turn individual virtue into social action, others discussed the process by which good men achieved social-political reform. Professors at the major urban southern universities and seminaries completely revamped their courses to fit their new beliefs. Many of them began to teach sociology, a subject they called the science of society. During the academic year 1900–1901 Wilbur Fisk Tillett, dean of the School of Religion at Vanderbilt University, established a Department of Applied Christianity in order to develop methods to ameliorate social ills. The emphasis in religious education, he insisted, should shift from polemics to ethics, "from rhetoric and imagination to logic and science." Another college instructor described the "sociological function of the ministry," as he called for a new professionalism among the clergy. The basis for reform became the study of public welfare.[21] That study also led clerical reformers to define one of their tasks as the need to clean up the instrument of reform, the government. Edgar Gardner Murphy called this "applied Christianity," a term he borrowed from his mentor, Dean DuBose. Murphy asked that the new science of faith be applied to the state's actions—"And by the state I here mean no merely artificial political entity, but the local organ and expression of our social responsibility."[22]

This group of reform clergy actually hoped to participate in state activities.

Beginning in the 1890s, Thomas Pearce Bailey, dean of the School of Education at the University of Mississippi and an ordained Episcopal priest, taught courses in moral philosophy for over twenty years to many of the reform clergy. In his lectures he exclaimed: "Will the church leave the study of the negro question to purely secular agencies that care nothing about the negro's soul? . . . Shall we do as one of our bishops advises—do as we are doing and leave results in the hands of Providence, or shall we take it that Providence expects us to be provident and foresighted and scientific in the Lord's work?"[23] For Dean Bailey the state itself became the instrument of providence.

But Bailey also issued a veiled warning about the means to achieve social reform. The state governments obviously had become the best instrument for the clergy to achieve their goals. Yet Bailey and others regarded that secular entity as a "corrupt vessel" that frightened those who wanted to use it. For if government could be a power for good, it could also be one for evil. That is why so many of those clergy reformers called for renovation of the state, for the church to cleanse the government.[24]

The reform clergy had found hope in their new theology for man's actions, one that allowed them to enter the public fray in order to help their fellow human beings. They had studied how to behave collectively. That study had led them to cross, although always reluctantly, the once sacred barriers between church and state to use government for reform. But what if the "vessel" turned out to be too corrupt for even the saints to use?

That question lay behind the support of the reform clergy for black disfranchisement. Its members were defensive of their new activist role in society and wary of their own activities. Their actions to remove blacks from political life appeared to contradict the role that they had claimed, justified, and carried out for themselves. Nevertheless, they used many of the tools of reform that they had developed for other social activities to combat black voting.

As southern state legislatures began to debate disfranchisement of blacks during the fateful 1898–1908 decade, many of the reform clergy openly supported their efforts. The Baptist minister and professor of English literature at the University of Georgia, Benjamin Franklin Riley, supported the Georgia legislature's disfranchisement debates in his many histories of southern Baptist life, most particularly the influential *White Man's Burden*, in his classes, and in his sermons. The famous education reformer, former political officeholder, historian, and Baptist minister, Jabez L. M. Curry, joined in the call for disfranchisement. He became a leader in the movement to repeal the Fifteenth Amendment. Curry also made an important speech to the Louisiana Constitutional Convention of 1898 in which he advocated the disfranchisement of blacks. The lay Baptist minister, son of a minister, and future United States Senator, Josiah William Bailey, used his editorial column and printed articles in the prestigious *Biblical Recorder*, to urge the North Carolina legislature to promote political reforms— among them the secret ballot, the initiative and referendum, and rigorous voting rules—that would effectively disfranchise most of the state's black men.[25]

Social-activist Episcopal church leaders also joined in the call for restrictions on black voting. The lifelong reformer Edgar Gardner Murphy wrote a letter to the 1901 Alabama Constitutional Convention, gave the opening prayer at that gathering, and preached from his Montgomery pulpit in favor of black disfranchisement. At times Murphy appeared to waffle about depriving blacks of their political rights. Yet, he most often took the position that all people, black or white, who had improper education should be barred from the political process. Thomas Pearce Bailey, another reform clergyman and educator, discussed in his classes the issues of voting rights, the role of blacks in the political process, and the very nature of the governmental process itself. He, too, spoke out against black suffrage. Even the northern-born Episcopal bishop of Arkansas, William Montgomery Browne, who would later be deposed because of his membership in the American Communist Party, called for all Episcopal priests in Arkansas to support that state's legislature as it effectively reduced black voting.[26]

At first the reform-minded Methodist clergy resisted debate in open forums on black disfranchisement. The Methodist bishop of Georgia, Atticus Greene Haygood, had long supported black rights, which included the right to vote. But in 1889 a then alcoholic and perhaps demented Haygood questioned the merits of black voting in a new edition of his *Our Brothers in Black*. By 1900 Warren Aiken Candler, the scion of an old Georgia plantation family, who later became president of Emory University, joined other mainline Protestant clergy in urging the Georgia legislature to adopt plans for the disfranchisement of blacks. Candler supported his views in the college pulpit and in his classroom lectures on moral philosophy and political economy. In a ringing defense of the right of clergy to participate in reform activity, President John Carlisle Kilgo of Duke University also took the stand against black voting. From his position as head of the Methodist seminary at Duke and in letters to clergy around the state of North Carolina, Kilgo by 1898 openly supported those who wanted to disfranchise blacks. Southern Methodism's foremost reformer activist, at least as reflected in his lectures and his publications, was Dean Wilbur Fisk Tillett of the Vanderbilt School of Religion. Yet, at the turn of the century he, too, called on both the many reform clergy he had taught and the faculty of his school to add their voices to the crescendo of clergy crying out to end black voting.[27]

Modern scholars have not hesitated to condemn these reform clergy for having turned on black people, for never having been serious about reforms, and for being the willing tools of white elites. They follow the judgment of H. Paul Douglas, who wrote in 1909 that "the Southern church shares the recognized conservatism of ecclesiastical institutions and has an additional measure of its own. It is not to discredit its ardent piety to say that it has shown itself the least adoptive of the reconstructive functions of its section." Dewey Grantham, at times somewhat sympathetic to the clergy, nevertheless asserts that they rarely participated in the progressive reform movement. For him the southern clergy's social gospel "was in considerable part a matter of conference and association rhetoric." Thomas Szasz comments that most so-called reform church leaders simply hid behind their religious traditions of non-involvement in politics to cover up their support for the economic and political status quo. Others claim that the clergy's racism determined their actions. David Reimers suggests that if blacks were believed inferior, "how could they be expected to participate in the political process, to hold office or even vote?" A few historians find proof of their arguments as to why the clergy participated in the movement for black disfranchisement in the 1904 assertion of the Methodist bishop Charles Galloway that "intelligence and wealth will and should control the administration of government affairs." For these scholars the clergy had always been agents of the southern white business elite.[28]

These many conflicting historical arguments neither convince nor get to the heart of the question of the clerical role in, and support of, black disfranchisement. Obviously, their pronouncements and the ways they supported disfranchisement give the lie to the argument that they had ceased to be, or had never been, activists. Even if they agreed neither on all reform issues nor on the tactics to be used, they did regard black disfranchisement as a reform activity. Perhaps their discussion of their actions—and they certainly attempted to explain themselves—should be heard in order to judge the motivation of those southern clergy who supported black disfranchisement at the turn of the century.

Some reform clergy explained their support for black disfranchisement in segregationist language that expressed their peculiar views of paternalist obligations. These reformers suggested that black people had to be removed from politics in order to protect them and to assist them to have peaceful lives. Separate black education, business, culture, and religion would then thrive under the tutelage of white paternalists. Social-political reformers such as Edgar Gardner Murphy clinched the paternalist rationale with the argument that social groups, not government, would serve as the principal instrument to guide and protect separate black life.[29]

Those who believed that reform capitalism or Social Darwinism, as they understood it, could help blacks also supported disfranchisement. Their reasons centered on making a competitive, business-minded black society. Successful black businesses, they argued, would impress the white middle classes and eventually lead them to accept a viable black presence in southern society. These white reformers, especially Wilbur Fisk Tillett, expected a separate, non-dependent black clergy to teach their people self-help, to rely less on government handouts, to develop self-discipline, and thus to lead in the movement to upgrade blacks' material life.[30] This free-enterprise argument, of course, also removed blacks from government, and government from black lives.

Other clerical reform leaders argued for a segregated and disfranchised black society in order to assist their poorer white constituents. Many of these clergy had long lamented the loss of poor whites from their congregations, the rise of poor-white violence toward blacks, and the inability of poor whites to compete in the new business world of the late nineteenth century. Black voters, those clergy claimed, competed with poor whites for public support. Poorer whites responded with violent outbursts, which not only disrupted the status quo but left them at the mercy of demagogic white politicians. Thus, with blacks out of the public eye through their removal from the political arena, the reform clergy could turn to the needs of white people. Of course, this form of paternalist argument led reform clergy such as Benjamin Franklin Riley to advocate disfranchisement of poor and uneducated white people also.[31] Again, the argument seemed connected to attempts at making clean government.

A few reformers, most notably Alexander J. McKelway and Wilbur Fisk Tillett, feared a decline in the quality and responsibility of political leaders, as agrarian unrest and irresponsible voters brought potentially unsatisfactory new leaders to the forefront of the political fray. That probably explains their seemingly elitist views on who should vote. A number of these clergy even turned on the few European immigrants to the South and accused them of inciting riots. They connected these riots to the new political leadership. Thus, their answer to the problem was simply to remove from all undesirables the power their votes gave to radical demagogues. After all, if reform clergy had to work with governmental officials, these leaders should represent the best men in their society.[32]

Most of these rationalizations for disfranchisement also turned on the reform clergy's analysis of educational levels, voter susceptibility to demagogues, and the resultant corruption of the political process. These qualities of an unrestricted southern electorate translated into corrupt governments that abused reform, coddled the people, and violated the clergy's historical religious beliefs. The justification for disfranchisement always seemed to relate to corrupt government, for all the clerical reformers—even those ostensibly opposed to using the state—linked government activities for themselves to some extent with the idea of clean government as an instrument for social action. A clue to the difficulty of these ministers' positions on the place of government in reform, and their attitudes toward reform itself, can be found in this apparent contradiction. In fact, it was central to their justification of black disfranchisement.

Clearly most arguments for disfranchisement developed a linkage between good government and social reform. With his distorted view of historical events, Edgar Gardner Murphy declared that during Reconstruction the black people had lost their true friends, the former planters, to public service, the result of which was the rise of political corruption in the South. In order to improve black life in the South, Murphy reasoned, corruption in government had to be erased. Others took a more state-rights line, asked that the Fifteenth Amendment be declared unconstitutional, and declared that state governments would be freed of corruption if only the federal government left them to police themselves. Edgar Young Mullins, for one, described a Christian paternalist government free of ignorance and corruption, prepared to lead in the quest for social justice and order.[33]

Those ministers who clung to beliefs in individual salvation and suspicion of the state were also convinced of the need to resort to the state as the instrument of reform. They merely reversed the central issue. Josiah William Bailey maintained that removal of black votes would indeed clean up government. But that meant reform no longer would be necessary, that clergy could leave their un-accustomed roles as social reformers and return to their true calling, the regeneration of individual souls through moral suasion.[34] Others baldly stated that black disfranchisement would remove the state from people's lives. Most explicit was the reluctant reformer Jabez L. M. Curry. Curry condemned the states for ever having defended inferior black voters and blamed those activities on the North. He claimed that new laws had "broadened citizenship beyond what the fathers had dreamed of." For him, activist church leaders who supported black disfranchisement actually wanted ultimately to diminish government interference in the lives of all southerners.[35] Thus, those whose religious beliefs called for a return to individual salvation united with those who wanted the church to be responsible for social reform in their support for disfranchisement, if not in their reasons for that action.

The often conflicting arguments that reform ministers offered to explain their support of black disfranchisement converged on a number of points. Some of the clergy insisted that they assisted black society by keeping it out of government. These leaders claimed that much of the political prejudice directed against black people related to white fears of continued government corruption. A few of the clerical reformers believed that the government had been forced into reform activity because of the continued presence of blacks in politics. To remove blacks from political activity, they believed, would ultimately allow reformers to separate their reform activities from government. That minority seemed to want to return to their historical duties of attending to individual souls. But the majority of reform clergy who described their reasons for support of black disfranchisement regarded the state as the major instrument of reform. If they were to continue as reformers, they simply had to clean up the state. The black voter became the victim of their reform.

These contradictory positions of reform and anti-reform clergy obviously give some plausibility to historians' claims about their culpability in support of business and political leadership. But this view does not give credit to a clergy that truly struggled with its role in society. The new social theology did expect to use the state as its instrument of reform. Although differences certainly existed, most reform-minded clergy were convinced that elimination of black voting was necessary to achieve a reformed state government. That belief best explains why they regarded black disfranchisement as one of their reform activities.

Modern southern clergy have continued to debate political action for social reform, with contradictions not unlike those of their predecessors. A natural tendency of many fundamentalist clergy has been to attempt to withdraw from social reform and to return to individual salvation. But the clergy have also wanted to use the state to confront the issues of prohibition, immigration restriction, child welfare, labor organizations, massive resistance to integration, and civil rights. Especially during the period of massive resistance in the 1960s, the old argument of the need to keep the clergy free from the temptation of social theology made many appear to support the sorry continuation of racial discrimination. Other members of the clergy, active in social reform, have continued to worry about the state's soul, because they still want to use it for reform.[36] At times this has worked to the benefit of those in need of social aid. At other times it has made activist clerics willing partners of the state in acts of repression. Perhaps this contradictory behavior reflects the mainstream southern ministry's inability to cope with conflict over its historical spiritual mission and its modern sense of social responsibility. Certainly the instrument of social action, the state, remains a source of concern for reform-minded clergy. To this day their conflicted view of the state impedes their efforts to achieve social reform.

NOTES

1. C. Vann Woodward, *Origins of the New South* (Baton Rouge, 1951), 321–395; J. Morgan Kousser, *The Shaping of Southern Politics* (New Haven, 1974), passim.

2. Rufus B. Spain, *At Ease in Zion* (Nashville, 1951), 212–13; Joel Williamson, *The Crucible of Race* (New York, 1984), 231, 237; Hugh C. Bailey, *Liberalism in the New South* (Coral Gables, Fla., 1969), 124.

3. See John Lee Eighmy, *Churches in Cultural Captivity: A History of the Social Attitudes of Southern Baptists* (Knoxville, 1972), passim.

4. Many studies have traced the origins of this relationship between individualistic theology and anti-statism. One recent analysis is Henry F. May, *The Enlightenment in America* (New York, 1978), 319–24.

5. Sydney E. Ahlstrom, *A Religious History of the American People* (New Haven, 1972), 360–84, 403–14; H. Richard Niebuhr, "The Protestant Movement and Democracy in the United States," in James Ward Smith and A. Leland Jamison, eds., *The Shaping of American Religion* (Princeton, N.J., 1961), 1: 20–71.

6. Stanley Elkins, *Slavery: A Problem in Institutional and Cultural Life* (Chicago, 1961), ch. 4; Ahlstrom, *Religious History of the American People*, 415–28.

7. Anne C. Loveland, *Southern Evangelicals and the Social Order, 1800–1860* (Baton Rouge, La., 1980), passim. Why the Southern clergy chose to begin their political and social activism with the Civil War is a topic that calls for more research.

8. Richard E. Beringer, et al., *Why the South Lost the Civil War* (Athens, Ga., 1986), 82–102, 268–93.

9. Beringer, et al., *Why the South Lost the Civil War*, 336–67.

10. See Charles Reagan Wilson, *Baptised in Blood: The Religion of the Lost Cause, 1865–1920* (Athens, Ga., 1980).

11. Paul Gaston, *The New South Creed* (New York, 1970), 191–92.

12. Dewey Grantham, *Southern Progressivism: The Reconciliation of Progress and Tradition* (Knoxville, 1983), 247, 255, 259, 316; Mark K. Bauman, *Warren Aiken Candler* (Metuchen, N.J., 1981), 65.

13. Williamson, *Crucible of Race*, 88–93; Bauman, *Warren Aiken Candler*, 48–65.

14. Williamson, *Crucible of Race*, 277, 331–32; Ronald C. White, Jr., "Beyond the Sacred: Edgar Gardner Murphy and a Ministry of Social Reform," *Historical Magazine of the Protestant Episcopal Church* 49 (1980): 51–69.

15. Herbert J. Doherty, Jr., "Alexander J. McKelway: Preacher to Progressives,"

Journal of Southern History 24 (1958): 177–90; Bauman, *Warren Aiken Candler*, 73; Edgar Young Mullins, *The Axioms of Religion* (Boston, 1908), 307.

16. Samuel S. Hill, Jr., *Southern Churches in Crisis* (New York, 1967), 120–27.

17. Mullins, *Axioms of Religion*, 17, 204, 305.

18. *The Baptist Review and Expositor* 1 (1904): 362–63; Wilbur Fisk Tillett, *The Hand of God in American History* (Nashville, 1922), 4.

19. William Porcher DuBois, *Turning Points of My Life* (New York, 1912), 30, 41, 42.

20. DuBois, *Turning Points of My Life*, 30, 137. Also, see Theodore DuBose Bratton, *An Apostle of Reality: The Life and Thought of the Reverend William Porcher DuBois* (London, 1936), 69, 79, 101.

21. *The Baptist Review and Expositor* 7 (1910): 22–23; 5 (1908): 225.

22. Edgar Gardner Murphy, *The Basis of Ascendancy* (New York, 1909), xii, 17.

23. Thomas Pearce Bailey, *Race Orthodoxy in the Old South* (New York, 1914), 259.

24. Ibid., 11; Jerome Dowd, *Democracy in America* (Oklahoma City, 1921), 265–99; Lester Hubert Colloms, *Wilbur Fisk Tillett* (Louisville, 1949), 152; John Carlisle Kilgo, *Willam Wallace Duncan* (privately printed, 1908), 58.

25. Benjamin Franklin Riley, *The White Man's Burden* (Birmingham, Ala., 1916), 20, 22, 227; Jabez L. M. Curry, *Principles, Utterances, and Acts of John C. Calhoun* (Chicago, 1898), 23; Jabez L. M. Curry, *Civil History of the Government of the Confederate States* (Richmond, Virginia, 1901), 307; John Robert Moore, *Senator Josiah William Bailey* (Durham, N.C., 1968), 13–18.

26. Edgar Gardner Murphy, *Open Letter on Suffrage Restriction* (n.p., 1901); Hugh C. Bailey, *Edgar Gardner Murphy: Gentle Progressive* (Coral Gables, Fla., 1968), 59–62; Grantham, *Southern Progressivism*, 239; William Montgomery Browne, *The Crucial Race Question* (Little Rock, 1907), 111–18.

27. Atticus Greene Haygood, *Our Brothers in Black* (Miami, 1969), 81–83; Williamson, *Crucible of Race*, 265–67, 280–81; Bauman, *Warren Aiken Candler*, 153; Tillett, *Hand of God in American History*, 16.

28. H. Paul Douglas, *Christian Reconstruction in the South* (Boston, 1909), 58; Grantham, *Southern Progressivism*, 22; Thomas Szasz, *The Divided Mind of Southern Protestantism, 1880–1930* (University, Ala., 1982), 62; David M. Reimers, *White Protestantism and the Negro* (New York, 1965), 38, 49. See also Paul D. Escott, *Many Excellent People: Power and Privilege in North Carolina, 1850–1900* (Chapel Hill, N.C., 1985), 259–61; and Frederick A. Bode, *Protestantism and the New South* (Charlottesville, Va., 1975), 44–45.

29. Browne, *Crucial Race Question*, 113, 134; Edgar Gardner Murphy, *Problems of the Present South* (New York, 1904), 11–13, and *The White Man and the Negro at the South* (Montgomery, Ala., 1900), 28, 31.

30. Murphy, *White Man and the Negro*, 36; Bode, *Protestantism and the New South*, 70; Tillett, *Hand of God in American History*, 16.

31. Riley, *White Man's Burden*, 20, 22, 227; Mullins, *Axioms of Religion*, 307.

32. Doherty, Jr., "Alexander J. McKelway," 188; Eighmy, *Churches in Cultural Captivity*, 46; Tillett, *Hand of God in American History*, 9.

33. Murphy, *Problems of the Present South*, 11–13; Curry, *Principles, Utterances, and Acts of John C. Calhoun*, 23; Mullins, *Axioms of Religion*, 207. See also Hugh C. Bailey, *Edgar Gardner Murphy*, 40–59, for the most thoughtful analysis of Murphy's arguments for black disfranchisement.

34. Moore, *Senator Josiah William Bailey*, 13.

35. Curry, *Civil History of the Government of the Confederate States*, 180–81; Mullins, *Axioms of Religion*, 307.

36. See Hunter Dickinson Farish, *The Circuit Rider Dismounts: A Social History of Southern Methodism* (Richmond, Va., 1938), passim, and, especially, Francis M. Wilhoit, *The Politics of Massive Resistance* (New York, 1973), 256, 259, 260, 262, 265, 267.

5

CITIZENS AND BELIEVERS: ALWAYS STRANGERS?

Harvey Cox

> I promised to write of the rise, progress and appointed end of the two cities, one of which is God's, the other this world's, in which, so far as mankind is concerned, the former is now a stranger.
>
> St. Augustine, *The City of God* 18: 1

Must the citizen of the City of God always be a stranger in the City of Man? Is there any legitimate way the believer can be a full and first-class citizen in a kingdom of this passing age? In seeking to address this question in late twentieth-century America, this essay is divided into two parts. The first deals with historical obstacles that have hindered the development of what might be called a Christian theology of citizenship. The second argues why these obstacles no longer have the weight they once did and thus suggests that it may now be more feasible to forge such a theology.

The topic is the recurrent one of the relation of the secular to the sacred—"recurrent" because the topic keeps reappearing *whatever* the reigning theory of how the sacred and the secular relate to each other. Every time the discussion seems dead for sure, the rising moon of a new theory of sacred and secular stirs the cadaver to life. The coffin lid creaks open, and the question once thought dead stalks abroad once more.

In the relatively short span of one scholar's career, at least four theories about the relation of the secular to the sacred have come and gone. The first held that secularization was a massive aberration—a falling away from a normative religious or Christian culture. Consequently it interpreted the various expressions of secularization in the light of this larger picture. Next came the theory of secularization as a relentless and unidirectional movement. This linear theory of secularization was related to cognate theories of the stages of economic development and the alleged stages of political maturation. Then came the more sophisticated theory of a dialectical relationship between secularization and revivalism. This theory, ably defended by William Bainbridge at Harvard, amasses considerable data to prove that secularization stimulates a revival of religion, which in turn looses currents of secularization, and so on. The movement continues in a challenge and response pattern. More recently, even more complex and nuanced theories have emerged. They hold mainly that there can be no global theory of secularization. They contend that patterns of secularization and re-sacralization have to be studied in very particular and local settings, and that it is misleading to make universal generalizations.[1]

Despite all these theories, one of the most persistent forms the question takes in the modern world is this: *What is the appropriate role of those persons who are at once both believers and citizens?* It immediately becomes evident that this is a question that has a very different meaning in Japan than in Iran and that the question has yet another valency when asked within the context of Western Europe and the United States. Nonetheless, the question keeps reappearing. There is a very good reason why it reappears. One may separate church from state by constitutional dictum; one may delineate the religious from the profane in analytical categories; but the dilemma of the ''citizen'' of a nation state, who is also a religious believer, is not thereby alleviated.

Looking at this dilemma from the perspective of Christianity, one is led to observe that ultimately the most enduring tension between the secular and the spiritual runs straight through the soul of the individual, that person who is a citizen of both the kingdom of God and one of the kingdoms of this world. Furthermore, the decisions such citizen believers must make press in on them every day. They involve not simply an occasional choice of whether to pay taxes to Caesar. They include questions of the daily choices churned up by two overlapping realms, both of which make their demands and in both of which one lives out one's existence. Perhaps the most vivid example of such hard choices appears when civil authorities are also Christian believers. Mario Cuomo, the governor of New York, put the matter starkly in the famous speech he gave at Notre Dame University in September, 1983:

Must politics and religion in America divide our loyalties? Does the separation of church and state imply separation between religion and politics? What is the relationship of my Catholicism to my politics? Where does one end and one begin?[2]

In view of this continuing riddle faced by a citizen-believer, one might assume that a general principle would run as follows: The stronger any person's religious commitment, the weaker will be his or her identification with a national state. The evidence, however, does *not* support this hypothesis. Often quite the opposite occurs. One has only to think, for example, of the intense patriotism exhibited by many American evangelicals and fundamentalists, or of the widely recognized tendency among American ethnic Roman Catholics to underline their loyalty to the American nation. On the other side, one notices the large numbers of upper-middle-class people in the United States and elsewhere whose sense of belonging *either* to a national state *or* to a religious community seems increasingly attenuated. Obviously, whatever solutions are chosen to lessen the tension a given person feels when confronted with these two conflicting loyalties, that of identifying more strongly with one while lessening one's sense of belonging in the other is *not* one of the most common strategies for solving the riddle. The late Cardinal Spellman of New York was not a man who sensed very much tension between his Roman Catholic faith and his American patriotism—not, that is, until he began to clash with Pope John XXIII and Pope Paul VI about the war in Vietnam. The question remains: How can one be a full, not half-hearted, citizen as a well as full believer?

In a recent paper John Coleman, S. J., has suggested that Christianity has never developed an adequate theology of citizenship. Christian theology has always emphasized, Coleman says, a certain "eschatological reserve." That certainly is an important element, he says, but the question must be asked, what next? What is the *positive* content of being a Christian citizen?[3] Christian theology has never dealt adequately with the relatively modern question of the positive significance of one's participation, as a believer, in one of the national states. Theologies exist to guide one's behavior in other aspects of the secular: theologies that instruct about being a husband or a wife, about one's professional or vocational work in the world. A vast literature of guidance and admonition has accumulated on the Christian's participation in economic organizations, labor unions, and business life. If Coleman is right that an adequate theology of citizenship in the nation state never appeared, one might well ask why?

This essay argues that the reason an adequate theological understanding of the appropriate role of the believer in the public sphere has not developed is that the concept "citizen" is itself an *ideological* construct. This has created two historical obstacles. However, neither obstacle seems to be as weighty in the present as it once was in the past. This, in turn, may now clear the way for the development of a positive theology of Christian citizenship.

The two historical obstacles are both fused with the concept of citizenship itself. As such, they obscure an important tension between the classical idea of the *civitas* and the more modern bourgeois idea of the *citoyen*. This fusion is due first to the special historical circumstances under which the concept of the national state appeared in the West, a context that generated claims to a higher and prior loyalty. It is also due to the way these same conditions shaped the view of something that came to be called the "public realm" as an area purged of religious references.

THE NATIONAL STATE

In the eighteenth and nineteenth centuries a tense rivalry developed in the West between church and state, especially in countries within the Catholic realm.

The forces representing the state spoke for the interests of a particular and newly emergent class, the bourgeoisie. The increasing tempo of national state development meant that individuals were faced with conflicting claims on their loyalty from the national community on the one side and the religious community on the other.

It is interesting to recall that the victory of this concept of the national state did not occur without considerable opposition and debate. Several highly significant figures in the international scene opposed the idea vigorously from different perspectives: Lenin, following the teachings of Marx, taught that an international revolution would eventually lead to the withering away of national states; Woodrow Wilson proposed a League of Nations to which various national states would gradually hand over increasing amounts of their sovereignty; and from Pope Leo XIII to Pius XII the papacy taught a vision of a new Christendom in which national states would diminish in importance within the family of the church, a vision that has continued to influence European thinkers.

Post-revolutionary France and late-nineteenth-century Italy are the two prime examples of the bitter clash between church and state in previously Catholic countries. The development in Roman Catholic theology of ultramontanism, culminating in the definition of the infallibility of the pope, represented one response to this rivalry. Historians now largely agree that the infallibility doctrine arose more as the result of an effort to counter the emergence of national state churches than it did for any particular ecclesiological reason within the church.

This conflict between national states and the international community of the Catholic Church continued unabated with various ups and downs until the work of Eugenio Pacelli, first as Vatican secretary of state and then as Pius XII. He tried to secure treaties with the various national states that recognized the claims of those states but that also sought to ensure the rights of the church. In the 1930s these so-called concordats were worked out even with Fascist Italy and National Socialist Germany. After World War II, it proved difficult but not impossible to negotiate and ratify such arrangements even with states having communist governments. The undergirding theological position in forming the concordats was that Catholics *could* be *both* loyal citizens of their various nation states and *also* loyal Catholics insofar as the rights of the Catholic Church to exercise its pastoral ministry and its authority over such matters as family and religious education were respected by the national state. In return, the church accepted the national state's authority over believers *as citizens*. But this was a *formal* arrangement. Its actual content varied from country to country and from time to time. The tensions have never been fully resolved, as can be seen in such figures as Cardinal Sin of Manila, the late Archbishop Romero of El Salvador, and the role of the church in Poland.[4]

In the Protestant realm the effort to define the relationship between the religious community and the national state, and therefore to clarify the predicament of those who were both believers and citizens, largely took the form of various constitutional arrangements to disestablish or "separate" church and state. This separation restricted the power of religious bodies in the public realm and denied them any kind of official status, but it also at least technically delimited the powers of the state and forbade government to intervene in the internal affairs of religious bodies or to impair their right to exercise their religious convictions.

THE PUBLIC REALM

The second historical development that loaded "citizenship" and made it difficult for the church to develop a Christian theology of citizenship was the understanding of the "public realm" that arose during the appearance of the national states, especially after the French Revolution. As recent commentators such as Karl Adorno and others have pointed out, the idea of such a "public realm" emerged only with the bourgeois revolutions that created the concept of the national state. It bears definite marks of its historical origin.[5] The triumphant bourgeoisie wanted to make the public sphere free of religion. They claimed that the public realm could be one of "rational" politics and of social emancipation. Therefore, by definition there could be no specifically religious participation in the public sphere. It was to be a realm where only open debate, rational argumentation, and logical persuasion were to be employed in discussion of public policy issues. It was to be a "value-free" realm, based on the economic concept of a free market of ideas, in which authoritarian, superstitious, or religiously legitimated ideas were excluded by their very nature. It is significant that the Declaration of Independence and Adam Smith's *Wealth of Nations* both appeared in the year 1776.

The result of this bourgeois definition of the public sphere was that citizen-believers were forced to develop a kind of "bilinguisticality." In order to speak in the public realm they had to learn the language of that sphere, a tongue that was formed by the anti-clerical and "non-religious," sometimes anti-religious, philosophies of the bourgeois thinkers who had created it. Any participant in the public realm who could be accused of bringing some kind of religious bias or theologically grounded opinion into that arena risked being excluded or silenced for not following the established rules of the game.

The result of the historic process that created the national state and the public realm was that "citizen" came to mean one who (a) *belongs* to a *national state*, and (b) *participates* in policy debate in a *public realm*. The trouble was that the two colossal historical formations that underlay the concepts of the *national state* and the *public arena* placed those who were both believers and citizens in a doubly difficult situation. Seemingly they could participate in both the sacred and secular spheres of life, but only by donning different hats and operating from different sets of premises. Within the religious community they could assume a set of shared beliefs and symbols nurtured by that community. But in the national community and its public sphere they had to assume a different set of symbols and values. Of course, in some instances, there was a certain overlapping. This area of overlapping came to be known in the United States as the "civil religion." But the problem with the civil religion then as now is that it is neither completely civil nor completely religious. At points it contradicts the symbolic universe of those in religious communities and even risks a form of idolatry. At the same time, it evokes images and values with which most secular participants in the civil community understandably feel uncomfortable.

One result of these developments is that there is no positive Christian doctrine of citizenship. The modern bourgeois concept of citizenship conceals within itself an ideology that is deeply inimical to many Christian and religious values. But all this is now changing. The last decades of the twentieth century have radically altered the global context within which the status of the national state in the public realm exists. Therefore, the problem of the citizen-believer must be worked out in a new setting. This has happened because of the subversion of precisely the two historical formations just described. A new situation has thus been created, one not without its own dangers but also replete with new possibilities for elaborating a theology of Christian citizenship. It will be argued shortly that such a project can best proceed by reclaiming the earlier classical idea of the *civitas* that was displaced by the more recent notion of the *citoyen*. But, first, it is necessary to examine *why* these dislocations in the role of the "national state" and the nature of the "public realm" have occurred.

First, the hegemony of the national state as the only accepted way of organizing the international community has suffered severe slippage. The dreams of Wilson and Lenin and the popes have not materialized, but some believe that the national state has reached a certain "crisis of legitimacy." The legitimacy of the national state has been based primarily on two pillars: its capacity to promote the welfare of its citizens and its power to protect them from foreign invasion or attack. But on both these fronts national states now find their legitimacy severely questioned. As for the "general welfare," the internationalization of the market economy has meant that national states are no longer able to guarantee to their citizens the basic necessities of life. Current panicky efforts to curb "free trade" while extolling its merits vividly reveal this inability. At the same time the advent of nuclear weapons and intercontinental delivery systems means that states are not able to offer their citizens even minimal protection from foreign foes. The Star Wars fantasy is the last gasp of the dying myth that the national state can protect its citizens from external attack.

The second reason why it is now possible to venture a new and positive theology of Christian citizenship is the massive "return" of religion to the public realm. Commentators on the future of religion not many decades ago frequently conceded that religion might continue to exist for decades or even centuries, but they insisted it would be contained within the private or familial circle. It would have only a lessening impact on public policy formation. This, of course, has not happened. Instead, there has been a massive reappearance of religious personages and institutions in the public political realm in areas as disparate as Japan and Poland, Brazil and Iran, the United States and Israel.

Much of the current discussion about the relationship of religion to the political order in the United States is cast either in terms of the need for more religion and morality in public life *or* of the danger posed to the commonwealth by fanaticism, bigotry, and divisiveness. But it is possible to examine the issue in a mood that is at once more modest and more positive. Religiously motivated citizens can possibly make a positive contribution to the restoration of the reality of *citizenship* by reclaiming *civitas* in a republic where much evidence indicates it is faltering. If religious believers understand and respect the religious *pluralism* of the United States, and the fragile fabric by which persons and groups with different spiritual orientations are bound together in society, then they may be able to bring a gift that will strengthen and deepen citizenship in a democracy rather than diminish it.

At the start one should recall that the word "citizen" or *citoyen* stems from the same root as "civility" and "civilian." It goes back to the notion of the *civitas*, the classic polity in which each person played a role not as a cleric or as a soldier but as a participant in a publicly defined order.

Civitas is also the source of the word "civility." In its original meaning, civility meant that form of participation appropriate to this civic community, that is, pertaining to one's citizenship. Only in recent years has the word "civility" taken on the diminished meaning now normally attached to it: that of being deferential or polite, or cultivating the habit of speaking in moderated tones. In its classical sense, however, civility does *not* mean mere propriety. It means that set of skills and commitments appropriate to participation in the *civitas*.

At the same time that the idea of the "public sphere" is a recent reductionist redefinition of the much older notion of the *civitas*, dating only from the bourgeois revolutions of the late eighteenth century, it is also a distortion of *civitas* because it subtracts something vital and important away from the notion of *civitas*. It did so originally by trying to make the public sphere a realm free of religious rhetoric, and does so more recently by trying to cleanse it even of values or moral discourse and by declaring it to be an arena governed by a technical expertise that consists of the art of compromise plus an increasing body of administrative science. This is a sharp reversal of what the *civitas* meant to classical thinkers and to the great political philosophers and theologians of Western history. They also lauded skill and patience in civil debate, but they saw it primarily as a realm of *moral discourse*.

The proposition that the public realm should be free of value commitment or religious motivation is, in fact, a bourgeois ideology. It was an understandable product of the insistence by the bourgeoisie that their enemies—especially entrenched traditional religion and the customary aristocratic values of their day—should be prevented from dominating the realm of public debate. What has happened, however, is that the ideology of a "value free" public realm has become a vehicle for the new ruling elites of complex urban industrial societies to secure *their* power. It is an ideology that serves the interests of those elites and subverts justice by often preventing the participation of the less privileged sectors of the society.

The ideological function of the idea of a public sphere becomes particularly clear if one notices *where* a re-fusing of religious and political values and rhetoric takes place most often, although not always today: it is among oppressed peoples or captive nations or marginated ethnic or racial groups. In Latin America it is the poorest people, organized in base communities, who have created liberation theology, a powerful religious rhetoric, as a way of criticizing the allegedly neutral, technical, secular, and modern ruling elites of their impoverished nations. In the United States the picture is more confused since, despite the legal separation of church and state, the public square has never been "naked." Yet, even in the United States the most "visible" presidential candidate. for more reasons than one, has been Jesse Jackson, who freely combines religious and political language and who represents the social group in the United States that has endured the longest history of oppression and discrimination. If one thinks of "captive nations," obviously the country where Catholicism and national liberation are most thoroughly yoked is Poland, which labors under the yoke of an illegitimate and imposed Soviet-sponsored regime.

Because the existing notions of the nation-state and the public realm are now undergoing such severe questioning, the concept of citizenship is in crisis also. This crisis has opened the door to yet another reconsideration of Augustine's old, old question. In the United States itself in recent years a growing chorus of observers has lamented the decline of participation in the American political system. There are various theories of why this decline has set in—a decline suggested, for example, by the relatively small percentage of eligible voters who participate in national elections. Perhaps the increased visibility of religious groups and persons in the American political scene is to be attributed not simply to their growth, which seems statistically insignificant, but as a response to this progressive enfeeblement of the *civitas*.

Fifteen years ago Wilson Carey McWilliams wrote in his book, *The Idea of Fraternity in America*:

The great concern of American political philosophy has been the development of "democratic theory." That concern has focused on formal institutions and organizations, even when it rejected "formalism." In so doing, it has neglected the fact that democratic theory must also be a theory about a *demos*, about the character and relation of citizens.[6]

McWilliams is surely right. The earliest founders of the United States insisted that only with "an informed and active citizenry" would the new republic survive. But, increasingly, recent decades have witnessed a decrease in the level of participation at the polls.

Conservatives trace this decline to the growth of a gigantic national-state apparatus that is said to warp and undercut the possibility of genuine citizen participation. This conservative analysis has elements of novelty. Traditionally, conservatives have *opposed* broad participation in the polity. They have feared the excesses of majorities. Therefore, the Moral Majority is something of an anomaly. It is a conservative movement that claims to speak the mind of the "real majority." However, conservatives continue, as they have traditionally, to oppose measures that would genuinely extend voting rights to other sectors of the society, by simplifying registration or by other means of enlarging voter participation. Advocates of this view would like to diminish the size of the state so that citizen participation presumably can be increased.

A more "radical" perspective attributes the decline in citizenship to the enormous and growing power of the corporations whose influence on the *civitas* is to evacuate citizenship and to transform the *polis* into a market, not a "free" market except in strictly formal terms, but one in which money talks and wealth controls politics. It is argued from the second perspective that such an evacuation of citizenship removes it from either its classical or its modern definition, and transforms citizens into customers and eventually into consumers.

Whichever of these two diagnoses one accepts as the principal explanation for the decline in participation in the *civitas*, the result of the decline has been to deepen the chasm between the political world and the world of moral discourse. One institutional expression of this split is the so-called science of public policy formation and the rise of schools to train specialists in public policy. But the idea that public policy formation can be an administrative science from which genuine value conflict has been purged is itself clearly a version of the bourgeois myth of the "public sphere."

During the 350th anniversary of Harvard College in 1986, faculty members were asked what in their view was the most serious question facing the university in the future. Among those who responded, Prof. John Kenneth Galbraith acutely observed that in his mind the university's most dangerous current illusion is that "public policy" can be a value-free, neutral specialization. He insisted that public policy is always "political" and that pretending it is not merely obfuscates the actual political powers and motivations that operate within it.

Politics is, of course, always a moral activity. For Aristotle, politics and ethics were two volumes in a single book. The Hebrew prophets directed their polemics against rulers and rich landholders.

When politics is removed from the realm of moral discourse, it becomes a spurious kind of engineering or advanced policy plumbing—or at least that is the image it presents. When ethics and morality are removed from policy formation, they become trivial and marginal. This diminution of the meaning of ethics can be seen if one looks at the pathetic status of the "ethics commission" in most city and state governments. It monitors elementary honesty on the part of state and city officials, mainly at the level of avoiding obvious conflicts of interest. Ethics commissions never touch the morality of the larger issues these bodies debate. This allows the ideology/myth of a value-free public realm to proceed unchallenged.

Some way must be found to restore the link between morality and politics, and between politics and public policy formation, lest a further enfeeblement and weakening of the American *civitas* take place. Since for most people in America morality is perceived to have something to do with religion, this will obviously require a new link between *fides* and *civitas*. Otherwise large numbers of would-be citizens, who are also believers, will find themselves functionally disenfranchised.

America is religiously pluralistic. Even though the various traditions of Christianity and of Judaism form the majority tradition, any mode of relating religious and moral discourse to public policy formation has to be one that respects the fragile fabric of pluralism that has been created and sustained in this country. Will it be possible to evolve modes of political discourse that draw on *various* religious traditions and bring their insights to bear in the formation of the policies that guide the common life? In recent years various attempts have been made to do this—some more respectful of that pluralism than others. Examining some of these actual attempts may help to clarify the question about citizen-believers.

The Rainbow Coalition and the Jackson candidacy for president represent a remarkable maturation on the part of the black churches in their mode of relating to the American *civitas*. True to the history of these churches, the Rainbow Coalition focuses on a person, the preacher who "goes downtown to meet the man," and who represents and speaks for that community to the larger society.[7] But there is an irony. The main impact of the Jackson campaign has been to increase the number of registered black voters and also the number of black citizens who hold public office on local, county, and state levels. Consequently, there is now a statistically larger chance that when one finds the "man downtown," he may be black. But the Rainbow Coalition has also gone beyond the personal embodiment stage. The *content* of its program is a constructive and coherent criticism framed in a religious mode of discourse, directed against the main contours of American domestic and foreign policy over the last decades, and presenting credible alternatives. Jesse Jackson may turn out to be the Norman Thomas of the 1980s and 1990s: never elected to office but watching his ideas and programs taken over by the major parties.

On the so-called "religious right," fundamentalists and evangelicals have become increasingly active in electoral politics and in other forms of public policy. Although some would argue that they have not yet learned the necessary art of civility, even to each other, it is interesting to observe that they are in the process of learning. They are beginning to notice that in order to accomplish anything in politics one needs to build coalitions and find allies. One cannot insist on a "pure" position unless one is seeking a glorious defeat rather than a partial victory. The Pat Robertson campaign may turn out to be a salutary lesson for his followers in the dynamics of American political life.

Perhaps the most instructive example of a religious community enlivening the public policy realm without imposing a narrow denominational view is represented by the recent pastoral letters issued by the American Roman Catholic bishops on nuclear war and on the economy. The bishops set other religious groups a fine example by circulating drafts of their two letters and encouraging widespread discussion before they were edited in their final forms and published. Also, the perspective the bishops took skillfully combined pluralism and particularity. They insisted that the realm of public policy is *not* a value-free one of merely technical arrangement. It is one in which moral perspectives (indeed moral perspectives based on underlying theological visions) *are* relevant and appropriate. They presented their own perspective, however, to enrich, deepen, and broaden the discussion rather than to dominate it. The most positive result of their encyclicals was to demystify the realm of economic and military policy discussion, thus inviting large numbers of people to engage once more in the activity of being informed citizens.[8]

In each of these three examples, believers are moving beyond either being Augustine's stranger, or embracing a bifurcated or schizophrenic bilinguisticality. Both the Roman Catholic bishops, and Jesse Jackson and the Rainbow Coalition break taboos of the national state and the public realm. The Catholic bishops do this by reclaiming the biblical ideas of creation, covenant, and world community. Jesse Jackson reaches into the Hebrew prophetic tradition, seeing the United States in relation to Third World peoples and emphasizing God's initial "preferential option for the poor." Both the Rainbow Coalition and the Catholic bishops represent attempts to let a particular tradition speak to a pluralistic community. They go beyond bilinguisticality. The underlying assumption they embody is that the pluralistic community will ultimately profit from a variety of particularities.

All this in turn means that a Christian theology of citizenship must be based on what has traditionally been known as "confession" or "testimony." The Christian can be a full citizen both of his or her national state and of the emerging international community. Indeed, a Christian can help reclaim an older and more wholesome idea of citizenship in the *civitas*. The believer-citizen may always be a stranger, but in one sense all are always strangers. Still, even strangers can participate, *along with others* who also testify to the stories of their own particular communities and bring them to the common fund of wisdom. Further, the Christian citizen's particular story has mainly to do with the rights of the oppressed and excluded, the care of the helpless, and a utopian vision that can bring hope even to the darkest hour.

The two major obstacles that have heretofore prevented the development of a credible theology of citizenship have begun to crumble. The once unquestioned legitimacy of the national state as the only sensible way of organizing the international community is waning and is rightly questioned. Other forms of belonging, including communities of faith, are both invaluable in themselves and also vital to the health of national and international communities. Also, the bourgeois notion that the public realm is or should be one free of values or moral argumentation based on religious assumptions is being exposed as merely one ideology among others.

Is America ready to allow, even welcome, into the public arena a form of argument about public policy drawn from those moral traditions based on religious world views? Some fear this entrance would fan bigotry and fanaticism. The evidence of the reception of the bishops' letters and the Jackson candidacy suggests this need not happen. Indeed, these two events in national life have helped to mitigate the lethal fanaticism of an unchecked nationalism, a heresy that has already exacted a heavy toll in the twentieth century. They have presented a reasonable alternative to the ideology that tries to perpetuate the power of technocratic elites by keeping the public realm pure of religious and moral language and thus deprive citizens whose opinions stem from religiously based moral visions from the opportunity of contributing to the conversation. Must Christians always be strangers in the city of this world? The answer to Augustine's question is "yes," at least until the kingdoms of this world become the kingdoms of our Lord and of his Christ. But a stranger can also be a citizen while he or she is passing through, indeed, perhaps an invaluable citizen. A Christian can serve the state, as Luther and Calvin once so eloquently argued, by preventing it from drifting into idolatry. A point has been reached that makes a new step both necessary and possible. The way is now open for the elaboration of a positive theology of citizenship, one that sees the whole family of God as the highest earthly community, that respects and nourishes religious pluralism, and that makes a contribution to the linking of morality and politics in the activity of public policy debate.

NOTES

1. See William Sims Bainbridge and Rodney Stark, *The Future of Religion: Secularization, Revival and Cult Formation* (Berkeley, Calif., 1985); Bryan Wilson, "Secularization: The Inherited Model," in Phillip E. Hammond, ed., *The Sacred in a Secular Age* (Berkeley, Calif., 1985), 9–20; Daniel Bell, "The Return of the Sacred?" in *The Winding Passage: Essays and Sociological Journeys, 1960–1980* (Cambridge, Mass., 1980), 324–54; and Peter L. Berger, "From the Crisis of Religion to the Crisis of Secularity," in Mary Douglas and Steven Tipton, eds., *Religion and America: Spirituality in a Secular Age* (Boston, 1982), 14–24.

2. Mario Cuomo, Text of Notre Dame Speech, September 13, 1984, p. 1.

3. John A. Coleman, "The American Civil Religion Debate: A Source for Theory Construction," *Journal for the Scientific Study of Religion* 20 (1981): 51–63.

4. Derek Holmes, *The Papacy in the Modern World* (New York, 1981). See chapters 4, 5, and 6 for Pius XII and his successors. Also, see Oscar Romero, *Voice of the Voiceless* (Maryknoll, N.Y., 1985).

5. Karl Mannheim, *Man and Society in an Age of Reconstruction* (New York, 1951).

6. Wilson Carey McWilliams, *The Idea of Fraternity in America* (Berkeley, Calif., 1973), 96.

7. James Baldwin, *Going to Meet the Man* (New York, 1965).

8. For example, see the full text of the bishops' letter on the economy entitled "Economic Justice for All: Catholic Social Teaching and the U.S. Economy," in Thomas M. Gannon, ed., *The Catholic Challenge to the American Economy* (New York, 1987), 297ff.

6

WOMEN AND CHRIST: THE TRANSFORMER OF CULTURE

Page Putnam Miller

In 1804 Isabella Graham, a committed Presbyterian and the founder of the Female Society for the Relief of Poor Widows with Small Children, reflected on the pioneering work of the society, one of the first such female benevolent organizations in the United States. She proclaimed, ''A new thing is on the wheel in the city of New York.'' Although Graham cautioned her followers that ''care must be taken not to obtrude in any respect'' and marshalled the support of leading Presbyterian ministers for the society, she was well aware that women were moving into unprecedented territory. Graham instilled in her followers a sense of their Christian responsibility for addressing social problems, an appreciation of their capabilities, and an awareness of the inequities and vulnerability of women's status.[1]

The transforming dimension of Christianity enabled Graham and other early nineteenth-century Presbyterian women to challenge cultural norms. This essay examines the writings of five antebellum Presbyterian women who, by taking active organizational roles in the Protestant churches, not only transformed their own lives but contributed to an emerging movement to expand women's public roles. These women, who predated the beginnings of the women's movement in America, found in their Christian experience a means to question basic social structures. After examining the religious experiences of these early-nineteenth-century women, this essay argues that the typology established by H. Richard Niebuhr in his classic work, *Christ and Culture* (1956), is the best means to interpret their experiences.[2]

Throughout the centuries, Niebuhr noted, Christians have struggled with the intersection of their life in Christ and their lives in culture. And in a variety of ways Christians have dealt with the problems presented by the differing claims, authorities, and experiences of Christ and culture. ''What is ultimately in question,'' Niebuhr stated, ''is the relation of the revelation in Christ to the reason which prevails in culture.''[3] Niebuhr developed in *Christ and Culture* a five-part typology of major motifs in what he described as the many-sided and enduring debate over the relationship of Christ and culture. Of these five—Christ against culture, the Christ of culture, Christ above culture, Christ and culture in paradox, and Christ the transformer of culture—it is the last that provides the perspective for this essay.

The early-nineteenth-century Presbyterian women examined in this essay clearly understood the claims of their Christian faith in dealing with questions of culture such as meaningful work, familial and community structures and obligations, and viable social orders. And, for Christians who function under the rubric of Niebuhr's fifth motif, Christ the transformer of culture, Christian faith is inextricably bound up with an activist and optimistic approach to dealing with cultural problems.

Central to these women's success in creating new organizational structures and adopting new social roles was a whole array of early-nineteenth-century economic, political, social, and religious developments in the United States. The Second Great Awakening, with its emphasis on revivals and lay leadership, urbanization, democratization, and industrialization, worked to create an environment conducive to new opportunities for women's endeavors. However, to justify their new roles, women turned to the authority of Scripture. That Scripture was frequently used, then as now, to prescribe restricted activities for women did not prevent these women from discerning in Scripture an alternative authority to expand their role. The themes of the New Testament that were particularly important to women were the accountability of all Christians for the wise use of one's talents and the inclusiveness of all people—whether Jew or Greek, slave or free, male or female—in the Christian mission and community.

The five antebellum Presbyterian women whose lives exemplify Niebuhr's typology of Christ the transformer of culture are Ann Breese, Charlotte Chambers, Louisa Wilson Lowrie, Joanna Bethune, and Hannah Murray. They based their right to transform culture and carve out new roles for women on Biblical authority.[4] By stressing the very fundamental doctrine of the New Testament that all Christians have a responsibility to carry out the commands of Jesus, these women, in fact, launched a subtle attack on patriarchy. Challenging the monopoly of male ministers, they found in Christian doctrine a priesthood of all believers and support for a belief in a discipleship of equals.

The leadership and expansion of women's role in the Presbyterian church and in the public arena came primarily from middle-class and upper-class women about whom relatively little is known. Only fragments of diaries and correspondence of antebellum Presbyterian women are extant. By far the largest body of material available on these women is printed reports of their organizations' activities and memoirs written by their male contemporaries. Few reports included more than the most elementary information about the organization. And ministers who wrote about women imposed their ideas of appropriate female conduct on their subjects. Yet, ministers who wrote memoirs primarily to extol women's piety did intersperse them with letters and diary entries that are a valuable source of information about these women's lives.

In one of the few extant speeches by a Presbyterian woman in the early nineteenth century, Ann Breese, the president of the Female Missionary Society of the Western District of New York, addressed the doubts of those who felt that the new female association and women's exertion of public leadership were inappropriate activities for women. In her "Address," published in 1817 as a part of *The First Annual Report of the Trustees of the Female Missionary Society of the Western District*, she began by extolling the work of the society in employing male missionaries and in expanding the membership to over 1,500 women and the number of branch societies to 28.[5]

In her address she invoked a litany of questions and statements to rally women to the missionary work of the society. She first focused on the issue of women's responsibilities as Christians for missions. If women shared equally with men in redemption, Breese argued, women should bear equal responsibility "to diffuse the grace of the Redeemer." Instead of viewing Eve, "the first in transgression," as a symbol of women's inability to conduct missionary work, Breese stressed the redemption of women by Jesus. Calling upon women to be confident in their own work, she stated, "tell us not [that] you feel on this subject, and are prepared to act, but the object of missions pertains exclusively to the other sex." Breese appealed to examples from the Bible often cited by women and asserted, "Say not the thing is unexampled. Who ministered to the wants of him who 'had no where to lay his head?' " Then referring to Jesus' appearance to Mary Magdalene after the resurrection, she asked, "Who fired the zeal, and roused to increasing exertions, the first heralds of the Gospel?" Despite the fact that the apostles and many ministers through the years have rejected this witness and proclamation of Mary Magdalene, this episode clearly encouraged women to assert a larger role in the church.[6]

Breese urged women to move beyond their long tradition of engaging only in private religious and benevolent activities and to participate in an organized effort to expand Christianity. She sought to dispel the notion of those who "prefer disposing their own bounty" rather than working through an organized society and stressed both the superiority of collective action and the capabilities of women, who, she asserted, possessed "no inconsiderable knowledge of the field." She discreetly noted that the society could seek the counsel of men. However, she emphasized that women had the experience, skill, and knowledge to operate a missionary society. If anyone doubted women's abilities, Breese asked that "facts be consulted" and referred them to the considerable accomplishments of the Female Missionary Society.[7]

The initial experimentation of women in the United States with the formation of women's organizations occurred during the first decades of the nineteenth century. Women such as Breese, with the support of some sympathetic ministers, presented carefully considered arguments to support women's innovation of forming female societies. Although most of the early women's societies adopted modest goals and a simple local organizational structure, the Female Missionary Society of the Western District was an ambitious regional organization with a sizable budget used to hire missionaries. Yet, whether the organizational structures were simple or complex, the women who founded the early female societies defended and promoted an expanded public role for women.

Charlotte Chambers, a leader in the interdenominational Dorcas Society in Cincinnati, relied, as Breese did, on the authority of Scripture to legitimize the reform of women's lives and society. Many female charity societies in the early nineteenth century took the name of Dorcas, a New Testament figure known for her good works. In 1818 Chambers, on behalf of the Dorcas Society, wrote to the mayor and town council of Cincinnati and urged the reform of the inhuman conditions in the local prison, particularly as they affected women prisoners. "How can those who profess to be the followers of Jesus suffer such things to exist?" she asked. "Can they expect at the last day to have the encouraging words addressed to them, 'I was in prison and ye comforted me?' "[8]

From Chambers's letters, which were saved by her daughter and later published, one is able to appreciate how Christianity transformed her life. Chambers spent her life rallying women throughout the midwest to leave the private sphere and to form Christian organizations and, as she said, "to be zealous in promoting what it is our glory and honor to profess and obey." Instead of being preoccupied with "extravagance in dress" and "all other frivolous diversions," Chambers challenged women to "be aroused" to participate in the "great work of civilizing and evangelizing the world." She frequently reminded her friends that Jesus loved Martha and Mary as well as Lazarus, and she affirmed that "His religion, wherever it extends, elevates women from degradation and misery." A letter in 1819 to a woman in Louisville—a "fellow laborer" in this cause—illustrates Chambers's conviction that Jesus called women to undertake a new and important public role and that women were capable of this demanding task. Women must, Chambers urged, "rightly estimate the privilege they possess in the opportunity of doing good and make the exertion of which they are capable." Chambers lamented that women did not have a greater esteem for their own abilities and a greater desire to engage in meaningful work. The transformation that Chambers sought was, therefore, of women's self-perceptions.[9]

In 1836 the minister Ashbel G. Fairchild wrote the *Memoir of Mrs. Louisa A. Lowrie*. At the age of twenty-one Louisa Wilson joined the Presbyterian Church in Morgantown, Virginia. Three years later, in 1833, she married John Lowrie, who had just been commissioned by the Western Foreign Missionary Society of the Synod of Pittsburgh to northern India. Louisa, commissioned by this same society as a "missionary assistant," sailed to Calcutta with her husband. She died in her mid-twenties after being in Calcutta only a few years. Two letters, included in Fairchild's memoirs of Louisa Lowrie, reveal her perceptions of Christianity as an agent for change.[10]

In 1830 in an exchange of letters with her brother, who was also a minister, she reflected on how to respond to the claims of Christianity on her life. She began by stating that she was writing for advice on a subject that has "for some time been bearing with weight on my mind." She revealed that she had been preoccupied for more than a year with concern for the condition of the heathen world. "My heart has been deeply affected when I have read and reflected upon their darkness and degradation," and, she insisted, "I have felt strong desires to do them good." But, she lamented, she knew of no way to benefit them but by her prayers. "Afterward an opportunity was afforded me to contribute to the support of missionaries," she recalled, but "my desires for their salvation became still stronger, and I began to inquire whether I had not some additional duty to perform in relation to them." Then, changing her inquiry to an assertion, she informed her brother that she believed it was the duty of every Christian to do all possible for the conversion of the heathen. She concluded, "In asking myself what I ought to do for them, as I had not much to give, I know of no other way than to give myself to the work—to go to them."[11]

In a second letter, also printed in the *Memoir*, Lowrie elaborated on the theme of the equal responsibility of men and women for Christian ministry. Although the content of her brother's reply is unknown, clearly she was not pleased with his response. "I must confess, dear brother, that I was much disappointed in your answer to my letter," she wrote. She reminded him that he had left home at an early age to pursue the ministry and that he had "laboured in the vineyard of Christ" until falling ill. "That you should be anxious for me to do good only where I may live at ease is to me indeed a sore disappointment." Coming to the crux of her argument, she exclaimed, "How, dear brother, are the heathen to be converted. Is not the command, 'Go ye into all the world, and preach the Gospel to every creature,' still binding? All shall be saved who call upon the name of the Lord. 'But how shall they call on him of whom they have not heard; and how shall they hear without a preacher?' " She concluded with a promise: "I do think, if God in His providence will open the way and makes me feel it to be my duty, that I will go to them and try to 'do them good.' The females especially are degraded to the level of brutes. I do feel for them."[12]

Louisa Lowrie clearly chafed at her secondary status within society and the church, and intended, despite her brother's hesitations, to explore options for moving beyond the limitations placed on women by a patriarchal society. Like Breese, Louisa Lowrie sought confirmation of her beliefs in Scripture and argued that the call of discipleship, and more specifically, the missionary ministry applied to both men and women. To shelter women from difficult situations deprived them of the opportunity to respond faithfully to God's will for their lives. She sought responsible and meaningful work as an alternative to a life of ease and pleasure. And Lowrie's concern for women who were degraded to the "level of brutes" reflected a reoccurring theme in the early missionary literature.

Thus in 1838 the report of the Presbyterian Board of Foreign Missions combined an account of atrocities committed against females in India with appeals for women's financial support. Referring specifically to female infanticide and the practice of suttee (the burning of widows on their husbands' funeral pyres), the 1838 foreign mission report rhetorically asked its readers to account for differences between the status of women in the United States and that of women in India. "We need not tell you that it is the Gospel of Jesus Christ." The report then continued with a request for missionaries and money. "Men and women are wanted to carry it to them, and means must be afforded to enable the missionaries of the Cross to reach their fields of labor."[13]

In emphasizing the plight of women in India, Lowrie both expressed solidarity with abused women and, by implication, raised the issue of women's appropriate status. She did this by interspersing her pronouncements on the degradation of women in India with her statements expressing a reluctance to accept the secondary status assigned to woman by her church, family, and society. For Lowrie and for many other American women, the full implications of the rhetoric of human rights for Asian women tended to remain below the surface, but the language of concern suggested a spirit of international sisterhood. Though Presbyterian ministers may have highlighted the condition of Asian women to increase missionary donations, many Presbyterian women understood the degradation of Asian women as a mandate for women to become missionaries.

Lowrie was among the first women in the United States to become foreign missionaries. But her "missionary assistant" position depended on her status as the wife of a missionary. For many women such as Lowrie, marriage offered the opportunity for a missionary career. In the early nineteenth century, brief courtships frequently preceded commissioning services as male missionaries tried to find a co-worker and as women, such as Lowrie, waited and hoped that "God in his providence will open the way." Between 1837, when the Presbyterian Board of Foreign Missions was established, and 1850 the Missions Board commissioned eighty-five women, only eleven of whom were single.[14] Although the number of women missionaries was not great, the missionary movement did provide a new career for women. Clothed in the respectability of the church, women could reject the role of "lady" and opt for the role of adventurer in the cause of Christ.

Of the five women under consideration, only Joanna Bethune could be characterized as a national leader. A pioneer in the establishment of Sunday schools in this country, Bethune also participated in the early stages of the infant school movement. It established schools to foster the moral and intellectual development of children from one to seven years old. Bethune relied heavily on biblical tradition to challenge cultural norms of female behavior and to justify the use of her skills in the establishment of new educational institutions. On March 21, 1826, she wrote in her diary, "This evening I expect a few religious friends, to converse on the subject of infant schools. I have often thought on the subject, and have prayed to the Lord, if it was His will, to use me as an instrument in promoting them, and now He seems about to answer my prayer." She then affirmed, "Thou art never at a loss for an instrument when Thou has work to do. Thou often chooses the weak things of this work to confound the wise."[15]

Despite the fact that women were often considered the weaker sex, Bethune had no doubt that God could use the insights and talents of women to put to shame the inaction of men. While working some years later on what turned out to be an abortive attempt to form a large-scale women's interdenominational missionary organization, Bethune responded to the ministers' request that the "ladies defer" with an often recalled exclamation: "Is the American Board afraid the ladies will get ahead of them?"[16]

Bethune's experiences also illustrated how the increased role for the laity that occurred during the Second Great Awakening was particularly helpful to women who sought to legitimize their participation in the priesthood of all believers. The elevation of the laity was a central feature of the expansion and revitalization of American churches during the early nineteenth century. Bethune's diary reveals the power that the laity generally, and women especially, felt from having a direct relationship to God, a relationship that was not dependent on the directives of a hierarchy. She described her thoughts on attending a worship service and hearing the reading of John 20:16—"Jesus said to Her, 'Mary.' She turned herself and said, 'Rabboni! Master!' " In reflecting on her reaction to these words, Bethune recorded, "When Mr. M'Cartee [her minister] read the verse, and paused on the word *Mary*, it went to my heart, and I could not help claiming my Savior as much as if he at that moment said *Joanna*! and in the sweet confidence of faith my heart responded 'Rabboni! Master!' " Significantly, in this same diary entry she wrote about her trials as a public leader. "However discouraged at the difficulties I have had to encounter, both public and private, a feeling that my Redeemer cared for me, and that the Lord Himself upheld me with His arm, has sustained me."[17]

Certainly Bethune's location at a hub of evangelical activity in New York City, the friends of her family and business acquaintances of her husband, and her visits abroad where she observed the English Sunday school movement all contributed to her innovative leadership. Yet the source she called upon finally for her authority to use her talents and challenge the social customs of a restricted sphere for women's activities was the Bible, which authenticated and sustained her work.

The Memoirs of the Late Hannah L. Murray, written by Gardiner Spring, a prominent New York Presbyterian minister, included an excerpt that focused on the measure in which scriptural citations could be an underpinning for change for women. The unmarried daughter of a wealthy New York merchant, and a coworker with Bethune, Hannah Murray was well aware that her participation in the new women's organizations conflicted with the prescribed behavior for women. She wrote in her diary, "My earnest desire is to do all things to God's glory; and now having associated myself with some others for the purpose of administering to the necessities of my fellow creatures, I humbly pray that I may be influenced by a love to Him." The themes of human community and accountability permeated Murray's thoughts. In summing up her convictions about her innovative work, she concluded, "It is better to obey God than man, and to be willing to become a fool for Christ's sake.'' Reliance on biblical teachings about the responsibilities of discipleship provided the needed support for challenging accepted cultural norms, particularly patriarchy.[18]

Because American women in the early nineteenth century were primarily confined to a private sphere and had no experience as religious leaders or as organizers of associations, women who wished to venture forth into new public roles had to legitimize their activity and then had to convince others that they were capable of performing public roles. Yet, within Christianity there were passages of Scripture that enabled women to justify a new perception of themselves and to give themselves confidence to pursue public roles.

In trying to assess the meaning of the religious experience of these early-nineteenth-century women, H. Richard Niebuhr's typology of Christ the transformer of culture in *Christ and Culture*, as well as his definition of culture, are most pertinent. Niebuhr developed a broad definition of culture. "What we have in view when we deal with Christ and culture," he stated, "is that total process of human activity and that total result of such activity to which now the name culture, now the name civilization, is applied in common speech." Drawing on the work of anthropologists, Niebuhr fashioned what he referred to as a layman's definition of culture. Without trying to define the "essence" of culture, he identified four major characteristics of Christian culture: the organization of people into distinct groups, human achievements that people have purposefully accomplished, values that reveal the intended ends that human achievements serve, and pluralism—a recognition that there are varied values in any time and place.[19]

It is precisely these aspects of culture that Louisa Lowrie, Charlotte Chambers, Ann Breese, Joanna Bethune, and Hannah Murray wanted to transform. They wanted a transformation of the social groupings that placed women in restricted private roles outside the arena of public action. They wanted to have an opportunity to participate in the human achievements that had previously been reserved for men, to be missionaries, reformers, organizers, and educational leaders. They hoped for a regeneration of values that recognized women's skills and abilities to function in a variety of new roles and within new social groupings. Specifically they wanted women to assume a new measure of self-worth and dignity and a new appreciation of inclusiveness and of equality in discipleship, to replace patriarchy's dehumanizing role for them. Finally, they wanted women, as well as men, to be able to exercise the options available in a pluralistic society and to move beyond the restricted and private roles previously prescribed by their culture.

Seeking to transform culture through obedience to the Christian faith, these early-nineteenth-century women stood solidly within one of the major strains of Christian tradition. Niebuhr described in *Christ and Culture* how these five great motifs have appeared and reappeared in the long wrestling of Christians with their enduring quest for answers to the question of the relationship of Christ and culture. There have been Christians in many periods of history who have exemplified the fifth motif and emphasized the expectation of the transformation of human societies through the creative energies of Christ working through the achievements of men and women. The divine vision of the healed and renewed human society combines with the possibility of human actuality. The exploration of Christ and culture involves, Niebuhr stated, the "total process of human activity" and comprises habits, ideas, beliefs, customs, social organization, technical processes, and values. All, he affirms, are subject to the great conversion that ensues when God makes a new beginning for man by causing man to begin with God.[20]

Niebuhr identified the nineteenth-century English theologian F. D. Maurice as one of the major exponents of this motif. Writing about Maurice's views of the Kingdom of God as transformed culture, Niebuhr noted that transformation comes through humiliation and exaltation, "through the humiliation which comes when members of the body willingly accept the fact that they are not the head, and through the exaltation which results from the knowledge that they have been given their own particular, necessary work in service to the head of the body and to all its other members."[21] This idealized perspective of Christ as the transformer of culture has no room for patriarchal structures or values.

Breese, Chambers, Lowrie, Bethune, and Murray sought through biblical authority to challenge accepted norms of appropriate female behavior. Of course, they made only initial inroads into the accepted norms of society. Nonetheless, their experiences shed light on two very basic questions that have confronted women throughout the centuries: What do women want, and what tactics are appropriate for achieving the desired ends? In the broadest sense these particular nineteenth-century women wanted a transformation of culture that replaced strict hierarchical structures with greater egalitarianism. Within the Bible they found the authority to raise this challenge effectively.

On the other hand, the Bible contains a number of proof texts that have been used to keep women in subordinate roles. However, if one considers the broader and most basic themes of the New Testament, and not a few selected verses, the New Testament message is not one of hierarchical structures.

One of the most insightful contemporary commentators on the issues of feminism and the Bible is Elizabeth Schussler Fiorenza. She readily acknowledges that various readings of the Bible are both death-dealing and life-giving. Death-dealing passages have given license for the persecution of Jews, the burning of witches, the torture of heretics, and the subhuman conditions of slavery. These were all carried out under a banner of biblical authority. Recognizing that many feminists have chosen to abandon the Bible because of certain texts that serve to legitimize women's subordinate status, Fiorenza has urged women to reclaim their scriptural heritage. This other scriptural heritage, she argues, presents a powerful theology of liberation, of the solidarity of humanity, and of the oneness of life. These are the very passages cited by nineteenth-century Presbyterian women.[22]

The writings of these nineteenth-century women reflect the basic longings and needs of human beings to confront the essential questions of life. The Christianity of Breese, Chambers, Lowrie, Bethune, and Murray offered a means of modifying their society by transforming, in their own limited ways, the traditional structures. Christianity could be a powerful force for liberation and for challenging the most dehumanizing aspects of patriarchy.

NOTES

1. *The Power of Faith Exemplified in the Life and Writings of the Late Mrs. Isabella Graham of New York* (New York, 1816), 73.

2. H. Richard Niebuhr, *Christ and Culture* (New York, 1956), 32–34.

3. Ibid., 11.

4. Page Putnam Miller, *A Claim to New Roles* (Metuchen, N.J., 1985) offers an extensive account of the ways in which Presbyterian women in the early nineteenth century moved into new roles in the church.

5. *The First Annual Report of the Trustees of the Female Missionary Society of the Western District* (Utica, N.Y., 1817), 17–19.

6. Ibid., 21.

7. Ibid., 21–22.

8. Lewis H. Garrand, *Memoir of Charlotte Chambers* (Philadelphia, 1856), 95.

9. Ibid., 104–6.

10. Ashbel G. Fairchild, *Memoir of Mrs. Louisa A. Lowrie* (Pittsburgh, 1836).

11. Ibid., 112–13.

12. Ibid., 116–17.

13. *Foreign Missionary Chronicle* 6 (1838):194.

14. Arthur Judson Brown, *One Hundred Years* (New York, 1936), 1096–1134.

15. George W. Bethune, *Memoirs of Mrs. Joanna Bethune* (New York, 1863), 163.

16. Mary E. A. Chamberlain, *Fifty Years in Foreign Fields* (New York, 1925), 7.

17. Bethune, *Memoirs of Mrs. Joanna Bethune*, 163–64.

18. Gardiner Spring, *The Memoirs of the Late Hannah L. Murray* (New York, 1849), 142–48.

19. Niebuhr, *Christ and Culture*, 32–34.

20. Ibid., 32.

21. Ibid., 226.

22. Elizabeth Schussler Fiorenza, *Bread Not Stone: The Challenge of Feminist Biblical Interpretation* (Boston, 1985).

creation and control of modern industrial society. The legacy of that monument is, as much as anything else, the belief that popular culture must have an acceptable didactic content and a properly maintained environment.

But the secular Fair in no way exhausted the events of Chicago during the summer. It was not the only vision of modern urban culture proposed for the edification of visitors. The city was also aroused by an evangelical campaign led by the great preacher Dwight Moody. In open competition with the Fair and its Parliament of Religions he offered his vision of a more celestial city. He proposed a sanctified culture as a solution to the problems that touched the imagination of the Fair planners. Like them he set his hopes in an urban environment. Like them he focused on the problems of technology, enterprise, and social and cultural diversity. He, too, articulated a strategy for controlling modern consumer/industrial culture. But his proposal demanded nothing less than infusing evangelism into secular popular culture—to face up to and transform the new world that was being born on the Midway.

The World's Fair Evangelization Campaign led by Moody in 1893 suggests an attempt to use popular culture as a tool of social engineering. Moody refused to distance himself from popular institutions, however much he might disapprove of them. Nor did he, like the designers of the Fair, maintain two visions of culture (the White City and the Midway) bound together in tension and competition. Instead, he attempted to evangelize the institutions he saw around him and graft a middle-class business ethic and ideas of social control onto some of the newest instruments of mass culture and communication that he observed (with suspicion) in the modern city. The result was perhaps more complicated than he imagined—an influence that flowed in two directions. He helped to open popular institutions to contemporary evangelical ideas. At the same time, he altered the nature of evangelical Protestantism, to make it more accommodating to modern popular culture. If this did not amount exactly to the secularization of evangelical religion, neither did it result in the sanctification of secular institutions. Indeed, a new word is required for the syncretism Moody and his assistant Ira Sankey achieved—some term that can capture the reciprocal, transforming process that occurred as they renewed and revived the fusion between religion and popular culture. Of course, Moody would never have enjoyed much success in bringing about this revival without the strong religious sensibility already present in most places in American culture. Nonetheless, his achievement was significant.

Perhaps the most intensely felt problem that spurred Moody into urban evangelism can be discovered in his parable of the Prodigal Son and in one of his and Sankey's favorite hymns, the "Old Ninety and Nine." An early observer of Moody and Sankey wrote:

When you hear the "Ninety and Nine" sung, you know that down in this corner, up in that gallery, behind that pillar which hides the singer's face from the listener, the hand of Jesus has been finding this and that and yonder lost one, to place them in his fold.[1]

7

THE CHICAGO CAMPAIGN

James B. Gilbert

During the summer of 1893 much of the attention of Chicago and the nation was fixed upon the great Columbian Exposition constructed south of the city on the shores of Lake Michigan. With its central core of fanciful neo-classicism (the White City) and its Midway (a collection of ethnic delights) the World's Fair was an enormous and influential experiment in modern mass culture. Its planners hoped to demonstrate their vision of a perfect urban world. Cognizant of the immense problems of the contemporary city, they offered a resolution: the planned utopia of the great White City and the commercialized entertainment center appended to it. Knowing full well some of the critical problems of the new industrial and consumer society springing up around them, they proposed a cultural solution for rebuilding the city. This aesthetic vision of universal truth even influenced the way the Fair presented religion. Over the summer the Exposition hosted a number of international conferences, among them the World Parliament of Religions. At this meeting representatives from various important world religions explained their beliefs. The purpose was to underscore the universality of religious experience, just as the White City expressed a generalized aesthetic vision.

What the designers of the Fair created must be considered one of the important landmarks of modern culture. Attracting millions of visitors to the disposable utopia at Jackson Lagoon, the creators of the Fair displayed the new consumer/industrial culture that they foresaw. In designing this world of the future they had three problems very much in mind: the challenge of modern science and technology, the risks of unfettered enterprise, and the controlling of diverse populations. For the planners of the Fair, each of these problems had a special cultural dimension and peril, and each required a cultural solution. In some respects the Fair represented the articulation of a strategy, an experiment in the

The theme of this hymn and the parable is "lost and found," straying from home and community, and being rescued through God's burning desire to gather in His lost flock. Reverend H. B. Hartzler, in his extensive account of the campaign and report on Moody's Chicago Fire Anniversary Sermon in October 1893, spoke poignantly of this modern state of estrangement:

With this closing appeal the speaker turns to God with a fervent prayer of thanksgiving, consecration, supplication, and tearful intercession for the city and for the multitudes coming up to the Fair. Then once more the people unite in singing, and are dismissed with the benediction to meet again no more until all the earth shall stand before the judgement-seat of God.[2]

In these words the anguish and loneliness of urban life leach into and color an account that Hartzler had obviously intended to be a positive portrayal of Moody's mission.

In a curious, autobiographical way, Moody could himself be the subject of such sermons on alienation and restoration. Born in Northfield, Massachusetts, he grew up fatherless yet he imbibed the typical Protestant virtues of his day. As a young man he set out for Boston in 1854 to become a shoe salesman. Moving shortly afterward to Chicago, he plied the same trade, with considerable skill and success. But the lure of evangelism proved too strong. Neither trained minister nor theologian, he joined lay institutions such as the YMCA and eventually organized Sunday schools, prayer groups, schools, a church, and a major evangelical institute. If not completely rootless (he often returned to Northfield where he established a summer camp and missionary school), he did lead a peripatetic life similar to others who searched for new callings at the turbulent end of the century.[3]

Moody's burden, as he described it, was to evangelize the city. Like many contemporary reformers he let his particular passions shape a very personal response to the new urban America. In his experience he discovered the secret key to the converted city. The problems of industrialism and urban culture he responded to were those that other observers certainly recognized. But he expressed his vision in the particular language of a new sort of popular evangelism. Reacting to strikes at Pullman in 1884 and at his benefactor Cyrus McCormick's plant in 1885 (culminating in the 1886 Haymarket Riot), Moody warned: "Either these people are to be evangelized or the leaven of communism and infidelity will assume such enormous proportions that it will break out in a reign of terror such as this country has never known."[4]

Certainly not always so engaged, focused, or topical, Moody apparently became more and more pessimistic toward the end of his life. He spoke of a world "getting darker and darker" and grown "worse and worse." Most of the time this anxiety aimed beyond specific political or economic considerations at the more general problem of a church grown "cold and formal" and an urban society filled with strangers and alien, threatening cultures. In the city luxuriant modernism expressed itself in the profligate growth of theaters, Sunday newspapers, drinking, lust, worldly amusements, and threatening science like Darwinism. Through it Moody picked his way, a man who in his own itinerant search for career and ministry reproduced the experience of many Americans in their late-century rush into the city with its daunting new mass culture, industrialism, and consumerism.[5]

Marshalling his forces against a church grown cold, the proliferation of institutions beyond the hegemony of Protestantism, and a population strayed from home and mission, Moody took his evangelical message directly to those questionable institutions and populations. He sought to meet and master them on their cultural grounds. This strategy caught the attention of a Catholic satirist who was outraged by Moody's first great American crusade in 1876 in Philadelphia. The satirist mocked "Reverend Eliphalet Notext," who was neither theologian nor minister, but a modern businessman who "had been originally the business manager of a circus." This vulgar and blasphemous performer, he continued, made religion into a sideshow. "When he was at a loss for words to continue one of his disjointed discourses, he took refuge in music and hymns."[6]

Of course, the critic was right—at least from his learned perspective. But he failed to appreciate that Moody's immersion in popular culture, which so offended him, was, in fact, one explanation for the great evangelical's success. It made his message relevant. By directly engaging modern popular culture, about which he certainly had grave reservations, Moody touched his audiences, and offered a clear and important pathway for future revivals to follow.

Of the aspects of modern industrial society that perplexed middle class observers in 1893, the most worrisome to Moody were the morally disintegrative effects of urban life that he had experienced. Heterodox beliefs and populations appeared to adulterate religious faith and allow disorder to flourish. The evangelist understood that religion and order sat on the same tray of the social balance—or at least he understood the appeal of linking them together when he solicited funds from wealthy benefactors. As he wrote a Chicago businessman in 1889, "there can be no better investment for the capitalists of Chicago than to put the saving salt of the gospel into those dark homes and desperate centers from which come the criminals."[7]

Reverend Hartzler, the chronicler of the campaign, offered a perceptive account of what it was about the city and the World's Fair that inspired and disturbed Moody:

But the aggregation of individuals in the cities creates perils on the one hand and offers opportunities on the other, which call for evangelistic effort on a larger scale, of a more comprehensive character not alone for the salvation of the individual sinner and the edification of the individual believer, but also for the salvation of society itself.[8]

To Moody the World's Fair especially exemplified, in its promiscuous mixing of uprooted populations and competing religions, all the dangers of the urban environment. But its bad effects only compounded its opportunities. The ambiguity of the city and its institutions refracted doubly from the Fair, and, as Hartzler noted, Chicago in 1893 filled up with diverse sorts of groups, Americans and foreigners, and especially "vicious" people. As one Methodist publication put it, the campaign intended to "neutralize to the greatest extent, the bad influences which beset World's Fair visitors."[9]

Moody recounted his decision to conduct the Chicago campaign in a parable. In London in 1891 the revivalist had visited a specialist who confirmed an earlier diagnosis of serious heart disease. Then the ship returning home was struck by a dangerous storm. Moody promised in a prayer that, if he survived, he would "come back to Chicago and at the World's Fair preach the gospel with all the power He would give me."[10] Whether it was God's bargain fulfilled, or as Moody explained elsewhere, the "opportunity of the century" to convert a wicked city, does not much matter. By 1892 planning was well under way, and by May 1893, Moody and his specially recruited staff of ministers and gospel students prepared to meet the challenge.[11]

When it came to providing an alternative spiritual "city" to the secular Columbian Fair, Moody's organization enjoyed the advantage of long experience. One particularly competitive note was struck in arguments over the Parliament of Religions. The evangelist was alternately urged to join or denounce the proceedings. But his aloof strategy proved to be more effective, as one of his lieutenants wrote:

When the ecclesiastical menagerie gathered from all quarters of the globe made its appearance, Mr. Moody was asked again and again to take part, he only replied that he had his hands full of work and declined to go. When it seemed to some of us that our Lord was belittled and disgraced by the motley crew who disported themselves upon the platform day by day in the wonderful "Parliament" we suggested that we should attack them all along the line. Mr. Moody was very emphatic in his instructions. "Preach Christ," said he, "hold up Christ, let the Parliament of Religions alone, preach Christ." And he was right.[12]

To win Chicago and its summer visitors for Christ, the revivalist decentralized his ministry, carrying the crusade to a variety of churches, and then into those places of the city—the pleasure resorts—where visitors might wander seeking amusement. He divided Chicago into districts and designated a church headquarters in each. He further segmented his "congregation" by holding special services for selected populations: young men, young people, children, foreign visitors (in their native languages), and even survivors of the Civil War. By the end of the campaign in October, his organization was sponsoring as many as 125 services and meetings on a single Sunday.[13] Although many of the principal services occurred in churches, Moody appeared to prefer the confrontational environment of theaters and public halls, such as Tattersall's where Buffalo Bill performed and where political conventions took place. In fact, his favorite spot appeared to be the notorious Haymarket Theater in downtown Chicago, located, as Reverend Hartzler put it, "in the midst of a very hell of saloons and vile resorts of all kinds."[14]

Because Moody spent considerable time preaching in secular amusement centers, he concluded that he should advertise his meetings in the Announcements section of Chicago newspapers. There, amidst notices for performances at the Trocadero, Buffalo Bill's Wild West Show, cycloramas, theaters, and World's Fair events, Moody listed his evangelical meetings. As he told a *Chicago Tribune* interviewer, he had "taken a new departure by advertising his meetings in the amusement columns of the newspapers, and found that it paid. It brought in the crowds." The result convinced him of the virtue in "advertising, even in the service of the Lord."[15]

Perhaps the most striking of these descents into the resorts of popular culture was Moody's meeting before an audience of 15,000 at Forepaugh's Circus. Speaking to jaded circus workers "used only to rough words and oaths and condemned to a life of hurry and bustle," Moody inspired listeners to allow their "thoughts to wander away to the old home"—or so the *Tribune* imagined it. "The trapeze wires were pulled up to the top of the amphitheater; where the performing lions do their turn, was the pulpit from which the great preacher was to tell his story." Attempting to cash in on this success, the owners asked Moody to lend them an evangelist to travel with the circus and preach on Sundays.[16] Clearly, the Forepaugh management saw an advantageous kinship between their performance and Moody's, although the evangelist refused the offer.

With this offer Forepaugh insinuated that both revivalism and popular performances shared some of the same perspectives and audiences. Moody's borrowing of certain elements of popular culture made his preaching seem comfortable and appropriate to the audiences that attended circuses. So it was on that special circus Sunday. Sentimental and simple in his message, he again preached the parable of the Prodigal Son. Other elements of the evangelical production were familiar. Moody understood the emotional power of music and used it extensively. The harmonium, massed choirs, congregational hymn-singing, and Ira Sankey's melodies and words particularly appealed to popular audiences.

Observers had long associated Sankey's hymnody with popular culture. In 1876 the *Nation* wrote: "Determine the pleasure you get from a circus quick-step, a negro-minstrel sentimental ballad, a college chorus, and a hymn all in one, and you have some gauge of the variety and contrast that may be perceived in one of these songs." Later historians have also commented on Sankey's technique, finding it scarcely distinguishable "from the ordinary secular songs of the day"—that is, similar to music hall and vaudeville styles.[17]

Inevitably, this practice was also the source of criticism. An accusing letter to Moody admonished: "You are not a Christian. You are serving the money god. You are preaching to please the people. You are no Christian." That Moody made this letter public testifies to his confidence that every observer would see that the charge was patently false. His intent was always to Christianize secular institutions and culture, although the writer was perceptive to imply that influence could flow in the opposite direction too.[18]

One last strategy rounded out this energetic campaign. Equipping wagons with lanterns and a small organ and drawing them with two horses, he assigned young students to advertise his services in tough sections of the city, such as "Little Hell." These "Gospel Wagons," the "flying artillery of the evangelical forces," as Moody dubbed them, later became the basis for his Colportage Society, which also sent out wagons equipped with evangelists and a supply of religious works to peddle throughout the countryside.

Despite his remarkable experiments in modern communication and advertising, Moody's social views remained remarkably unextraordinary, even conservative. Unlike many of his Social Gospel brethren, he believed the answer to unemployment, immigrant adjustment to urban life, and the venality of modern culture lay in individual conversion. Still democratic and catholic in wishing to unite all denominations and classes, he wrote, "The churches can be crowded full and the masses reached if we go about it in the Spirit of the Master."[19] Yet the impulse he followed, both theologically and sociologically, helped create a great schism in Protestantism between fundamentalism and modernism. Moody's social beliefs were conservative and traditional. He firmly believed in the work ethic, temperance, Sabbatarianism, and individual—not social—regeneration. He feared the growth of urban Catholicism and secularization. While he located the Bible at the very center of his teachings, it was an American Bible resonant with meanings and analogies already established in popular culture. It was not the Bible of theologians, who sought their contexts in classical learning and philological science.[20]

Ironically, Moody's attention to modern urban problems and his repeated attempts to evangelize the city exacerbated his pessimism and caused him to turn more and more away from the corrupt, secular world. For all his efforts in 1893, the World's Fair campaign probably signalled the decline of his efforts to mobilize the city for conversion. Increasingly he grew uncertain about the outcome of his struggle to evangelize the world. This pessimism placed him close to the camp of the premillennialists, whose ideas would emerge full-blown in the fundamentalist movement of the early 1920s.[21]

Nor, perhaps, were his apparent successes as deep as he presumed. Great numbers of Protestants flocked to his campaigns. But many of those he touched he only reconverted; certainly they could not be counted among the newly saved. Still, thousands were undoubtedly affected by the experience in ways that Moody may not have suspected. What they heard was a redefinition of modern religion based upon an affinity between evangelical ideas and popular culture.[22]

What was this urban vision? Despite his confident air, Moody was thoroughly ambiguous about modern society. For example, there is his attitude to technology. Here, Moody seemed both engaged and aloof. Certainly he was enthusiastic about adopting the tools created by modern communication technology. He had a telegraph machine installed at his headquarters, and toward the end of his life had his voice recorded. More than tinkering with inventions, however, he seriously adapted to his evangelical operations the culture of modern communication technology as it was being invented and developed for American business. His urban crusades borrowed advanced forms of organization from corporate enterprise, and, in particular, Moody shared the modern penchant of business for identifying its products and purposes with familiar and universal symbols of popular culture. As Martin Marty has aptly noted, Moody was "able to exploit modern technology [but] he was ambivalent about its ethos and content."[23]

While Moody enthusiastically borrowed what he wanted from modern technology, he tended to ignore the implications of modern scientific theories, especially Darwinism. As George Marsden has written, the fundamentalism that sprang up behind Moody relied upon an older science derived from Common Sense philosophy. This philosophy assumed an affinity between the facts of nature and the verses of Scripture; consequently, it dismissed contemporary scientific theories that implied a disjuncture between natural and divine law. The historian Marion Bell has on this basis concluded that "Moody preferred to ignore evolution as a divisive force, and this refusal to deal with modern science alienated revivalism from contemporary intellectual currents of thought and ultimately estranged it from the mainstream of society."[24] The first part of this evaluation is undoubtedly correct; revivalism did swim against contemporary scientific intellectual currents. But it is wrong to conclude that modernism swept throughout the mainstream. Mainstream American culture is more complex than this suggests; it is not one stream but many coexisting and related attitudes. One of these—certainly shared in Moody's attitudes—separated science and technology, rejecting, ignoring, or simplifying science but adopting technology without hesitation.

Of course, even Moody's cautious adoption of modern communication practice and technology and his use of business methods had its critics. Some contemporaries scored the evangelist for relying on "un-Christian," modern techniques. But in doing so they ignored the impact of Moody upon popular culture. By turning these tools to evangelical purposes Moody simultaneously linked revivalism and popular Christianity with vital new forces in mass culture.[25]

About the question of regulating enterprise, the evangelist also picked his way through a serious contemporary debate. He was an enthusiastic friend of American entrepreneurs, in part because of his experience and success as a salesman, and in part because they supported his efforts. It is perhaps an apocryphal tale that Moody started his first great American revival in a temporary tabernacle built on a portion of land in Philadelphia where his friend John Wanamaker located his famous department store.[26] This shared terrain only symbolized the sympathy of both men for the competitive enterprise system.

Moody was nothing if not ambiguous here too. While he celebrated a business ethic and exemplified it in his own organization, he did not approve of unlimited cultural enterprise—the freedom that characterizes modern society. Far more than the planners of the White City, he protested developments in popular culture—the other culture sported on the Midway. Yet his strategy was neither to ignore it nor to confine it. Moody insisted on meeting this culture on its own ground. He hoped to transform the leisured resorts of American urban life and turn them to his own purposes. While he denounced saloons and theaters, this did not deter him from preaching in them to capture their audiences. This aggressive rivalry made Moody's World's Fair Campaign into the remarkable event that it became. It also accounts for Moody's lasting contribution to the creation of modern mass culture.

By the time the five-months' campaign ended in October, the Moody organization had probably spent about $60,000 in additional funds. It employed a roving staff of 220 men and women. By the organization's own estimate, it reached close to 2,000,000 people (compared to 21,000,000 at the Fair). Moody was encouraged to believe that he had converted thousands of new people. To maximize this possibility, his organization issued tickets to meetings—to prevent the same audience from following him around the city. He also began asking crowds if they were Fair visitors. He was satisfied by a show of hands that most were. By his estimate he had preached to the nations of the world through their representatives visiting the Fair. He also claimed practical results such as a cut in the consumption of whiskey; he also prevented crowds from attending the Fair on Sundays. He had, finally, helped to educate "the common people."[27]

On all these grounds, Moody's optimistic appraisal is probably unwarranted. By any measure Chicago remained a wicked city after his efforts. But evaluations based on numbers, conversions, attendance, or the immediate elimination of moral corruption cannot measure his or any revival's impact. What Moody developed throughout his career, and summed up in this spectacular crusade, was a unique approach to problems of modern industrial and urban society—a bold use of culture to overcome disunities, to affect behavior, and to control technology and enterprise. His was no mere accommodation of traditional America to the modern world. He discovered how traditional ideas might be heated in evangelical emotions and poured into the mold of a developing new popular culture in order to assure their continuing importance and relevance. "He is," wrote a supporter, "a great advertiser. He is one of the children of light, who have learned from the children of this world. The newspapers, streetcars, bill-posters, and ticket distributors are all brought into requisition."[28]

If Moody requisitioned the inventions of the "children of this world," then they, in turn, borrowed some of his light. The tone of such middle-class attitudes to popular culture is often censorious. But that does not mean that their effects are only astringent or controlling or irrelevant. Moody used the technology of an emerging popular culture to communicate his religious ideas. It would be incorrect to say that he alone was responsible for creating a pathway between mass culture and evangelical ideas. The history of this conjunction is far more complex, and his role less pioneering. Yet the great evangelist was a noteworthy player in the great cultural drama that has kept and still keeps religious ideas and emotions on the center stage of American popular culture.

NOTES

1. H. M. Wharton, *A Month with Moody in Chicago: His Work and Workers* (Baltimore, 1894), 80. The verses of the hymn call the lost back home:

> There were ninety and nine that safely lay
> In the shelter of the fold,
> But one was out on the hills away
> Far-off from the gates of gold—
> Away on the mountains wild and bare,
> Away from the tender Shepherd's care.

2. H. B. Hartzler, *Moody in Chicago or the World's Fair Gospel Campaign* (New York, 1894), 201. Hartzler was called especially to Chicago to help Moody in the campaign.

3. James F. Findlay, Jr., *Dwight L. Moody, American Evangelist, 1837–1899* (Chicago, 1969), 30ff; George Marsden, *Fundamentalism and American Culture: The Shaping of Twentieth-Century Evangelicalism, 1870–1925* (New York., 1980), 36.

4. Findlay, Jr., *Moody*, 327.

5. William G. McLoughlin, *The American Evangelicals, 1800–1900, An Anthology* (New York, 1968), 184–85; Findlay, Jr., *Moody*, 183; John Charles Pollock, *Moody: A Biographical Portrait of the Pacesetter in Modern Mass Evangelism* (New York, 1963), 292; and Marsden, *Fundamentalism*, 35.

6. Author unknown, "A Revival in Frogtown," *Catholic World* 22 (1876): 700–706.

7. Dennis E. Graf, "Dwight L. Moody and the 1893 Chicago World's Fair Campaign" (M.A. thesis, Wheaton College, 1965), 90. See also Sandra S. Sizer, *Gospel Hymns and Social Religion: The Rhetoric of Nineteenth-Century Revivalism* (Philadelphia, 1978), 142. Sizer relates revivals to political crises and sees them, in part, as "strategies of pacification."

8. Hartzler, *Moody in Chicago*, 15.

9. Ibid., 17; Graf, "Dwight L. Moody," 46.

10. Wharton, *Month with Moody*, 12–13.

11. Hartzler, *Moody in Chicago*, 20.

12. Pollock, *Moody*, 279–80.

13. Graf, "Dwight L. Moody," 33, 43, 75. Apparently there was violence when ministers tried to move the crusade into the tougher parts of the city.

14. Hartzler, *Moody in Chicago*, 70. See also Pollock, *Moody*, 284. Graf lists the following as the principal centers for Moody's crusade: Central Music Hall, Empire Theater, Haymarket Theater, Institute Hall (owned by Moody), and the Standard Theater. Graf, "Dwight L. Moody," 96.

15. *Chicago Tribune*, 1 November 1893, p. 6.

16. *Chicago Tribune*, 12 June 1893, p. 1.

17. *Nation* 22 (1876): 157. See also Marion L. Bell, *Crusade in the City: Revivalism*

in Nineteenth Century Philadelphia (Lewisburg, Pa., 1977), 208; Graf, "Dwight L. Moody," 48–49.

18. Quoted by *Chicago Tribune*, 1 November 1893, p. 6.

19. McLoughlin, *American Evangelicals*, 255, 174.

20. Findlay, Jr., *Moody*, 296ff, 270, 281. Findlay argues that Moody created an "effective bridge for many people between the old and the new in American society" (p. 300). It would be better to argue that Moody linked old ideas to a new cultural context. Findlay's formulation makes it seem as if the "people" abandoned the old in favor of the new.

21. McLoughlin, *American Evangelicals*, 185; Findlay, Jr., *Moody*, 245ff; Marty, *Modern American Religion*, vol. 1, *The Irony of It All, 1893–1919* (Chicago, 1986), 210–12. Premillennialism is the belief that before the second coming of Christ there will be a long period of turmoil, strife, and sin.

22. On reconversion see Findlay, Jr., *Moody*, 267.

23. Marty, *Modern American Religion*, vol. 1, 209.

24. Marsden, *Fundamentalism*, 5ff; Bell, *Crusade in the City*, 225.

25. Graf, "Dwight L. Moody," 33.

26. Bell, *Crusade in the City*, 229. Moody tried to enlist Wanamaker in revivalism.

27. Hartzler, *Moody in Chicago*, 106, 211.

28. Wharton, *Month with Moody*, 13. It is probably not necessary to point out how similar Moody's campaign and techniques were in spirit to modern popular evangelism. See Ben Armstrong, *The Electric Church* (Nashville, 1979).

8

KING TUT AND THE SCOPES TRIAL

Mary Sheila McMahon

The Scopes trial was one of several events that made 1925 a tumultuous year for religion in America. In the same year as the trial, Billy Sunday launched a much-publicized crusade against vice in Chicago, and Bruce Barton published the extraordinarily popular *The Man Nobody Knows*, in which he depicted Christ as a businessman. Sunday and Barton reached for a national audience, that consumed rather than participated in the rituals of religion and the marketplace.[1] The supporters of anti-evolution, however, feared that the relationship between religion and the scientific order resembled the hostile takeover of a local concern by a rich, impersonal national one. Compared with Sunday or Barton, the anti-evolutionists seemed socially vestigial, fearful of urban life, and desperate in their reliance on legislation to halt social change.[2]

By contrast 1925 was a quiet year for international relations in America. One of its most significant events, in fact, lay in the efforts of John D. Rockefeller, Jr., to promote archaeology as a means of achieving international harmony.[3] Above all Rockefeller hoped that archaeology would stimulate a sense of common ancestry that would encourage current cooperation among peoples.[4] In seizing on archaeology as a vehicle to resurrect a sense of a common global civilization, Rockefeller chose a subject with popular appeal. The discovery of King Tut-ankhamon's tomb had occurred two years before, but stories of the excavation continued to attract attention. It seemed to add to knowledge about the primitive origins of man, an enterprise that had been popularized earlier by the book of the Egyptologist James Breasted, *Ancient Times* (1915), and by the discovery of Piltdown Man in 1911.[5]

On the surface, the Scopes trial and Rockefeller's interest in archaeology have even less in common than the trial and Sunday's crusade and Barton's book. They are separate events with separate narratives, connected in a linear sense only by the coincidence of time. Nevertheless, connections can be made between business-Christianity, the Scopes trial, and archaeology in 1925, specifically between the trial and a Rockefeller-backed project to protect the relics uncovered in the tomb of King Tut.

In part, the nature of culture itself connects these separate phenomena. Traditionally historians have relied on contemporary elites—privileged interpreters of culture—to provide insights into the structures of thought of any given society. In other words, they have relied implicitly on a notion of hegemony: that dominant groups articulate and shape the world views of subordinate groups. In this light it always makes sense to focus only on those whose ideas "succeeded."[6] In this context the particular cultural symbolism surrounding Tut and Scopes would appear as efforts by parochial localists to halt the progress of knowledge. However, this trickle-down type of cultural authority is difficult to identify in modern society, where people are exposed to a multitude of competing signals that defy total organization and definition. In the course of daily life people are bombarded with cultural signals from which they construct meaning. Elites are still important, but the signals must be examined too, for insights into the cultural messages they transmit. In order to recreate the meanings available to people at an earlier time, historians must cast a wide net over these cultural signs and include ones that have only limited linear relations.[7]

If Tut and the Scopes trial are juxtaposed as part of the universe of cultural signals bombarding Americans in 1925, then common threads emerge in spite of their lack of linear connection. Both dealt with clashes between assertions that religion provided the bases of national identity and the claim that modern civilization rested on the universal techniques and skills of science. The Tut controversy centered on an international conflict between Egyptian nationalism, defined in religious and cultural terms, and American efforts to protect the treasures of Western civilization. The Scopes trial reflected an intra-national struggle between those who sought to retain the definition of American character as localist, religious, and exceptional, and those who sought to replace that character with one that was urban, secular, and cosmopolitan.[8] In both instances, albeit in different contexts, there was a struggle between culture and science for authority to define social habits and structures.

Even beyond that, though, is the perception of what "science" meant. Both fundamentalists and Egyptian nationalists feared that it connoted control of society by a few extremely wealthy industrialists or by an elite class of managers and experts. They suspected that the rhetoric of science obscured the danger that such control would limit popular participation in public affairs. In this sense the comparison between Tut and the Scopes trial concerns not only the clash between religion and science, but perceptions about what constituted public affairs, who was judged competent to participate in the public life of society, and who established the criteria for participation.[9]

The Scopes trial, of course, has received far more attention as an emblem of religious and constitutional controversy. In 1924 Tennessee became one of four states to forbid the teaching of evolution and other doctrines not compatible with the Bible.[10] Many people, in both North and South, immediately identified this law with the resurgence of the doctrine of states' rights and as a challenge to the Constitution. Opponents of the law in Dayton, Tennessee, decided to challenge it so that the courts could judge its legality. John Scopes, a young teacher (though not of biology), publicly averred that he had taught evolution, and his friends duly swore out a complaint against him.[11] It is important to note that Scopes volunteered to be the defendant. The law was not being enforced by Tennessee, and the penalties attached to it were not particularly punitive.[12] Nevertheless, it theoretically was enforceable. Scopes asked for support from the American Civil Liberties Union (ACLU), which agreed, in anticipation of a quick journey through the federal courts. All these assumptions changed when Clarence Darrow volunteered his services to the ACLU.

In 1925 Darrow's name was notorious. He had started his legal career in a small town not unlike Dayton, but had quickly abandoned it for the vitality of Chicago's political and intellectual life. Darrow had literary aspirations; his apartment near the University of Chicago was a congenial gathering place for activist scholars, lawyers, and journalists.[13] However, his fame derived from his legal connections with cases that shocked conventional thinkers, for he had defended a number of radical labor organizers who were accused by industrialists of trying to destroy "American civilization," by which they meant the system of private industry unhampered by government regulation or unions representing employees. In these cases Darrow had perfected an argument that turned industry arguments upside down. Countering their image of radicals conspiring to attack society, he charged that corrupt conspiracies of private interests and government power threatened to silence individuals who tried to expose the myths by which the common people were restricted. In the Scopes case, Darrow saw religion as yet another private interest that kept the majority in conditions of ignorance, divided from their own best interests. He styled himself the defender of reason, who could expose the repressive cabal of local government and fundamentalist faith.[14]

His defense of radicals alone undoubtedly would have made Darrow suspect to many small-town observers. In 1924, though, he defended two wealthy Chicago youths, Leopold and Loeb, who had confessed to murder following an attempt to commit the "perfect crime." This case made Darrow a household name, for it was exhaustively covered by the press as the "crime of the century." The title was deliberately double-toned. It was among the most scandalous crimes of the period, but it also reflected fears that the side effects of urbanization and industrialization included the loss of morality and human sociability.

Darrow's defense of Leopold and Loeb underlined those observations. He had no hope of winning acquittal for the youths, so he focused instead on the question of culpability. The courts could condemn the crime, but not the criminals, who were merely products of their environment and heredity. Neither boy, indeed no one, exercised free moral judgment. Leopold and Loeb were certainly mentally diseased, but they were no more or less to *blame* than their wealthy but neglectful parents, the University of Chicago, or various book publishers who had provided them with the opportunity to read Nietzsche and his philosophy of the *Übermensch* and the will to power.[15] Society and the law should not condone such behavior, but neither could it damn the doers. The only proper punishment was imprisonment, not execution.[16]

Darrow's defense of determinism contradicted his earlier record on behalf of the voices of protest. If society inevitably was shaped by powers beyond individual control, the function of reason was reduced to describing those powers rather than shaping them, an important but nonetheless passive role.[17] Darrow's justifications themselves were inconsistent. He opposed capital punishment out of distaste for the lurid bloodthirstiness of the mob mentality, but by no means believed that society should not punish crime. Indeed, he supported very strict measures of social control. However, such measures did not defend any abstract sense of justice or morality, for Darrow believed such abstractions were shams manipulated by demagogues. Society should control criminals, but this function should be recognized for what it was: the interest of the dominant classes in maintaining order.[18]

Darrow's defense disturbed many people, even those who shared his commitment to social reform, for it was read as a recantation of his earlier radicalism. If individual protestors served only to disrupt society without hope of changing it, their efforts did seem purposeless and thus appeared to justify corporate accusations of radicalism.[19] The ACLU seriously considered refusing his offer to defend Scopes because it feared he was vulnerable to charges of elitism and amorality, which would confuse the constitutional issue of First Amendment rights.[20] Of course, Darrow did confuse the case, although in an unanticipated way. His appointment as counsel for the defense prompted William Jennings Bryan to accept a similar position for the prosecution. Bryan, too, was a figure who elicited both admiration and contempt. For thirty years he had roiled the Democratic party with his insistent celebration of the virtues of small-town community, as opposed to the patronage organization of urban politics.

Bryan was not ignorant, but he was a simple man and, in 1925, in ill health and increasingly withdrawn from American society. More important, though he was deeply pious, he was not a Biblical literalist. Still, he was the orator deemed most capable of withstanding Darrow's withering courtroom tactics. He agreed to appear in order to support once again his political faith in the virtues of the small community as the model for American society.[21]

Bryan and Darrow's conflict was echoed in a quiet exchange of correspondence in the same year between Tarrytown, New York, and Cairo, Egypt. In New York John D. Rockefeller, Jr., followed with interest the arguments between Western archaeologists and the Egyptian government over the disposition of the treasures unearthed from King Tutankhamon's tomb in 1922–23. Excavations in Egypt had been conducted predominantly by Americans and Europeans; Tut's tomb was discovered by an Englishman, Howard Carter. In the 1920s, however,

Egyptian nationalists of the Wafd' party charged that Western archaeologists were colonialists who exploited Egypt's sacred dead while ignoring Egypt's living populace. They demanded greater local control over excavations.[22]

To Rockefeller these arguments fit a pattern of social conflict for which he had a solution. The nationalist demands seemed similar to American unrest on the part of the working classes. In years past, industrialists had dealt harshly with such demands, but Rockefeller believed it was more enlightened to encourage a sense of community of interests between the wealthy and the rest of society.

This approach reflected Rockefeller's religious beliefs, which were not remarkably different from those of Bryan. Both expressed faith in social harmony. Both believed that violence and unrest resulted from the loss of the religious values that in the past had preserved social harmony. Rockefeller, however, did not believe that Bryan's small community could be preserved in the twentieth century. He aimed instead to substitute corporate relations for community ones. Social unrest was a failing of the businessman as well as the worker, for the businessman had abandoned his duty to set a Christian example. Rockefeller adopted a new responsibility, that of corporate citizen. This citizen had a new definition of public virtue: to use the products (money and material goods) and methods (decentralized organization, public relations, managers trained in similar techniques and social outlooks) of business in order to create social consensus and a peaceful world civilization.

Egypt's unrest particularly resonated with Rockefeller because he linked archaeology with the recovery of Christian sentiment. In this he followed the ideas of one of his beneficiaries, James H. Breasted, an Egyptologist at the University of Chicago.[23] Breasted had studied with William Rainey Harper, a dominant force in the organization of American education and a charismatic figure who had spread a particular idea of modern religiosity. Harper believed that education was a spur to an individual's religious devotion. He equated faith with truth-seeking, with inquiry, and believed deeply that a religion based on ignorance was hypocritical and anti-democratic.[24] He had exercised a strong influence on Breasted and helped to foster what became Breasted's major theme: that the people of ancient times had created the values, specifically mercy and justice, that were essential as well for modern life.

To Breasted the ancients' discovery of social responsibility was a spiritual achievement of far more miraculous proportion than obedience to revealed laws. In particular, he admired the Pharaoh Ikhnaton, the heretic who abolished the Egyptian pantheon and replaced it with worship of the Sun-god Re. Earlier researchers believed that he had left a legacy of chaos and internal divisions to Egypt and its next Pharaoh, Ikhnaton's stepson, Tutankhamon. In Breasted's eyes, though, Ikhnaton was the world's first monotheist. He represented the first break in a religion dominated by superstition, by challenging priestly authority in an effort to spread a gospel that proclaimed a relation between one individual and one god.[25]

In a series of lectures in 1912, Breasted had stressed ancient Egypt's relevance to American society. Religion initially had been imposed upon people by rulers and priests. However, the emergence of an individual moral sense among the non-priestly intelligentsia gave the first impetus to individual free will and a moral community. These individuals did not disrupt order, but created it by breaking away from the "drift of tradition."[26]

He clearly identified with Ikhnaton. Here was a model for moderns, for he "appeals to no myths . . . to no customs sanctified by centuries—he appeals only to personal and visible evidence of his god's dominion, *evidence open to all.*" Instead of folkways or sacerdotalism, Breasted introduced "the rule of ideas" and a belief in the power of individual reason to affect the world.[27] He implored his audience not to dismiss the lesson of Ikhnaton's legacy; not Ikhnaton's ideas but the weakness of his successor, Tutankhamon, allowed the old priests to abolish the reforms. Without Ikhnaton as a guide the common people fell back into folk religions and magical views of life, and the Egyptian empire faded into moral and political decline. Ikhnaton's ideas survived only among Bedouin tribes, who carried them to the Hebrews. Christianity's development merely repeated a pattern that was tied to the broader rise and fall of civilizations.[28]

Breasted's faith in the reforming power of heretics superficially echoed Darrow's justification of radicalism. Both believed that individuals who broke from traditional society were prophets for future progress. Darrow seemed willing to accept a great degree of disorder as an accompaniment of prophets, though, while Breasted suggested that acceptance of iconoclasm would solve unrest in American society. His warnings about the similarities between the ancients and American society captured the attention of a broad public when the popular version of his lectures, *Ancient Times*, was published in 1915. It proved especially interesting to Rockefeller, who sought to foster projects that underscored his views about the relation between religion and social cooperation as an alternative to social revolution. The belief that Ikhnaton sponsored "a vision of social idealism and altruistic human conduct" that began the development that would lead to Christian social cooperation appealed to Rockefeller. He funded Breasted's Oriental Institute at the University of Chicago as a center for research on the development of ancient thought and society. Work on behalf of the institute kept Breasted in Egypt for much of the following five years, so that he was in the Valley of the Kings in November 1922, when Howard Carter asked him to be present at the opening of the tomb of Tutankhamon.[29]

The discovery of King Tut was electrifying. For archaeologists, who long had suspected that the tomb was hidden in the Valley of the Kings, it was a triumph of scientific method and persistence.[30] For Breasted it was also an opportunity to confirm theories about society and religion. He was emotionally overwhelmed by the tomb. He wrote to Rockefeller, "All about us lay a totally new revelation of ancient life, transcending anything we had ever known before."[31]

Breasted was thrilled by the chance to establish the basis for modern religious ideas, but Carter's description of Tut expressed the public's fascination. "All about us," he wrote of his first entrance to the antechamber, "there was the glint of gold."[32] News of the discovery's splendor captured the attention of the world, and, literally overnight, Egypt swarmed with visitors and press. While Breasted assisted in the task of cataloguing and repairing the objects, Carter occupied himself with negotiations with Egyptian authorities over ownership of the treasures.

Carter's haughty attitude strained his relations with the Egyptian government. The acrimony peaked when Egypt withdrew Carter's excavation permit and closed the tomb to all scientific work for a year. This act scandalized archaeologists, who felt that the petty nationalist concerns of the government were endangering the salvage of the most significant discovery in Egyptology.[33] As Carter's difficulties with the Egyptians mounted, he asked Breasted to mediate.

Breasted was not neutral in his sentiments; he referred to Egyptians as "arrogant, self-conscious" nationalists. But he agreed to help. He spent the next year growing increasingly disgusted with both the Egyptians and Carter, who refused most offers of compromise and who persisted in insulting the very officials Breasted tried to placate. By 1925 Breasted was willing to abandon both sides and try a new solution, one based on his vision of social cooperation and educational guidance.

Rather than arguing with the nationalists, he proposed that Rockefeller offer an ingratiating compromise. Egypt was determined to retain control of the Tut undertaking, but scholars were equally adamant that such precious artifacts required expert conservancy. He suggested that Rockefeller could underwrite a new museum that would house the collection and also be a training center for Egyptian curators and archaeologists under Western guidance. It would serve the dual purpose of appeasing nationalism while protecting the relics of early society.

Rockefeller was intrigued. The need clearly existed, for the decrepit Cairo Museum was flooded annually by the Nile.[34] While Rockefeller's attorneys drew up a trust agreement that gave power over the museum administration to a group of international trustees, including two Egyptians, he encouraged Breasted to begin quiet negotiations with the more "responsible" Egyptian authorities.

Breasted was delighted with the opportunity to publicize the United States as the new source of enlightenment. The idea of completing the circle of education begun by Ikhnaton was immensely appealing. He felt this was

a powerful illustration of the new mission of America and American civilization. Here in the ancient valley where men of the Nile first taught the world . . . the wealth of a new continent will return to the ancestral shores to raise a shining symbol of Western enlightenment and friendship.[35]

Rockefeller used these ideas in his offer to King Fuad of Egypt and cited links between the newest land of the West and the oldest land in history as impetus for his profound interest in the development of Egypt.[36]

If Rockefeller's gesture was stunning in its generosity, it also was carefully constructed to keep control of the museum in the hands of the trustees outside Egypt so as "to make it easier to manage in the event of any political situation arising." Even as he formalized the offer, the political situation did deteriorate when the assassination of the British governor in Egypt led to a rout of the nationalists. However, Breasted felt that this represented an opportunity to negotiate with officials not attached to the more radical Wafd' party. He formally offered a ten-million-dollar museum to King Fuad in February 1926.[37]

The Americans were disconcerted by the King's cool reaction. They blamed Egyptian ignorance of art and the peevish and vain character of Egyptians in general for the delays in solidifying the deal. One negotiator concluded it was evident that Egyptians would be helpless in independence, as they stubbornly focused on details rather than the "big picture." The King lacked common sense, he added, for he objected to the strings attached to the museum rather than praising the splendor of the gift. Negotiations continued into April, but Egyptian reluctance to meet the terms and the threatened return of the Wafd' to power finally led Rockefeller to withdraw the offer.[38]

The Americans were genuinely shocked at the rejection, and discounted the Egyptian argument that Western control was an affront to the Egyptian public. Breasted personally blamed "a few anti-foreign bigots," who spoiled the opportunity for all Egyptians.[39] Americans never accepted the Egyptian argument that Tut was a peculiarly Egyptian matter and that any guidance by Westerners was interference in national affairs. They believed that their own motives of safeguarding the heritage of civilization were reasonable, indeed inevitable. In contrast, they derided Egyptians as ignorant demagogues, whose appreciation of Tut's aesthetic masterpieces remained at the low level of fascination with amulets, charms, and fears of the mummy's curse.[40]

The charge of ignorance figured also in the Scopes trial, where it was important for Darrow's strategy that Bryan and religion appear profoundly ignorant. He combined two assertions into one argument, which he defined as the defense of reason. Initially he used the ACLU argument that the First Amendment disallowed efforts to impose any one religious view on Americans.[41] This is the argument for which Darrow has been praised, for he evoked the classic Jeffersonian concepts of individualism that continue to provide the core of defense of rights in the United States.[42] However, he tied those rights to more personal prejudices that equated religion with ignorance and coercion. It was impossible, he said, for Tennessee to build a Chinese wall around the state in order to keep out knowledge. This was a forceful argument but a fearsome one as well. Walls not only exclude but contain. If there was a possibility that "ignorance" could seep out to infect others, those attitudes could not just be controlled; they had to be defeated.

Bryan's argument, like that of the Egyptian nationalists, simply pursued a different agenda: an anti-colonial argument writ small. He repeatedly emphasized that "foreigners" from Illinois should not be able to compel Tennesseans to do anything. We do not invade your communities in an effort to change your beliefs, he contended, so we ask that you leave us in peace as well.[43] He also objected to Darrow's efforts to rest the case on the testimony of experts as if they had a privileged monopoly on truth. The trial was indifferent to issues of science and education. Instead, it went to the heart of the issue of citizenship: Who was allowed to participate in questions of concern to a public community and who set the values for it?

Bryan argued that he had nothing against education. God did not despise the learned, but God did not attend exclusively to the learned either. A religion that appealed only to the educated, to those with the inclination to contemplate their place in the cosmos, would ignore ninety-nine percent of the people. It would be exclusionary and elitist, an ethical sacerdotalism rather than a religion of the common man. Darrow's type of scientific expertise was destructive of American cultural codes of equality and public citizenship. If citizenship had educational preconditions, community was replaced by hierarchy. If a community's values were separated from everyday life, an individual had no reason to acknowledge moral codes. Bryan acknowledged the value of education for modern life but said, "the God I worship is the God of the ignorant as well as the God of the learned man."[44]

These are serious issues, which have been obscured by efforts to depict Darrow as the heroic defender of liberty and Bryan as an ignorant fanatic. Indisputably, Darrow's arguments on behalf of the right to think and speak are landmarks in the defense of civil liberties in the twentieth century. Bryan's fundamentalists supported "community" but ignored the idea that community participation meant the whole community, not just those members who agreed with them. However, Darrow also grossly exaggerated the threat posed by the Tennessee law. He borrowed a tactic from his labor law cases and charged that there was a dread conspiracy aiming to separate people from all their rights. In essence, he concocted a domino theory of civil liberties. The Dayton trial was but the first battle in the war against repression. It could be won by forcing religionists to concede that only scientific thinkers were competent to establish laws.

Darrow clearly saw that Bryan's democracy could be a form of tyranny of the majority. He recognized, too, that the symbols of religion might be far more coercive if used by someone who was not as tired and ill and honest as Bryan. However, Darrow's argument left no room for measuring whether religious emotions were genuine or were being manipulated by charlatans. His eloquence on behalf of evolution was bound tightly to his cynical view of all religion as delusion.[45]

He left no room either for the crucial issue of participation. By lampooning fundamentalists as lunatics, he dismissed their argument that society was capable of weighing moral choices. By implication, only scientific knowledge was capable of guiding society, but this distorted the nature of science as inquiry and left positivist science vulnerable when it was unable to produce perfect social solutions.[46] Darrow himself knew that experts could and did disagree and that a clever lawyer could pick and choose among facts to create an aura for a jury, but he chose to obscure this point in order to paint a stark portrait of religion and science in a struggle for authority.[47]

In this sober discussion of battles within American culture, it seems almost flippant to note that Darrow mentioned Breasted and King Tut at the Scopes trial. Darrow's expert witnesses were not allowed to testify before the jury, but in a publicity-grasping move Darrow called Bryan to the stand as an "expert" on the Bible.[48] Bryan accepted in anticipation that his testimony would underscore the need for society to be attentive to New Testament morality. However, Darrow emphasized the Old Testament and questioned the link some fundamentalists had made between specific historical dates and the stories in Genesis. In the process he brought up Tut and ancient civilization. Bryan asserted that the Bible was unfailingly correct as a guide to moral behavior, though not to all knowledge. Darrow ignored the distinction and asked Bryan if he was familiar with Breasted's views that the Bible was not revealed truth but a reweaving of Egyptian tales. Bryan professed indifference, but Darrow persisted and asked him about the disparities between geology, archaeology, and the supposed dates of the Flood and Creation. Bryan fell into Darrow's trap when, after some fulmination, he admitted that the Book of Genesis need not be accepted in temporal terms. Darrow retorted that if one day did not equal a literal twenty four hours, then creation could have taken a week, or a month, or millions of years, thus making it compatible with evolution as taught by Scopes and technically not in violation of state law.[49]

The jury did not hear this testimony. The judge ruled it inadmissible, and, when the court reconvened on the following day, Darrow changed Scopes's plea to guilty in order to move quickly to the appeal process. Although this was a technical concession to Bryan, it was Bryan who was a triple loser. Darrow had succeeded in caricaturing him as dogmatic and indecisive, yet had avoided being put in a position to explain his own views. Bryan's fundamentalist supporters had been dismayed and alienated by his admission that the Bible need not be taken literally. Most important, Darrow had obscured his real argument, which was encapsulated in the final point of comparison between Scopes and Tut, the "ascent" versus the "descent" of man.

Bryan believed that Darrow ignored the extent to which Christianity had made the United States an exceptionalist society. Darrow's argument to replace Christianity with science as the arbiter of the American character meant to Bryan that the United States would become as exploitative and cynical as any other industrial nation. He tried to illuminate this by reference to Leopold and Loeb and argued that they represented the depths to which society could descend when it relied solely on intellect as a measure of social morality. Bryan suspected that in the guise of his defense of science Darrow really was arguing for a limit on political and social participation.[50]

Darrow objected sharply to this comparison of the two trials and accused Bryan of cheap sensationalism; but in a bumbling, half-conscious way, Bryan had focused on a disturbing issue. Darrow, too, was an admirer of Nietzsche. His closest political allies had been men of great will but few scruples. They had enormous faith in their righteousness and capacity to act on behalf of the people, but they also denigrated people's capacity to know their interests. Darrow's was an eloquent plea for liberty for iconoclasts who had risen above the common views, but he never established standards by which to judge true or false prophets.[51]

In comparison, Egyptian nationalists rejected the American offer because it deprived *them* of a personal, exceptionalist symbol from which they as a unique people had descended. Tut was an incontestable image of solely Egyptian culture and "help" from Americans was just another example of Western arrogance. Rockefeller and Breasted felt this was narrow and unreasonable. They, too, styled the passage from localism to modernity as an "ascent" from ignorance. The museum would have served as a symbol of their brand of guidance, which united nations by an appreciation of their common heritage.

Bryan believed that to give in to modernism would be to abandon social morality and the peculiar identity of American community. Darrow felt that fundamentalism threatened the possibility of moving beyond tradition. Small wonder then that they both saw the trial as "the death struggle between two civilizations."[52] A superficial glance would suggest that Bryan's civilization lost; his technical victory was hollow, and his efforts to defend a small community from outside contamination was exactly as Darrow described it—a futile attempt to stop the future.[53] In a similar manner Breasted and Rockefeller successfully opposed the nationalists, though in a negative way. Rather than negotiate with them, they withdrew the museum offer and turned their attention to archaeology in Palestine, where British control seemed more stable.[54]

But ultimately which values predominated? Who defined American "civilization" for the future? In 1925 there were not two but three views in conflict. Bryan, like the Egyptian nationalists, defended the virtues of a particularistic community against any innovation from outside. Breasted and Rockefeller praised a cosmopolitan civilization that was creating global harmony, but that regarded diversity as ignorant and destabilizing. Significantly, neither Bryan nor Rockefeller envisioned a civilization that permitted conflict. Although they held very different views of belief and community, both hoped for social harmony rather than dissension. In this they differed from Darrow, who defended the right to dissent, the right to be different.[55] On the basis of his earlier labor cases, he might have sympathized with the efforts of small communities to stand against the impersonal force of industrializing power. In 1925, though, he rejected the hope that such protest could be exercised on behalf of any definable sense of community.

However, there are important comparisons between Darrow's and Rockefeller's views, too. The museum aimed to placate nationalist demands for autonomy by offering the opportunity to acquire skills necessary to replace Western tutelage. The American proposal was the only "real" alternative to colonial domination, but Egyptians should be satisfied because it connected the Egyptian heritage to the rest of civilization. There was room in the American mansion for King Tut as an ancestor of all Western men. The gift of a museum is a startlingly appropriate metaphor. The Egyptian heritage would be neatly catalogued, assorted, and displayed as an interesting but dated relic, confined to experts for protection because it had outlived its capacity to inspire passion and belief.

Darrow's arguments attempted a similar enclosure. Properly configured, science and Christianity could dwell in mutually exclusive but compatible spheres of thought. Darrow asserted that he was not interested in destroying the Bible as a good book, but he wanted to confine it to its proper realm, namely, individual choice instead of community mores. The only true universal was science. Scientific experts—those called as expert witnesses anyway—professed Christianity, but they did so for personal reasons, not because its teachings were particularly relevant or binding.[56] Christianity could be a part of modern American culture, but it must relinquish its claim to define the public character of America.

Any criticism of Darrow must be blunted by an understanding that American society in 1925 was peopled by individuals of many faiths. When he argued that Christianity no longer could dictate policy, he made a path for the ideal of tolerance for a multitude of viewpoints. But in his earlier cases, his defense— that no one social interest should dictate policy—was directed against corporations that attempted to proclaim social harmony based only on business desires.

In the Scopes trial, however, he used language that came very close to echoing that of Rockefeller; attempts on the part of a community to defy the civilization of which science was the foundation were ignorant or even subversive. Rockefeller and Breasted couched their definition of civilization in scientific and educational terms, but they clearly envisioned an international harmony based on American methods. In their catechism, "expertise," "consensus," and "civilization" substituted for "good." When Egyptian nationalists refused to accept the museum, they were described in the only language this catechism could imagine: "ignorant," "divisive," "barbaric."

In similar fashion Darrow confronted Bryan with the vocabulary to which his years as attorney for unpopular causes had enured him: "conspiracy," "persecution," "ignorance." He, too, defended his views in terms of science, but he was inspired by a sense of social dissonance to emphasize the dangers of fundamentalism. Like Rockefeller, though, he failed to make a distinction between "reason" and what he considered "reasonable."

After 1925 the modernist vocabulary did emphasize "civilization" and "reason" as primary values. The definitions, though, resembled those of Rockefeller: consensus and social harmony based on the benevolent guidance of scientific expertise. Fundamentalist and communitarian discourse did not disappear, but its inclusion into public discussions remained confusing and divisive unless "community" came clothed in a corporate rhetoric that exalted a silent majority who accepted what experts offered. Yet, in 1928 Walter Lippmann commented on the Scopes trial. He observed that fundamentalists had been asked to submit to the destructive effects of scepticism and indifferent tolerance. Lippmann warned that asking any culture "to smile and commit suicide" led not to a universalization of culture, but to more and more drastic challenges to the modern ethos.[57] Lippmann certainly was neither a defender of ignorance nor a partisan of particularistic religious identity. His comment was a warning that the codes of "civilization" and "science" could be problems in the future if they formed a truncated language that could explain *all* expressions of community only as vestigial, ignorant, or subversive, or that took "reason" to be the property only of educated elites. To say this is not to ignore the problems with participation that Breasted and Rockefeller saw: divisiveness and instability, *or* the problems that Darrow exposed: complacency with "things as they are" and invitations to demagoguery.

It does suggest, though, that there might have been a fourth view of American civilization possible in 1925, one that legitimated argument over issues of morality and participation as part of the quest for a "great society." This view might have developed from Darrow's earlier vision of American society as one that did not merely submit to structures of industry and technology but that substituted inquiry for authority as the character of American civilization: the freedom to question rather than to obey. Despite structural problems—whose questions would be valued and whose discounted, who would choose the criteria—this vision had faith in the creative tension between an outsider, a protestor who tried to awaken people, and the ability of a community to judge that protestor's message.[58] In previous cases Darrow had defended such protestors, but in Dayton he was more purely destructive in his efforts to expose religious authority as a fraud.

In the Scopes trial the outsider remained the stranger, capable of understanding a community's structures but ultimately indifferent to its life. Darrow the radical, who had used Rockefeller, Sr., as an image of all that oppressed American society in 1902, had become Darrow the cynic. He had not changed his belief about the dangers of a rhetoric of "consensus," but he implicitly extended that sense of danger to any definition of "community."[59] He seemed to succeed, but in doing so he also succeeded in identifying scientific thought with a certain determinism and elitism, a sense that it was useless to oppose science or, at least, those who identified themselves as scientific experts. Ironically, the dissenter became part of a majority, which could hear only threats and conspiracies in fundamentalist voices of protest because it could not separate the issue of participation from the conflict between religion and science.

NOTES

1. William McLoughlin, *Billy Sunday Was His Real Name* (Chicago, 1965); Bruce Barton, *The Man Nobody Knows* (Indianapolis, 1925); Donald Meyer, *The Positive Thinkers* (New York, 1965); George Marsden, ed., *Evangelicalism and Modern America*

(Grand Rapids, Mich., 1984); James Hunter, *American Evangelicalism: Conservative Religion and the Quandary of Modernity* (New Brunswick, N.J., 1983).

2. William Leuchtenburg, *The Perils of Prosperity* (New York, 1958), 217–23, is sympathetic to the pressures on fundamentalism and notes that it made sense in a rural atmosphere, but nevertheless dismisses it as profound ignorance, akin to prohibition and nativism.

3. The use of economics and culture is discussed in Frank Costigliola, *Awkward Dominion* (Ithaca, N.Y., 1984), and Melvyn P. Leffler, *The Elusive Quest* (Chapel Hill, N.C., 1979).

4. For some of Rockefeller's activities, see Charles Harvey, "John D. Rockefeller, Jr., and the Interchurch World Movement of 1919–1920," *Church History* 51 (1982): 198–209.

5. Breasted, *Ancient Times* (New York, 1915). Piltdown Man, of course, was a hoax, exposed in 1953. Nevertheless, experts of the 1920s took it quite seriously. Joseph Weiner, *Piltdown's Forgery* (London, 1955), and Ronald Millar, *The Piltdown Men* (New York, 1972).

6. Friedrich Engels, *The German Ideology*, C. J. Arthur, ed. (London, 1977); Antonio Gramsci, *Selections from the Prison Notebooks of Antonio Gramsci*, Quintin Hoare and Geoffrey Nowell Smith, eds. (New York, 1972); Thomas R. Bates, "Gramsci and the Theory of Hegemony," *Journal of the History of Ideas* 36 (1975): 351–66.

7. Edmund Leach, *Culture and Communications* (New York, 1976), 9. "We must know a lot about the cultural context . . . before we can even begin to decode the message."

8. One could argue that "civilization" became a substitute for "mission." The approach of New Left historians, such as William Appleman Williams, *The Tragedy of American Diplomacy* (New York, 1959) and Walter LaFeber, *The New Empire* (Ithaca, N.Y., 1963), rejected "mission" as anything more than the gloss for geopolitical concerns and material interests. Frank Ninkovich, "Ideology, the Open Door and Foreign Policy," *Diplomatic History* 6 (1982): 185–208, points toward a corrective by re–introducing the concept of culture. See, also, Raymond Williams, "Base and Superstructure in Marxist Cultural Theory," *New Left Review* 82 (1973): 3–16, and Clifford Geertz, "Ideology as a Cultural System," in Geertz, *The Interpretation of Cultures* (New York, 1973), 201–3.

9. There are many interesting, if superficial, comparisions between Egypt and the American South. Both were cotton cultures, economically backward relative to an industrial North, but in the midst of the industrializing tensions that previously had gripped the North. Both were also objects of Rockefeller philanthropy. See Rockefeller Foundation, *Annual Reports*, 1925–30.

10. See Leuchtenburg, *Perils of Prosperity*, 204–24; George Marsden, *Fundamentalism and American Culture: The Shaping of Twentieth-Century Evangelicalism, 1870–1925* (New York, 1980); Ernest R. Sandeen, *The Roots of Fundamentalism: British and American Millenarianism, 1800–1930* (Chicago, 1970); and William R. Hutchinson, *The Modern Impulse in American Protestantism* (New York, 1976).

11. John T. Scopes and James Presley, *Center of the Storm* (New York, 1967), 57–64. This account makes clear how formal the challenge was. It also notes that Dayton was interested in acquiring the trial in order to help its businesses.

12. Ibid., 187–88. *Inherit the Wind*, the play by Jerome Lawrence and Robert E. Lee (New York, 1955), greatly exaggerates the threat to Scopes, who in fact was offered his job back once the trial was completed.

13. Clarence Darrow, *The Story of My Life* (New York, 1932). Kevin Tierney, *Darrow, A Biography* (New York, 1979), is the most recent and objective study, but see, also, Irving Stone, *Clarence Darrow for the Defense* (New York, 1941); Abe C. Ravitz, *Clarence Darrow and the American Literary Tradition* (Cleveland, 1962); and Victor S. Yarros, *My Eleven Years with Clarence Darrow* (Girard, Kans., 1950).

14. Tierney, *Darrow*, 105–6, 150–51. His more famous defenses included those of Eugene Debs (1894), the coal miners (1902 hearings), the IWW leader William Haywood (1906), and Communists involved in the Seattle shipworkers' strike (1919). See Alan Trachtenberg, *The Incorporation of America* (New York, 1982), 234; Arthur Weinberg, ed., *Attorney for the Damned* (New York, 1957), 267–488; and Darrow, "The Right of Revolution" (1895), in Arthur and Lila Weinberg, eds., *Verdicts Out of Court* (Chicago, 1963), 57–64.

15. Weinberg, ed., *Attorney for the Damned*, 16–88, especially 70–77; Francis X. Busch, *Prisoners at the Bar* (New York, 1952), 163–64; and Hal Higdon, *Crime of the Century* (New York, 1975).

16. This conformed to Darrow's long-held beliefs about capital punishment. See Darrow, *Crime: Its Cause and Treatment* (New York, 1922); Darrow, "Is Capital Punishment a Wise Policy?" in Weinberg, ed., *Attorney for the Damned*, 89–103; Darrow, "The Futility of the Death Penalty," in Weinbergs, eds., *Verdicts Out of Court*, 225–32.

17. Peter Conn, *The Divided Mind* (Cambridge, Mass., 1983), 49–82, describes the cynicism of muckraking journalists of the time. They exposed corruption but offered no alternative vision.

18. "Crime and Criminals," Address to the Prisoners, Cook County Jail (1902) in Weinberg, ed., *Attorney for the Damned*, 3–15; "The Hold-Up Man," *International Socialist Review* (1909) in Weinbergs, eds., *Verdicts Out of Court*, 219–24.

19. Tierney, *Darrow*, 318, 346–47, 352–53.

20. Jerry R. Tompkins, *D-Days at Dayton* (Baton Rouge, 1965), 19–20.

21. Bryan and Darrow had nursed animosity toward one another since 1896, when Darrow, as a political advisor to the Illinois Democratic party, felt Bryan's simple pieties had alienated the urban working classes. Tierney, *Darrow*, 125–27. For Bryan's political career, see Louis Koenig, *Bryan, A Political Biography* (New York, 1971).

22. Thomas Hoving, *Tutankhamon, The Untold Story* (New York, 1978), 109, 137, 155–63, 226–29; Charles Breasted, *Pioneer to the Past* (New York, 1943), 335–68. See also James H. Breasted to John D. Rockefeller, Jr. (JDR), 4 September 1925, Office of Messrs. Rockefeller (OMR), Record Group (RG) III, 2 E, B.25, F.258, Cultural Interests, Cairo Museum 1924–43, Rockefeller Archive Center (RAC), Tarrytown, New York

23. Charles Breasted, *Pioneer to the Past*, is a lively biography by James Breasted's son. It provides a fascinating picture of the relation between Egyptology and American politics and society in the early twentieth century. Also, see John A. Wilson, *Signs and Wonders Upon Pharaoh* (Chicago, 1964).

24. William R. Harper, "Bible Study and Religious Life," in Harper, *Religion and the Higher Life* (Chicago, 1910), 141–72; Robert Funk, "The Watershed of the American Biblical Tradition: The Chicago School, First Phase, 1892–1920," *The Journal of Biblical Literature* 95 (March 1976): 4–22. Harper is best known for his role as the first president of the University of Chicago, but he is also a quite interesting figure in the history of the popularization of religious education. See Leonard Sweet, "The University of Chicago

Revisited: The Modernization of Theology 1890–1940,'' *Foundations* 22 (October–December 1979): 338.

25. Wilson, *Signs and Wonders*, 142.

26. Charles Breasted, *Pioneer to the Past*, 135–38. The lectures were subsequently published as *The Development of Religion and Thought in Ancient Egypt* (New York, 1912), 3–117, 165–98, 339.

27. Breasted, *Religion and Thought*, 339–42. Other Egyptologists dispute Breasted's interpretation, and feel that he imposed his own beliefs and hopes onto his translations of inscriptions and papyri. See Wilson, *Signs and Wonders*, Introduction.

28. He analyzed a series of political tracts that criticized the corruption of Egyptian society and described it as ''shackled by its own inertia, incapable of discerning its own misery, or . . . without the initiative to undertake its own regeneration.'' Such criticisms could ''find appropriate place in the mouth of a morally sensitive social observer of our own times.'' But these Egyptian jeremiads also held out hope that evil could be ameliorated, and perhaps could provide clues for American social reformers as well. Breasted, *Religion and Thought*, 166, 202, 306–70.

29. Charles Breasted, *Pioneer to the Past*, 229–34. Breasted-Rockefeller correspondence is to be found in the James Breasted Papers, Oriental Institute, University of Chicago, Chicago, Illinois. See, especially, Breasted to Rockefeller, 16 February 1919; Rockefeller to Harry P. Judson (President, University of Chicago), 2 May 1919; Breasted to Rockefeller, 25 September 1931; Rockefeller to Raymond B. Fosdick, 23 November 1938, for a recapitulation of the Rockefeller grants to Breasted and the Oriental Institute. Also, see an Oriental Institute catalogue, *John D. Rockefeller, Jr., A Centenary Exhibition* (December 1974).

30. Carter had methodically plotted his search and had been engaged in the process for a decade. It added to the romance of the discovery that the tomb was discovered during the last season for which Carter was able to secure funding. Hoving, *Tutankhamon*, 73–89.

31. Charles Breasted, *Pioneer to the Past*, 336. Breasted to Rockefeller, 2 February 1923, OMR, RG2, B.111, F. Envelope #1, RAC. In fact, the tomb never yielded a wealth of information about society and social thought for, though rich in artistic treasures, it contained few papyri that described the period in which Tut was Pharaoh.

32. Herbert Winlock, the Metropolitan Museum of Art's Field Director, who was also present, reiterated this view. It was ''a fairy tale, an enchanted property room from the opera house of some great composer's dreams.'' Charles Breasted, *Pioneer to the Past*, 335.

33. Hoving, *Tutankhamon*, 155–63, 226–29; Charles Breasted, *Pioneer to the Past*, 368. Breasted to Rockefeller, 4 September 1925, OMR, RGIII, 2E, B.25, F.258, Cultural Interests, Cairo Museum 1924–43, RAC.

34. He mused that it was preferable to encourage the government to sell the relics to pay its national debt. However, if Egyptians were insistent, Tut had to be protected. Rockefeller to Fosdick, 24 October 1924, B.25, F.258, RAC.

35. Breasted to Rockefeller, 8 February 1926, B.25, F.261, RAC. For the trust agreement, see Breasted to Rockefeller, 21 July 1925; Breasted to Fosdick, 26 February 1925; Thomas M. Debevoise to Chauncey Belknap, 13 June 1925; Debevoise to Robert W. Gumbel, 22 July 1925; Debevoise to Fosdick, 9 September 1925, B.25, F.261, RAC.

36. Rockefeller to King Fuad (Draft), 13 June 1925. Breasted used this phrase in his

official announcement to the Egyptian press. Breasted to Rockefeller (Telegram), 13 February 1926, B.25, F.261, RAC.

37. Breasted to Rockefeller, 19 November 1925; Rockefeller to Breasted, 8 December 1925; Breasted to Rockefeller, 10 February 1926, B.25, F.261, RAC.

38. Chauncey Belknap to Rockefeller, "Egyptian Museum Negotiations, 1925–26," 10 March 1926 (received); Breasted to Prime Minister Ahmed Ziwar Pasha, 8 April 1926 (Copy); Breasted to Rockefeller, 13 April 1926, B.25, F.261, RAC. Even among Egyptians there was disappointment at the loss of the museum. See articles in the Egyptian newspapers, *L'Espoir*, 8 April 1926, p. 1, and 1 May 1926, p. 1; and *Egyptian Gazette*, 5 May 1926, pp. 1–2. Tut reappears in American foreign relations in 1978, when the travelling exhibit (which was carefully orchestrated to generate a positive view of Egypt in the midst of the Camp David negotiations) pervaded popular culture. Carter Ratcliff, "Tut, Exxon and Anita Loos," *Art in America* 67 (March-April 1979): 95.

39. Breasted is quoted in Ivy Lee to Rockefeller, 4 March 1926, B.25, F.261, RAC. Rockefeller himself later wrote that though the United States was accused of selfishness, it really was founded on an appreciation of the same vital and eternal supremacy of universal values that were represented by the Egyptian ruins. Sadly, the United States also faced the same suspicion and greed that had contributed to the decline of Egyptian civilization. Rockefeller's comment in *Egypt*, transcript of his remarks while on a journey to the pyramids, Winter 1928. RG2, JDR, Jr.–Personal, B.10, RAC.

40. One Rockefeller retainer scoffed that "public opinion does not exist in a country 95% illiterate." Fosdick to Rockefeller, 4 March 1926. OMR, RGIII, 2E, B.25, F.258, Cultural Interests, Cairo Museum 1924–43, RAC. The low level of art appreciation on the part of the Egyptian *fellahin* was replicated in the American public's interest in movies about "the curse of the mummy," which provided fodder for the silent film industry. This had an ancestor in popular curiosity about "the lands of the Bible" that had existed in the nineteenth century and that had exerted influence on American culture. Erik Iverson, "The Canonical Tradition," in J.R. Harris, ed., *The Legacy of Egypt* (Oxford, 1971), 70; Donald B. Kuspit, "Our Egypt," *Art in America* 67 (March-April 1979): 86–93; Richard G. Carrott, *The Egyptian Revival: Its Sources, Monuments and Meaning, 1808–1858* (Berkeley, Calif., 1978), 62. Early examples of Egyptian influence include the obelisks of the Washington Monument and the Bunker Hill Monument, the Grove Street Cemetery in New Haven, and the pyramid and ankh (eye) on the Great Seal of the United States. Two early works on Egypt for American audiences were Edward Robinson, *Biblical Researches* (New York, 1841), and George Glidden, *Ancient Egypt* (New York, 1843).

41. Leslie H. Allen, ed., *Bryan and Darrow at Dayton: A Record of Documents of the "Bible-Evolution" Trial* (Freeport, N.Y., 1967), 7.

42. Weinberg, ed., *Attorney for the Damned*, 183–84.

43. Allen, ed., *Bryan and Darrow* 7, 66, 74–78, 185–93.

44. Ibid., 9.

45. He emphasized Bryan's sincerity in a later article. Bryan was a "fanatic... but there is a clear distinction between the fanatic and the charlatan." Darrow, review of *Bryan* by M. R. Werner, in *The New Republic*, May 15, 1929, 363–64.

46. As one example, his experts commonly relied on Piltdown Man as proof of evolution, a source that was later exposed as a fraud. Tierney, *Darrow*, 360.

47. Leopold and Loeb, for example, were examined by eighteen psychiatrists, fourteen for the defense in order support Darrow's claim that the youths suffered from mental

disease that rendered them incapable of human emotion. Darrow, ''How To Pick a Jury,'' *Esquire* (May 1936), in Weinbergs, eds., *Verdicts Out of Court*, 313–24.

48. Affidavits of the testimony were accepted. All the attorneys knew that the Dayton trial was only a formality for appeal to a higher court.

49. Charles Breasted, *Pioneer to the Past*, 230; Allen, *Bryan and Darrow*, 29. In a sense Darrow had prepared his brief against Bryan two years earlier. The 4 July 1923, edition of the Chicago *Tribune* carried his series of questions about the Bible, which he addressed to Bryan, on the front page. Tierney, *Darrow*, 356.

50. Allen, *Bryan and Darrow*, 74–78, 185–93. A pamphlet containing Darrow's summation in that case was on sale in Dayton during the trial.

51. For example, Darrow was a close adviser to John Altgeld and William Randolph Hearst. Tierney, *Darrow*, 67–77, 160–77, 201–5.

52. Allen, *Bryan and Darrow*, 15. Compare both with Breasted's urgency about the post-Ikhnaton imperial decline. Each seemed convinced that the United States faced disaster if his approach was not adopted.

53. Scopes was fined one hundred dollars, but the conviction was overturned on a technicality in state court. The Supreme Court did not rule on such laws until the 1960s. See *Epperson v. Arkansas* 393 U.S. 97 (1968). Mississippi repealed the last anti-evolution law dating from the 1920s in 1972. *New York Times*, 16 April 1972, sect. 1, p.18.

54. After the Cairo project collapsed, Rockefeller donated a smaller sum to the British protectorate in Palestine for a museum, which is now the Rockefeller Museum in East Jerusalem. Charles Breasted, *Pioneer to the Past*, 397–403. OMR: JDR Educational Interests, RG 2, B. 111, F. Collections—University of Chicago, Oriental Institute, Envelope 1, RAC.

55. Bryan's desire for consensus shaped his entire career. He clearly understood that modernity was changing the meaning of America, but could never articulate an alternate society that appealed to fundamentalists and non-fundamentalists alike.

56. Allen, *Bryan and Darrow*, 29.

57. Walter Lippmann, *American Inquisitors* (New York, 1928), 65–66.

58. For Lippmann's struggles on this issue, see David Hollinger, ''Science and Anarchy: Walter Lippmann's *Drift and Mastery*,'' *American Quarterly* 29 (1977): 463–75.

59. Weinberg, ed., *Attorney for the Damned*, 10–15.

9

Revive Us Again: Alienation, Hope, and the Resurgence of Fundamentalism, 1930–1950

Joel A. Carpenter

For the past sixty years people have been predicting the imminent demise of American fundamentalism. In 1926 the editors of the *Christian Century*, who were savoring liberals' recent victories in the fundamentalist-modernist controversies, tried to post the movement's obituary. "Anybody should be able to see," they asserted, that "the whole fundamentalist movement was hollow and artificial" and "wholly lacking in qualities of constructive achievement or survival."[1] Today, however, the heirs of fundamentalism and a variety of other evangelical movements and traditions are thriving, and their newfound prominence in American public life has to be regarded as one of the greatest surprises in recent American history.[2]

Among those who have sought to explain this phenomenon, the best general theory may well belong to Martin Marty. He has brushed aside the common notion that "old-time religion" is inherently anti-modern and dysfunctional, in favor of the view that evangelicalism is "the characteristic Protestant way of relating to modernity."[3] Evangelicals have adapted readily to modernity's compartmentalization of life because theirs is an intensely personal religious expression. Modern society is often structured to favor voluntarism and choice-making, and evangelicals have responded to this reality with aggressive recruiting and creative institution-making, while more established faiths have tended to take the church's place in life for granted. Because the modern temper is intense, impatient, and egalitarian, modern people commonly expect to have quick and personal access to knowledge and experience. By offering such to "whosoever will," Marty argues, evangelicals have provided a viable faith for millions of modern Americans.[4] These features apply to fundamentalists in particular, as well as to evangelicals in general.[5] Fundamentalists survived their defeats in the 1920s, regrouped, and came to a fresh understanding of their mandate for the years to come, thanks to their embodiment of these characteristically evangeli-cal—and modern—features.

These developments, which have been traced in a number of studies, dem-onstrate fundamentalism's longevity, but do not explain its expansiveness and activism.[6] Sectarian impulses grew strong in the movement after the controversies of the 1920s, so its institutional vitality and grass-roots support did not imply it would necessarily re-emerge as a public force. This vigor could very well have been a sign that it was building a religious ghetto in which to await the Second Coming. Although fundamentalism did cultivate a fortress mentality, it also produced Billy Graham, whose generation of "neo-evangelical" leaders set out in the late 1940s to reform fundamentalism, reassert its cultural responsibility, and take its message to the world. And, more recently, the militant separatist wing that rejected neo-evangelicalism as too worldly has produced Jerry Falwell, who led a large contingent of separatists into public activism.[7]

In order to understand fundamentalism's engagement with American public life over the past generation, as well as its survival, one needs to examine the vision that drives it. The vision in this case is an old one, but one fraught with mythic power. During the 1930s fundamentalists began to seek another Great Awakening. While they predicted the imminent arrival of the cataclysmic "end times," they also yearned for a spiritual revival that would restore their churches' vitality, bring salvation and healing to their society, and, by implication, restore evangelical Christianity's lost cultural influence in America. This "revivalist" view of history qualified the otherwise grimly millenarian outlook that funda-mentalists accepted by offering them a way out of their cultural and religious alienation. As a result, a recharged fundamentalist movement appeared in the late 1940s that was determined to bring revival to America and the gospel to the world. Some of its young scholars even dreamed of "remaking the modern mind." The growing expectations of a "surprising work of God" helped to produce a major resurgence of evangelical religion by the 1950s and explain much of the contemporary public role of fundamentalist evangelicals.

FROM ALIENATION TO HOPE

Many observers thought fundamentalism played out by 1930. Its dual interests of bringing revival to America and crusading against modernism in church and society lacked public support. In the wake of the failed crusades of fundamen-talism, Walter Lippmann observed that the movement had been defeated and discredited. It was no longer able to appeal to "the best brains and the good sense of the modern community."[8] By Billy Sunday's death in 1935 urban revival campaigns and "the evangelical type of piety," as the *Christian Century* put it, also seemed to be dying out.[9] Americans seemed to have lost much of their interest in being saved, at least in the evangelical sense.

Fundamentalists responded to this adverse climate with an alienated stance toward mainstream America during the 1930s. James M. Gray, president of the

Moody Bible Institute, counselled that fundamentalists should "expect to be fought, to be spoken against, to be boycotted and picked at," because the "offense of the cross has not ceased." They should stand firm in what were "fighting days" for them.[10] To be a fundamentalist was to bear the social and psychic burden of an outsider.

One of the most important shapers of the fundamentalist outlook in those years was dispensational premillennialism, a doctrinal system that was preoccupied with prophecies of the second coming of Christ. The upheavals represented by Zionism, the Bolshevik Revolution, the fundamentalist-modernist controversy, the Great Depression, and the rise of fascist dictatorships and anti-Semitism proved to fundamentalists that the last days of the present age were at hand.[11] They thus had to ask what were the prospects of the "true church" as the age neared its end. The church was "not a permanent institution in the world," insisted Arno C. Gaebelein, editor of *Our Hope*, a dispensational monthly. Its "prospects" were "not in earthly things but in the glory with Him."[12] Until Christ came for them, the faithful were to evangelize the lost, discern the signs of the times, keep themselves free from error, and "earnestly contend for the faith" (Jude 3)—while the majority of professing Christians, their churchly institutions, and indeed all civilization stumbled toward the abyss. This outlook, which dominated the movement in the early 1930s, resonated powerfully with fundamentalists' sense that they were now outcasts. It offered little promise for any reversal of the church's apostasy and the world's declension.[13]

Implausible as it may seem, however, fundamentalists were at the same time calling for, yearning for, and working for revival. For example, "A Call to Prayer for Revival," published in *Revelation* magazine in 1932, acknowledged that "the end of this age" was fast approaching, when the world would experience "distress of nations" and " 'men's hearts failing them for fear.' " Yet, it "still might please God to send revival."[14] Using some quaint Old Testament terminology to allude to the Spirit's stirring, another writer claimed that he heard "the sound of a going in the tops of the mulberry trees," the sign for Christians to be "crying out to God to break forth with mighty power . . . to the reviving of His Church."[15] More was involved in these assertions than an argument among fundamentalists about the church's future prospects. Some of those who seemed to place the most stock in Christ's second coming as the world's only hope were also quick to add that, as James M. Gray put it, "since the Church and the Holy Spirit are still here, . . . we see no reason why a general revival of the Church should not be prayed for and expected at any time."[16]

Given the firm grip that premillennial eschatology and expectations of growing apostasy had on fundamentalism, nearly everyone who called for revival felt compelled to address the question of whether an awakening was still possible in these "last days." J. Edwin Orr, a young Irish revival preacher who had toured the United States in 1935–36, offered one way of reconciling this apparent contradiction when he insisted that "the truest preparation for the coming of Christ is a quickening in the Body of Christ." Furthermore, he argued, the apostle James's allusion to a "latter rain" before the harvest (James 5:7) was a prediction that there would be a great revival before the Second Coming.[17] Most dispensationalists, however, interpreted the "latter rain" as a promise of blessing to the Jews, which would occur after Christ's return.[18] Nevertheless, as revival yearnings and expectations grew during the 1930s and into the 1940s, not one leading fundamentalist denied the possibility of another great revival. Harry A. Ironside, the pastor of Moody Church in Chicago and perhaps the most influential dispensationalist of his time, probably spoke for the majority when he declared that "if there is world-wide brokenness of spirit on the part of the people of God, if there is repentance and crying to Him, God will delight to do some mighty work before the coming again of His blessed Son."[19] Clearly dispensationalists were not about to let their apocalyptic predictions strangle their hopes for revival.[20]

REVIVAL: THE ANATOMY OF A DESIRE

Most promoters of fundamentalist revivals in the 1930s drew heavily on the ideas of Charles G. Finney, especially from his *Lectures on Revivals of Religion* (1835). Typically they started with Finney's simple definition of revival. It was, said J. Edwin Orr, "a time of extraordinary religious awakening." But, in fact, revivalists had inherited a full-blown morphology of revival that enabled them to interpret historic trends and expect certain social patterns. Borrowing from Finney the idea that revivals are prompted by hard times, spiritual and material, Orr and other revivalists stressed that revival begins when the church repents of her sins and seeks to have her spiritual health restored. Repentance leads to fervent, persistent prayer for renewal. Revival then follows and brings with it a new sense of restoration, healing, and empowerment. Finally, revival in the church can flow into society and result in a great religious and moral awakening and transformation.[21]

At first glance these formulas seem as least as old as Finney's *Lectures*, but there were some strikingly different elements as well. Whereas Finney stressed God's providential direction of *natural* means and methods to promote revivals, the new revival advocates insisted that revivals were extraordinary events, that in them the Spirit of God moved in surprising and sometimes shockingly *miraculous* ways.[22] Indeed, fundamentalists were expressing a striking and insistent need for some miracles, some profound assurances that the Holy Spirit was at work in the modern world and, more important, within their movement.

Throughout the 1930s and 1940s a number of internal critics were charging that fundamentalism, for all its vigor and conviction, had become spiritually arid. Vance Havner, a Baptist Bible teacher, confessed that "too much orthodoxy is correct and sound but . . . it does not glow and burn, it does not stir the wells of the heart, it has lost its hallelujah, it is too much like a catechism and not enough like a camp meeting."[23] Havner deplored the passive and complacent disposition that he encountered on the Bible conference circuit. He claimed that "there is a grievous malady amongst us, affecting thousands who go from meeting to meeting . . . absorbing information like sponges, but not really doing anything about it after they hear it."[24] Ernest M. Wadsworth, head of the Great Commission Prayer League in Chicago, sighed that "a revival is something more than an increase of religious activity." Through all the busyness, however, he thought that he detected "a deep yearning for reality in revival" among pastors and people. "They want something supernatural," he noted, "they crave a movement that can be called in very truth 'a work of God.' "[25]

The search for "something supernatural" in a secular age sent fundamentalists back to the inventory of beliefs inherited from their turn-of-the-century ancestors. One of these was their expectation, somewhat suppressed by a reaction against pentecostalism, of wonder-working power from the Holy Spirit.[26] By the 1930s and early 1940s fundamentalists again began to feature this teaching. Often they referred to the Pentecost and claimed that the church in the present age still had access to the power of the Holy Spirit in apostolic proportions. "What God did once He can do again," the Canadian fundamentalist Oswald J. Smith insisted, "and what God did following the outpouring on the day of Pentecost . . . He will repeat in this our day."[27] Repeatedly, advocates of revival pointed to the infilling of the Holy Spirit as the key to revival, if only a critical mass of Christians would receive it. William Bell Riley, the aged Baptist warlord from Minneapolis, said, "To raise up a generation of those who know the third Person of the Godhead, who appropriate the promises of His power, who possess that endue-ment—this is to see perennial revival."[28]

One cannot help but notice the constant reference to *power* whenever these speakers talked of the Holy Spirit. This emphasis had been a common theme in the movement's formative years at the turn of the century, but the debased status of fundamentalists seemed to give it new significance. Fundamentalists were not actually dispossessed people in their social and economic standing, but they now felt marginal in reputation, essentially powerless to influence national religious life, morals, education, and public affairs.[29] That they could recall a time when things had been different for evangelical Christians made their current status even more painful.[30] Thus, the promise of power in the revival was doubly alluring. Not only might they be revived personally and corporately in their churches, but this transformative power might eventually spill into society again and, they hoped, empower them to heal their land.

Fundamentalists drew this hope from revival history. They were the self-proclaimed heirs of the Anglo-American revival tradition, which they traced back to George Whitefield and the Wesleys. Their reading of this history taught that revivals had two-fold results: restoration of the spirituality, zeal, and effec-tiveness of the church, *and* benefits to society. They quoted their favorite Bible verse on revival, II Chronicles 7:14, to point this out: "If my people, which are called by my name, shall humble themselves, and pray, and seek my face, and turn from their wicked ways; then will I hear from heaven, and will forgive their sin, and will heal their land." During years of economic depression, social upheaval, and the nadir of evangelical influence, fundamentalist leaders eagerly appropriated this promise. After all, did not revival history suggest as much? Had not England been saved from something like the French Revolution by the awakening led by George Whitefield and the Wesleys? And had not the Prayer Meeting Revival of 1857–58 restored evangelical Christianity's moral and religious influence for another generation? Certainly God could do it again.[31]

Fundamentalists had not forgotten evangelicalism's near-hegemony in those days either, which in nostalgic retrospective took on the golden hue of a "Christian America."[32] In the twentieth century, of course, America had become markedly less evangelical, and "Bible-believing Christians," as fundamentalists termed themselves and other evangelicals, were a decided minority. But for the most part fundamentalists simply could not give up on America. "God has a stake in the nation," said one leader, which seemed to imply that fundamentalists had much at stake themselves in this idea.[33] Against all millenarian and sociological logic they hoped to restore the mid-nineteenth-century evangelical moral consensus. The "custodial" cultural impulses of evangelicals, as Grant Wacker puts it, simply would not subside until the Second Coming.[34] Reform crusades had failed, but perhaps that was because revival was God's answer. The history of revivals, many believed, showed a cyclical pattern of prosperity, declension, depression, and revival. And by the reckoning of a variety of fundamentalist revival teachers in the 1930s and 1940s, if Christians would humble themselves, confess their sins, and pray, then revival was on its way, and God would restore His blessing on America.[35] Perhaps the most striking illustration of this hope was a cartoon in the *Sunday School Times* in 1934 that portrayed Uncle Sam kneeling at the altar rail and praying for forgiveness.[36]

The history and theory of revivals, then, offered fundamentalists the chance to retake the offensive. It gave these discouraged conservatives the means to perform some "ideological judo" on their low status and cultural despair, for they knew that, as Finney put it, "a 'Revival of Religion' presupposes a declension."[37] Just when things seemed so bad that they could scarcely get worse was the time to pray and work for revival—and, indeed, to expect one. In choosing hope over despair fundamentalists were restoring the earlier impulse that had endowed their movement's turn-of-the-century founders with great dynamism.

MOBILIZING FOR A REVIVAL

Throughout the 1930s and the 1940s, as these hopes began to flicker and flare, a complex and varied movement for revival was stirring. By 1950 this trend would result in the rise of Billy Graham, which marked the beginning of one of the greatest spurts of religious enterprise in American history. This postwar resurgence of evangelicalism has received much attention, but its earlier roots are obscure. Fundamentalists began remobilizing long before the rise of Billy Graham, as their yearning for another Great Awakening drove them forward.

In the late 1920s and early 1930s, however, the agents promoting revival were almost invisible as they began their work.

One of the most remarkable of these was Grace Winonna or, as she preferred, Mrs. Henry Woods, who had been a Southern Presbyterian missionary to China. In 1924 and 1925 Mrs. Woods had taken part in a "prayer band" for world-wide revival and then in a remarkable revival in Shanghai. After she returned with her husband to the United States in 1926, Mrs. Woods in the following year compiled and distributed a book, *The Half Can Never Be Told*. This slim volume combined a short account of the "Prayer Meeting Revival" of 1857–58 with a narrative of the Shanghai revival. Mrs. Woods distributed it among missionaries and leading evangelicals around the globe, and to major magazines, such as the *Sunday School Times* in Philadelphia and *The Life of Faith* in London. The book produced a remarkable response. Eventually over 200,000 copies were sent out, and this was just the beginning. During the 1930s and early 1940s Mr. and Mrs. Woods circulated prayer letters and books on revival to the vast network they had created. The point of these activities, they made clear, was to encourage Christians worldwide to pray for revival, to spread the news of local revivals, and to point to signs of impending global revival.[38]

Other enterprises of similar purpose existed, most notably Ernest M. Wadsworth's Great Commission Prayer League in Chicago and George T. B. Davis's Million Testaments Campaign, which had its headquarters in Philadelphia.[39] The premise for such activities was that revival came as God's answer to prevailing prayer, but, even from a non-theological perspective, these efforts clearly did a great deal to raise people's consciousness about the need and prospects for revival, to heighten their expectations, and to enlist their commitment to the cause.

The revival message circulated in more personal form as well, by means of itinerant revival promoters, who made this one theme the most important part of their preaching. The most widely known of these was J. Edwin Orr, a young evangelist from Northern Ireland. In an astonishing feat, Orr toured Great Britain, the Middle East, northern Europe, Canada, Australia and New Zealand, the United States, China, and South Africa in the 1930s and published small books about each tour—all within five or six years. Well-received on the fundamentalist circuit in the United States, Orr apparently helped to prompt awakenings at Wheaton College and Columbia Bible College in 1936.[40]

Orr's account of his tour of the United States in 1935 and 1936 reads like a tour guide to the burgeoning fundamentalist movement. American fundamentalists at that point were expanding their institutional network of mission societies, magazines, Bible institutes, colleges and seminaries, youth ministries, summer Bible conferences, and radio programs, to name some of these agencies.[41] This was, in aggregate, an amazing amount of activity, but few were able to appreciate its scope, for fundamentalism had become fragmented and localized after the controversies of the 1920s.[42]

By the mid–1930s, however, a number of the movement's leaders were be-

ginning to comprehend the breadth of fundamentalist activity. Yearning for
revival, they strained to discern any signs of the Spirit's movement. What they
discovered was vastly encouraging. Donald Barnhouse, a Presbyterian fundamentalist pastor in Philadelphia and editor of *Revelation* magazine, announced
in 1934 that revival was beginning. He cited the more than 1,000 students enrolled
in Philadelphia's two Bible colleges, the "Spirit-filled young people in charge
of the city's Christian Endeavor," and the many "witnesses to the truth" on
the radio. He noted further that evangelical mission boards were meeting budgets
and sending out new missionaries in spite of the Depression, and that some
1,000 congregations belonged to a conservative evangelical movement called
the New England Fellowship.[43] J. Elwin Wright, the director of the New England
Fellowship, had also perceived this widespread vigor and was experimenting
with ways to collect and mobilize it. In early 1935 he sponsored an evangelical
rally at the Boston Garden. He was gratified when 16,000 people showed up,
for this meeting helped cement new friendships and bolster the courage of those
who, Wright said, "had been under the mistaken impression that only I am
left."[44]

The president of the Moody Bible Institute, Will Houghton, also sensed these
new opportunities and determined to get something started. He launched a nationwide campaign to celebrate the institute's fiftieth anniversary in 1936 and
the centenary of D. L. Moody's birth in 1937, with the goal of kindling desire
for an awakening.[45] The institute persuaded over 800 congregations to schedule
Bible teaching and evangelistic services in 1937, at which attendance totaled
over 400,000. In addition, some 2,300 churches held special "Moody Day"
services, and a rally at the Chicago Coliseum attracted a crowd of 15,000.
Encouraged by the success of the centenary, Houghton followed up with a radio
crusade. Using the Bible Institute's own WMBI and a hookup of eleven major
stations in the Mutual network, Houghton broadcast "Let's Go Back to the
Bible," a series of twenty-six sermons, in 1938 and 1939. He published these
messages and sent complimentary copies to mayors of major cities, corporate
leaders, governors, members of Congress, and even the White House. Encouraged by the 40,000 letters the institute received in response to this campaign,
Houghton planned a second series for 1939–40. He asked supporters everywhere
to pray that God would bring the nation to its knees.[46]

At the same time, Charles E. Fuller's "Old-Fashioned Revival Hour," a radio
program broadcast from Los Angeles, was capturing the imagination and support
of evangelicals across the continent. The program began in 1930 as a local
broadcast of the Sunday evening service at the independent fundamentalist church
of which Fuller was pastor. Just seven years later it was broadcast over the
Mutual Broadcasting System from coast to coast on eighty-eight stations during
prime time on Sunday evening. In order to expand along with Mutual, Fuller
had to find loyal supporters in new cities. He scheduled a series of rallies in
1938 and 1939 that featured live productions of his program. Large crowds

appeared in city after city: 14,000 at Olympia Stadium in Detroit, then 40,000 at Soldier Field in Chicago, a capacity audience of 8,000 at Mechanics Hall in Boston, and two packed houses at New York's Carnegie Hall.[47] No evangelist had exerted such drawing power since Billy Sunday's heyday. These rallies prompted the local groups that sponsored them to consider reviving mass evangelism.

Although the movement's evangelistic efforts were beginning to thrive, fundamentalist leaders were deeply impressed by the mood of despair that the long depression and the rising threat of war had produced. In the summer of 1939 Donald Barnhouse wrote that the liberal idea of "a gradually progressing world" was being "buried under the avalanche of current events."[48] Where could people turn when every measure had failed? Fundamentalists answered that only spiritual measures would save the nation's freedom. Earlier in the decade fundamentalists had responded with resignation, "even so come, Lord Jesus." But now they were calling for nationwide repentance and revival. Will Houghton launched a second "Back to the Bible" broadcast in the fall of 1939 to offer "a world gone mad" the faith in Christ that he thought "the only true solution to its multiplying woes."[49]

The apocalyptic climate of the early 1940s actually helped to lift fundamentalists' hopes for a national awakening as well as to convince them of its necessity. The editor of *The Sunday School Times* reported in March 1941 that Charles E. Fuller's "Old-Fashioned Revival Hour" had enrolled over 100,000 people to pray continually for revival.[50] And the editor of the *Watchman-Examiner* believed that the very despair of the world had "jolted it into stark realism" and compelled people to reconsider "the severities in the challenge of Jesus." Evangelicals must find a new solidarity, he urged, and join in a united front.[51]

In the meantime a cadre of leaders gathered by J. Elwin Wright had been recruiting support for a national evangelical association to carry the revival impulse forward. After two years of ceaseless promoting and negotiating, Wright convened a "National Conference for United Action for Evangelicals" in St. Louis on April 7, 1942. The following year the National Association of Evangelicals (NAE) was launched.[52] Harold J. Ockenga, the scholarly pastor of Park Street Church in Boston, was named president. He urged that the NAE spearhead "an invasion of the Christian consciousness" in the United States.[53] In the meantime organizers had helped to found thirty-seven local and regional NAE chapters to provide bases for urban evangelistic campaigns.[54]

By this time other evangelistic efforts were under way. One was the "Christ for America" campaign, an ambitious plan launched in 1943 to promote co-operative citywide evangelistic meetings. By the late forties "Christ for America" would organize more than fifty city- and countywide campaigns.[55] Another vigorous movement was the "Christian Business Men's Committees" (CBMCs). The first of these was formed in Chicago in 1930 by C.B. Hedstrom and other "born-again" businessmen, for fellowship and the pursuit of evangelistic projects. Although the movement grew slowly at first, it expanded rapidly in the 1940s, from 5 chapters in 1938, to 75 in 1944, and 162 by 1947. By the late 1940s the CBMCs were organizing citywide evangelistic meetings.[56]

These businessmen often sponsored evangelistic youth rallies, which were part of the Youth for Christ movement. Youth for Christ was an effort to minister more effectively to young people by adapting swing rhythms to gospel music, fast-paced variety show formats to revival services, and the intensity and eventfulness of radio news programs to evangelistic sermons.[57] The result was electrifying. In the spring of 1944 a former dance-band leader, Jack Wyrtzen, brought 20,000 to Madison Square Garden for a "Victory Rally" as part of his "Word of Life" campaign. Meanwhile, the Philadelphian Percy Crawford was broadcasting his "Young People's Church of the Air" over 400 stations nationwide. And on Memorial Day, 1945, "Chicagoland Youth for Christ" attracted 70,000 to Soldier Field. By 1946 the movement's leaders estimated that there were 700 weekly rallies, with perhaps 1,000,000 in attendance. The movement spread among American military personnel and soon was operating in forty-six countries.[58] The Youth for Christ phenomenon represented an important milestone for fundamentalists and the broader evangelical coalition that was now supporting these ventures. For the first time since the Scopes trial, conservative evangelicals were receiving national attention, and this time most of it was rather friendly.[59]

Such coverage in the secular press points to the other important ingredient for the postwar evangelical resurgence. At the same time that fundamentalists and other evangelicals were gaining confidence and pursuing new initiatives, Americans generally were growing more interested in religion. World War II was in many respects a tonic for Americans' faith in their nation's promises and ideals. Popular culture celebrated the "American Way of Life" in these years, and religious faith appeared to many as one of the values most worth remembering and conserving.[60]

Another part of this package was a resurrection of civil religion. As the nation faced new crises and circled the globe with its military forces, the old themes of "covenant people" and "redeemer nation" found their way back into public rhetoric. The motives behind the religious expressions of public officials are probably always very complex, but it is clear that during the 1940s presidents and statesmen were issuing calls for revival that sounded very inviting to fundamentalists and other evangelicals. In 1943, for example, Vance Havner eagerly quoted President Franklin D. Roosevelt as saying that "no greater thing could come to our land than a revival of the spirit of religion."[61] At the surrender ceremony in Tokyo Bay that ended World War II, General MacArthur warned that without fundamental change, "Armageddon will be at our door." In his opinion the crisis was "basically theological," and it called for a "spiritual recrudescence."[62] Only a day after Winston Churchill's grim Iron Curtain speech in 1946, President Truman remarked that without "a moral and spiritual awakening" America would be lost.[63] Shortly thereafter General Eisenhower commented that there was no hope for mankind "except through moral regeneration.''[64] Public officials carefully included all Judeo-Christian faiths in these speeches, but their remarks were interpreted by fundamentalists and other evangelicals as an invitation to contribute as revivalists to the American Way of Life.

In sum, by the late 1940s conservative evangelicals were discovering that by forming a broad coalition, adapting their message to the new popular styles, building upon the renewed public interest in religion, and using advanced communications technology, they could succeed at mass evangelism. All they lacked was a new prophet. Revival advocates had hoped that some new Moody would arise, and now there were a dozen promising candidates.[65] One of these young "sons of thunder," a star on the Youth for Christ circuit, would soon emerge as the favorite. His name was Billy Graham. Graham's emergence to national prominence in 1949–50 was thus the product of nearly a generation of internal development.

Indeed, at the same time that the urban campaigns of Graham and others were making news, less spectacular but perhaps more protean forms of revival were sweeping the movement. Prompted by the work of itinerant revival advocates such as J. Edwin Orr and Armin Gesswein, fervent citywide pastors' prayer meetings for revival emerged across North America, followed by stirrings in local churches and a chain reaction of awakenings on the campuses of evangelical colleges.[66] Harold Ockenga, the host of Graham's remarkable Boston campaign in 1950, breathlessly reported that year to the assembled National Association of Evangelicals: "Brethren . . . we have the evidences of revival . . . . You don't have to pray anymore, 'Lord, send a revival.' The revival is here!''[67]

Such claims must be treated with caution. Even by non-theological criteria the presence or absence of a religious revival is very much a judgment call.[68] In a pluralistic culture such as the mid-twentieth-century United States, in which Protestant Christian revivalism was a minority expression, it is difficult to conceive of a pervasive national awakening. The many popular and public expressions of piety during the 1950s did, after all, coexist with a variety of counterpoints, such as a rock-and-rolling youth culture, and the largely secular "culture of critical discourse" that prevailed at the nation's universities. Clearly, however, by the late 1940s fundamentalists and an emerging coalition of evangelicals were experiencing new vitality and a renewed sense of mission. Their goals, as the evangelist Torrey Johnson put it, were "the spiritual revitalization of America," and the "complete evangelization of the world in our generation."[69]

Spurred on by this vision, the "new evangelicals," as this coalition was eventually labeled, began to make their mark on American life. Billy Graham became evangelist to the nation and counsellor to presidents. Civic "leadership prayer breakfasts," organized by evangelicals, sprang up in Washington, D.C., and across the country, while a cadre of younger theologians with solid credentials breathed new intellectual life into the movement.[70] By mid-century, conservative evangelical foreign missions were engaged in a spurt of growth that would make them the dominant North American missionary force.[71] Perhaps a Great Awakening had not come, but certainly the fundamentalists and other evangelicals were experiencing a pronounced and surprising new surge of vitality.

CONCLUSION AND EPILOGUE

The question still remains why this resurgence of religion took place in a nation that, at least from some important cultural vantage points, seemed to be increasingly secular. The record of the new evangelicals can be made to illustrate Martin Marty's thesis about evangelicalism's symbiotic relationship to modernity. The United States entered a new phase of modernization by World War II, which featured "electronic communications, rapid transportation, mobile and kinetic styles of living, affluence, and a sense of entitlement in large publics."[72] At the same time a new generation of fundamentalists and other evangelicals creatively adapted their movements to these trends and rode the new cultural wave.

The point of this essay, however, has been something different. It has explored the internal resources of fundamentalism, the inventory of beliefs that its adherents found personally persuasive, satisfying, and challenging, and that gave them the motivation to be culturally engaged. It has focused on the most potent and energizing of these beliefs, fundamentalists' vision of another great revival. Through it they were able to shake off adversity and replenish their hope. At a time when they had little reason to expect a reversal of their low estate, outside of their "hope of His appearing," fundamentalists reached back into their revivalist inheritance and grasped a hope that their personal spiritual lives, their churches, their movement—and eventually their nation—could still be renewed with "fire from above." Their efforts to usher in such a revival contributed to the revitalization of their movement and to a more general resurgence of evangelical Christianity in America.

This protean, revivalist element is vitally important for understanding fundamentalist evangelicalism. It is not enough to characterize fundamentalism as a protest movement, as militant religious and cultural traditionalism or anti-modernism that lacks, as the *Christian Century* put it in 1926, "qualities of constructive achievement or survival." For built into the movement are what George Marsden has termed "paradoxical tensions," and one of these is the tension between cultural alienation and cultural custodianship. These have been articulated most often as a tension between a millenarian cultural and ecclesiastical separatism on the one hand, and an expansive, revivalist-reformist impulse on the other.[73]

This ongoing tension in fundamentalist evangelicalism helps explain the dynamic but troubled career of the movement's various descendants since the 1940s. The "new evangelical" party, represented by Billy Graham, Fuller Seminary, and *Christianity Today*, was confident that a revival was breaking and that its members were in the vanguard. They felt called to purge the debilitating features from their fundamentalist heritage and to pursue positive evangelism and a cultural mandate. The result has been both a great deal of success and a series of fratricidal conflicts, for the new evangelicals have argued repeatedly over where to strike a balance between fundamentalist separatism and a more positive, culture-engaging mission.[74]

Competing revivalist and sectarian impulses also help to make sense of other contemporary heirs of fundamentalism. Certainly they lie behind the astonishing turn to political action on the part of many separatist fundamentalists, led by Jerry Falwell.[75] And they help one understand the former fundamentalists of the radical evangelical Sojourners' movement, led by Jim Wallis. Separatist, left-wing, and communal in their witness, the Sojourners still work, pray, and hope for a "new American revival," as Wallis puts its.[76]

Any accounting, therefore, of resurgent fundamentalist and post-fundamentalist Christianity must consider this powerful propellant. Revivalism is a complex and volatile religious compound. It has been expressed in a variety of ways and has a variety of meanings and implications. Its treatment here, though only suggestive, points to three levels of meaning and application for fundamentalist evangelicals.

The first is personal. Experiencing revival in one's personal life is a way of expressing the deeply human need for spiritual reality, for sacred moments that certify God's presence, love, and power to the believer. Fundamentalists had reasons to feel especially dry in spirit during the 1930s, living as they were in an inescapably material-minded age with fewer means at hand for experiencing grace than either their pentecostal cousins or the more sacramental traditions. So they drew on their revivalist heritage to seek fresh "showers of blessing." Many found what they were seeking and felt encouraged to pass their blessing along.

Fundamentalists also sought resuscitation for their movement. Not only was the movement stricken by its defeats, it was also split by internal bickering. Revival promised to renew fundamentalists' unity, draw together a broader evangelical coalition, and give them all a more positive purpose. The outcome has been increased diversity and not some all-encompassing alliance of evangelicals. But this diversity has been a mark of vitality, not declension. In fact, it was the product of something like a revival.[77]

Finally, revival promised to restore the land and, implicitly, to restore fundamentalists' lost influence. It is wrong to reduce fundamentalists' desire for revival to a thirst for cultural hegemony or even a more altruistic regard for their nation's welfare, but these motives were certainly present. Fundamentalists had failed to stem what they saw as the nation's declension with their campaigns in the 1920s, but revival advocates in the following decades nearly always voiced hope that an awakening would accomplish what they had failed to achieve. Despite the deep cultural alienation fundamentalists felt, a revival-inspired vision of "winning America" aroused their latent sense of responsibility for the nation's integrity and their yearning to regain their former status. As a result they have contributed with other politically aroused evangelicals to the diverse yet increasingly important "evangelical factor" in American politics.[78]

Their calls to "save America" have struck a more responsive note than one might have anticipated, largely because among the "mystic chords" of American cultural memory and hope is a revivalistic strain inherited from the great awakenings of the past. A new swelling of this "civil revivalism" during and just after World War II seemed to invite conservative evangelicals to share a chaplaincy to the nation's civic soul. Thus, fundamentalist-inspired revivalism converged with broader calls for cultural renewal, nearly all of which had some relation, however distant, to earlier evangelicalism.[79]

Ever since the 1960s, however, the rules of public discourse have tilted increasingly in favor of those who argue that religious conviction and expression have no legitimate public place. So at the same time that evangelicals of many varieties are thriving and regaining some of the status and influence that their predecessors were denied, their revivalist hopes for a Christian America seem to be thwarted.[80] Many evangelicals, most dramatically those on the right, have responded not so much with new calls for revival as with pressure-group politics.

Revivalists' dreams of their land's healing have turned sour, and they have provoked a sharp conflict with the inhabitants of the more secular regions of American culture. This conflict has polarized and damaged national politics and has very nearly reached an impasse.[81] Pluralistic America cannot be herded into the "Christian nation" corral again, but neither will the majority of its citizens accept the secular doctrine that religiously infused values have no place in the public arena. Indeed, a variety of the nation's pundits sense that this conflict is leading to an important juncture, in which religion's public role will be redefined.[82]

And so, curiously enough, the strains of civic revivalism are swelling again, in diverse counterpoints and instrumentations that range from Christopher Lasch to Robert Bellah to Jesse Jackson, and that include Shirley MacLaine as well as Jerry Falwell and Pat Robertson. William McLoughlin argues that this strange ensemble is performing an improbable, conflict-laden fugue of cultural revitalization. They are part of the historic process of recreating America's cultural identity and mission.[83] The difficulty with McLoughlin's argument is that in a polyvalent nation such as the United States the contours of cultural revitalization, like those of a religious revival, are difficult to discern, and may never again encompass all in a unitary wave of transformation.[84] Certainly the outcome will not be anything close to the triumphal vision of the fundamentalist revivalists, unless some bizarre turn of events takes place.

The future may owe something to their visions, however, for good or for ill. Just as the American cultural fabric follows a complex pattern, so its transformations are never cut from wholly new cloth. And visions of a revival, like visions of a millennium or a classless society, are remarkably resilient. They can foster hopes scarcely bound by the conditions that make revival seem implausible. Such hopes can and do shape the course of history.

NOTES

1. "Vanishing Fundamentalism," *Christian Century* 43 (1926): 799.

2. Phillip E. Hammond, "In Search of a Protestant Twentieth Century: American Religion and Power Since 1900," *Review of Religious Research* 24 (1983):281; R. Laurence Moore, *Religious Outsiders and the Making of Americans* (New York, 1986), 150–72; and R. Stephen Warner, "Theoretical Barriers to the Understanding of Evangelical Christianity," *Sociological Analysis* 40 (1979): 1–9, are illuminating discussions of why scholars and others have been so surprised.

3. Martin E. Marty, "The Revival of Evangelicalism and Southern Religion," in David E. Harrell, Jr., ed., *Varieties of Southern Evangelicalism* (Macon, Ga., 1981), 9, 7–21.

4. Ibid., 11–16.

5. This essay examines the fundamentalist movement, strictly defined. It does not include all the diverse movements and traditions that comprise evangelical Christianity, although it refers to them on occasion. Concentration on fundamentalists does not result from the assumption that many fundamentalists made, that they represented the strategic center of American Christianity. Indeed, understanding of the cultural role of evangelical Christianity in its broader dimensions can proceed only as other evangelicals receive the same careful scholarly attention that has recently been bestowed on the old fundamentalists and their contemporary heirs. The best discussions of the definitions of "fundamentalist" and "evangelical" and kindred issues are in Timothy L. Smith, "An Historical Perspective on Evangelicalism and Ecumenism," *Midstream* 22 (1983): 308–25; George M. Marsden, "The Evangelical Denomination," in George M. Marsden, ed., *Evangelicalism and Modern America* (Grand Rapids, Mich., 1984), vii–xvi; and Cullen Murphy, "Protestantism and the Evangelicals," *Wilson Quarterly* 5 (1981): 105–16.

6. A superb new treatment of this movement is George M. Marsden, *Reforming Fundamentalism: Fuller Seminary and the New Evangelicalism* (Grand Rapids, Mich., 1987). On the recovery of fundamentalism, see Joel A. Carpenter, "Fundamentalist Institutions and the Growth of Evangelical Protestantism, 1929–1942," *Church History* 49 (1980): 62–75; "The Fundamentalist Leaven and the Rise of an Evangelical United Front," in Leonard I. Sweet, ed., *Evangelical Tradition in America* (Macon, Ga., 1984), 257–88; "From Fundamentalism to the New Evangelical Coalition," in Marsden, ed., *Evangelicalism and Modern America*, 3–16; "Youth For Christ and the New Evangelicals' Place in the Life of the Nation," in Rowland A. Sherrill, ed., *American Recoveries: Religion in the Life of the Nation* (Urbana, University of Illinois Press, forthcoming); and "Contending for the Faith Once Delivered: Primitivist Impulses in American Fundamentalism," in Richard T. Hughes, ed., *The American Quest for the Primitive Church* (Urbana, Ill., 1988), 99–119.

7. The militant separatist wing of fundamentalism is featured in David O. Beale, *In Pursuit of Purity: American Fundamentalism Since 1850* (Greenville, S.C., 1986); and Jerry Falwell, ed., *The Fundamentalist Phenomenon* (New York., 1981). Both works are sympathetic treatments by insiders. A perceptive outsider's examination is Nancy Tatom Ammerman, *Bible Believers: Fundamentalists in the Modern World* (New Brunswick, N.J., 1987).

8. Lippmann, *A Preface to Morals* (New York, 1929), 31–32.

9. "Billy Sunday, the Last of His Line," *Christian Century* 52 (1935): 1476. See

also Robert S. and Helen M. Lynd's discussion of evangelism's fortunes in *Middletown in Transition: A Study in Cultural Conflicts* (New York, 1937), 302–3.

10. "Fighting Days," *Moody Monthly* 34 (1934): 252.

11. Timothy P. Weber, *Living in the Shadow of the Second Coming: American Premillennialism, 1875–1982* (rev. ed., Chicago, 1987), 9–24, gives concise explanations of premillennial and dispensational teachings.

12. Arno C. Gaebelein, *World Prospects: A Study in Sacred Prophecy and Present-Day World Conditions* (New York, 1934), 163.

13. Weber, *Living in the Shadow*, 177–203.

14. "A Call to Prayer for Revival," *Revelation* 2 (1932): 205.

15. "In the Tops of the Mulberry Trees," letter from William Allen Dean to Donald Grey Barnhouse, published in *Revelation* 4 (1934): 381.

16. Grace W. Woods, *Revival in Romance and Realism* (New York, 1936), 213.

17. J. Edwin Orr, *The Church Must First Repent* (London, 1937), 84–86. See also Grace W. Woods, *By Way of Remembrance* (Atlantic City, N.J., 1933), 49–50.

18. Harry A. Ironside, *Notes on the Minor Prophets* (New York, 1909), 128–31, and *Lectures on the Book of the Acts* (New York, 1943), 46–49; Arno C. Gaebelein, *The Annotated Bible: The Holy Scriptures Analyzed and Annotated: The Old Testament* (New York, 1913–24), 5: 108; Edwin C. Diebler, "The Relation of the Church to the Kingdom," *Bibliotheca Sacra* 97 (1940): 359; and Merrill F. Unger, "The Baptism with the Holy Spirit," *Bibliotheca Sacra* 101 (1944): 366, 373–74.

19. Harry A. Ironside, *The Lamp of Prophecy* (Grand Rapids, Mich., 1940), 148.

20. Other examples of how dispensationalists resolved this matter include Armin R. Gesswein, "Revival versus Apostasy," in Grace W. Woods, ed., *Preparing the Way* (Atlantic City, N.J., 1941), 28; Ernest M. Wadsworth, *Will Revival Come?* (Chicago, 1937), 31–36; Paul W. Rood, *Let the Fire Fall* (Grand Rapids, Mich., 1939), 32–33; Orr, *Church Must First Repent*, 81–90; and Vance Havner, *Road to Revival* (New York, 1940), 57–58.

21. Orr, *Church Must First Repent*, 14, 14–17. Other examples of this morphology are in Wadsworth, *Will Revival Come?* 24–29; Vance Havner, *It Is Time* (New York, 1943); George T. B. Davis, "How Prayer Brings Revival," in Horace F. Dean, ed., *Christ for America: A Nationwide Campaign for Union Evangelistic Meetings by Cities* (New York, 1943), 27–34; Paul W. Rood, *Can We Expect a World-Wide Revival?* (Grand Rapids, Mich., 1940), 14; Armin Gesswein, "How Does a Revival Begin?" *Moody Monthly* 44 (1943): 61–62, 86; and Wilbur M. Smith, *The Glorious Revival under King Hezekiah* (Grand Rapids, Mich., 1937).

22. Havner, *Road to Revival*, 44–45; Oswald J. Smith, *The Revival We Need* (London, 1933), 47–49; Wadsworth, *Will Revival Come?* 17–19; and H. M. and G. W. Woods, "Letter No. 5," in Woods, *By Way of Remembrance*, 41–42.

23. Havner, *It Is Time*, 76.

24. Havner, *Road to Revival*, 57.

25. Wadsworth, *Will Revival Come?* 20.

26. Marsden, *Fundamentalism and American Culture*, 72–80; Grant Wacker, "The Holy Spirit and the Spirit of the Age in American Protestantism, 1880–1920," *Journal of American History* 72 (1985): 45–62.

27. Smith, *The Work God Blesses* (London, 1934), 14.

28. William Bell Riley, *The Perennial Revival: A Plea for Evangelism*, (3rd ed., Philadelphia, 1933), 97.

29. The most precise and helpful examination of fundamentalists' socio-economic status is in Walter E. Ellis, "Social and Religious Factors in the Fundamentalist-Modernist Schisms among Baptists in North America, 1895–1934" (Ph.D. dissertation, University of Pittsburgh, 1974).

30. Moore, *Religious Outsiders and Americans*, 150–172; Douglas Frank, *Less than Conquerors: How American Evangelicals Entered the Twentieth Century* (Grand Rapids, Mich., 1987), 138–41, 246–56; Joel A. Carpenter, "The Renewal of American Fundamentalism, 1930–1945" (Ph.D. dissertation, Johns Hopkins University, 1984), 39–45.

31. George T. B. Davis, *When the Fire Fell* (Philadelphia, 1945), 7–24; "Our Daily Meditations and the Moody Centenary," *Revelation* 6 (1936): 499; Grace W. Woods, *The Half Can Never Be Told* (Atlantic City, N.J., 1927), foreword, 19–21, 26–27, 69; Wadsworth, *Will Revival Come?* 7–8, 11–12, 15–16; H. M. and G. W. Woods, "Letter No. 9" in Woods, *By Way of Remembrance*, 77–80, 109; Frank G. Beardsley, *Religious Progress through Religious Revivals* (New York, 1943), 39–51; "The Year Closes," *Moody Monthly* 39 (1938): 171; "Revolution, Rapture, Revival," *Revelation* 2 (1938): 205; "A Call for Prayer for Revival," *Revelation* 2 (1932): 205; and Will H. Houghton, "Revival—Then and Now," *Moody Monthly* 39 (1939): 248–49, 275.

32. Frank, *Less Than Conquerors*, 167–72.

33. Wilbur M. Smith, *A Watchman on the Wall: The Life of Will H. Houghton* (Grand Rapids, Mich., 1951), 128–29.

34. Grant Wacker, "Uneasy in Zion: Evangelicals in Postmodern Society," in Marsden, ed., *Evangelicalism and Modern America*, 22–28. See also Sandra Sizer, "Politics and Apolitical Religion: The Great Urban Revivals of the Late Nineteenth Century," *Church History* 48 (1979): 81–98.

35. Vance Havner, *Amos: The Prophet with a Modern Message* (Grand Rapids, Mich., 1937), 6–13; Harold L. Lundquist, "Can America Be Saved?" *Moody Monthly* 40 (1939): 120–21; and Paul S. Rees, *America, Awake or Perish!* (Grand Rapids, Mich., 1940), 6–14.

36. "Where He Belongs," a cartoon by E. J. Pace, *Sunday School Times* 76 (1934): 662.

37. Orr, *Church Must First Repent*, 14.

38. Woods, *Revival in Romance and Realism*, 24–25, 41–50, 77–78, 110–13, 162–63, 213–14, 225–26; *Preparing the Way*, 9, 12; and *By Way of Remembrance*, 77–80.

39. Wadsworth, *Will Revival Come?* 3–4; Davis, *When the Fire Fell*, back page notices.

40. J. Edwin Orr, *This Is the Victory! 10,000 Miles of Miracles in America* (London, 1936), 37–39, 90, 113–128. For Orr's many travels in these years, see his other books: *Can God—? "10,000 Miles of Miracle in Britain"* (London, 1934); *The Promise Is to You: 10,000 Miles of Miracle to Palestine* (London, 1935); *Times of Refreshing: 10,000 Miles of Miracle—through Canada* (Grand Rapids, Mich., 1936); *Prove Me Now! 10,000 Miles of Miracle—to Moscow* (London, 1936); *If Ye Abide—10,000 Miles of Miracle in South Africa* (London, 1936); *All Your Need: 10,000 Miles of Miracle through Australia and New Zealand* (London, 1936); and *Through Blood and Fire in China* (London, 1939).

41. Carpenter, "Fundamentalist Institutions."

42. Ernest R. Sandeen, *The Roots of Fundamentalism: British and American Millenarianism, 1800–1930* (Chicago, 1970), 269; Marsden, *Fundamentalism and American Culture*, 189–94.

43. "Are We in a Revival?" *Revelation* 4 (1934): 135.

44. J. Elwin Wright, "Bible Demonstration Day," *New England Fellowship Monthly* 33 (May 1935): 9.

45. Smith, *Watchman on the Wall*, 191.

46. Smith, *Watchman on the Wall*, 128–31; "Report of the President of the Business Division," *Moody Bible Institute Bulletin* 19 (March 1939): 3, 8; and Will H. Houghton, *Let's Go Back to the Bible* (New York, 1939).

47. Daniel P. Fuller, *Give the Winds a Mighty Voice: The Story of Charles E. Fuller* (Waco, Tex., 1972), 82–137.

48. Donald Barnhouse, "Scientist Confirms Bible," *Revelation* 9 (1939): 231. Other examples are Rollin T. Chafer, "Disillusionment," *Bibliotheca Sacra* 96 (1939): 387–88; Paul W. Rood, "Spiritual Rearmament and Mobilization," *Sunday School Times* 81 (1939): 398; Rees, *America, Awake or Perish!*; Alexander Fraser, "The Indiscipline of the Era," *Moody Monthly* 40 (1939): 15–16; W. J. Mosin, "Moral Preparedness," *Watchman-Examiner* 28 (1940): 907; W. W. Ayer, "The Pastor Says," *Calvary Pulpit* 3, no. 3 (1941): 2; and "Dangerous Opportunity," *Revelation* 10 (1940): 444.

49. "Again America Hears," *Moody Monthly* 40 (1939): 2.

50. "May We Hope For Revival Today?" *Sunday School Times* 83 (1941): 225.

51. "Planning the Peace," *Watchman-Examiner* 29 (1941): 1240–41.

52. J. Elwin Wright, "An Historical Statement of the Events Leading Up to the National Conference in St. Louis," *Evangelical Action! A Report of the Organization of the National Association of Evangelicals for United Action* (Boston, 1942), 3–16.

53. Harold J. Ockenga, "Christ for America," in *United We Stand: A Report of the Constitutional Convention of the National Association of Evangelicals* (Chicago, 1943), 15.

54. "Forty-Nine Regional Conferences Planned for Fall and Winter," *United Evangelical Action* (hereafter, UEA) 1 (September 1942): 1, 4; "Fall Series of Regional Conferences under Way September 21," ibid., 4; "An Issue of the Present Hour," *UEA* 2 (January 1943): 2; J. Elwin Wright, "The World Council of Churches," *UEA* 2 (April 1943): 2; Wright, "Constitutional Convention of United Evangelical Action," *New England Fellowship Monthly* 41 (April 1943): 8–9; and "N.A.E.'s Supreme Objective," *UEA* 3 (January 1944): 2.

55. Horace F. Dean, "Introductory Word," in Oswald J. Smith, *The Fire of God!* (Philadelphia, 1948), inside cover; Dean, *Christ for America*.

56. David R. Enlow, *Men Aflame: The Story of Christian Business Men's Committees* (Grand Rapids, Mich., 1962), 5, 13–14, 17–21, 24, 35, 38–39, 47–48, 55.

57. Bob Bahr, *Man with a Vision: The Story of Percy Crawford* (Chicago, n.d.); Forrest Forbes, *God Hath Chosen: The Story of Jack Wyrtzen and the Word of Life Hour* (Grand Rapids, Mich., 1948); Frank Mead, "Apostle to Youth," *Christian Herald* 68 (September 1945): 15–16; Mel Larson, *Youth for Christ: Twentieth-Century Wonder* (Grand Rapids, Mich., 1942), 106–7, 112–13; and Torrey Johnson and Robert Cook, *Reaching Youth for Christ* (Chicago, 1944), 15, 18.

58. J. Elwin Wright, "Youth for Christ," *UEA* 6 (February 1945): 8; Larson, *Youth for Christ*, 20–23, 60–63, 69–71, 80–81, 84–95; James Hefley, *God Goes to High School* (Waco, Tex. 1970), 29–30, 34–49, 69, 84–94, 90–91, 94–95; "Youth for Christ Expands to Continent," *UEA* 4 (March 1946): 9; "Five YFC Leaders Will Fly to Europe," *UEA* 5 (February 1946): 10; "G.I. Missionaries to Manila," *Sunday* 7 (February 1946): 26–29, 49–52.

59. William F. McDermott, "Bobby-Soxers Find the Sawdust Trail," *Collier's Magazine*, May 26, 1945, 22–23; "Bobby-Sox Hit Sawdust Trail," *News-Views: The Chicago Daily News Pictorial Section*, 3 February 1945, p. 2; Clarence Woodbury, "Bobby-Soxers Sing Hallelujah," *American Magazine*, March 1946, 26–27, 121, 123, 124; "Youth For Christ," *Time*, February 4, 1946, 46–47; "Wanted: A Miracle of Good Weather and 'Youth for Christ' Rally Got It," *Newsweek*, June 11, 1945, 84.

60. The argumentation and evidence for these assertions admittedly deserve more attention than given here. See Geoffrey Perrett, *Days of Sadness, Years of Triumph: The American People, 1939–1945* (Baltimore, 1974), 196–99, 325–42, 350–56, 384–85, 407–9, 441–43; Charles C. Alexander, *Nationalism in American Thought, 1930–1945* (Chicago, 1969), 155–56, 190–201, 223–24, 229; Allan Nevins, "How We Felt About the War," Lewis Gannett, "Books," and Bosley Crowther, "The Movies," in Jack Goodman, ed., *While You Were Gone: A Report of Wartime Life in the United States* (New York, 1946), 3–27, 455, 516; Philip Gleason, "Americans All: World War II and the Shaping of American Identity," *Review of Politics* 43 (1981): 483–518, and, "World War II and the Development of American Studies," *American Quarterly* 36 (1984): 342–58; Richard Pells, *Radical Visions and American Dreams: Culture and Social Thought in the Depression Years* (New York, 1973), 141–50, 358–61; Catherine Marshall, *A Man Called Peter* (New York, 1951); and Fuller, *Give the Winds A Mighty Voice*, 140–41.

61. Havner, *It Is Time*, 58.

62. William Manchester, *American Caesar: Douglas MacArthur, 1880–1964* (Boston, 1978), 453–54.

63. Harry S. Truman, "The Need for Moral Analyzing," *New York Times*, 7 March 1946, p. 11.

64. "Honoring Evangelical Chaplains of Our Armed Forces," *New York Times*, 25 April 1946, sect. 5, p. 2.

65. For examples of this expectation of a young "prophet," see Havner, *Road to Revival*, 49–50, and Wadsworth, *Will Revival Come?* (2nd ed., Chicago, 1945), 125–26. For a survey of the evangelistic scene at the time of Graham's emergence, see John R. Rice, *We Can have Revival Now* (Wheaton, Ill., 1950), 161–77.

66. J. Edwin Orr, *Good News in Bad Times: Signs of Revival* (Grand Rapids, Mich., 1953), 32–44, 54–85, and *The Second Great Awakening in America* (London, 1952), 160–201.

67. Harold J. Ockenga, "Is America's Revival Breaking?" *Evangelical Beacon*, 18 July 1950, 5.

68. See, for example, the debate over the "great awakening" construct, in the "Symposium on Religious Awakenings," *Sociological Analysis* 44 (1983): 81–122. It featured the following essays: R. C. Gordon-McCutchan, "Great Awakenings?" 83–96; Timothy L. Smith, "My Rejection of a Cyclical View of 'Great Awakenings,' " 97–102; William G. McLoughlin, "Timepieces and Butterflies: A Note on the Great-Awakening-Construct and Its Critics," 103–10; John L. Hammond, "The Reality of Revivals," 111–15; John F. Wilson, "Perspectives on the Historiography of Religious Awakenings," 117–20; and "Response of Professor Smith on Cycles of National Awakenings," 121–22. See also Jon Butler's critique of the construct in his "Enthusiasm Described and Decried: The Great Awakening as Interpretive Fiction," *Journal of American History* 69 (1982): 305–25.

69. *Time*, February 4, 1946, 46–47.

70. John C. Pollock, *Billy Graham, The Authorized Biography* (New York, 1965);

Orr, *Good News in Bad Times*, 86–104; Rudolph C. Nelson, "Fundamentalism at Harvard: The Case of Edward John Carnell," *Quarterly Review* 2 (1982): 79–98; and Marsden, *Reforming Fundamentalism*, 31–93.

71. Ralph D. Winter, *Twenty-five Unbelievable Years* (S. Pasadena, Calif., 1970), 47–51; W. Ritchie Hogg, "The Role of American Protestantism in World Mission," in R. Pierce Beaver, ed., *American Missions in Bicentennial Perspective*, (S. Pasadena, Calif., 1977), 354–402.

72. Marty, "The Revival of Evangelicalism," 11.

73. Marsden, *Reforming Fundamentalism*, 43–85.

74. This is the major theme of Marsden's new work, *Reforming Fundamentalism*.

75. Several have puzzled over the apparent contradiction between Falwell's ecclesiastical and cultural separatism, and his "rebirth" as a leader of the New Christian Right, notably Frances FitzGerald, *Cities on a Hill: A Journey through Contemporary American Cultures* (New York, 1986), 168–201, and Jeffrey D. Pulis, "Jerry Falwell and the Moral Majority: A Study of the Relationship between Theology and Ideology" (Ph.D. dissertation, Emory University, 1986).

76. Jim Wallis, *Revive Us Again: A Sojourner's Story* (Nashville, Tenn., 1983), 190.

77. Carpenter, "Fundamentalist Leaven," and George M. Marsden, "Unity and Diversity in the Evangelical Resurgence," in with David Lotz, Donald W. Shriver, Jr., and John F. Wilson, eds., *Altered Landscapes: Christianity in America, 1935–1985* (Grand Rapids, Mich., Eerdmans, forthcoming).

78. Stuart Rothenberg and Frank Newport, *The Evangelical Voter: Religion and Politics in America* (Washington, D.C., 1984); Corwin Smidt, "Born-Again Politics: The Political Behavior of Evangelicals in the South and Non-South," in Tod Baker, Robert Steed, and Laurence Moreland, eds., *Religion and Politics in the South: Mass and Elite Perspectives* (New York, 1983), 27–56; Lyman Kellstedt, "The Falwell Issue Agenda: Sources of Support among White Protestant Evangelicals," in Monty Lynn and David Moberg, eds., *The Social Scientific Study of Religion* (Westport, Conn., JAI Press, forthcoming); and Kellstedt, "Evangelicals and Political Realignment," in Corwin Smidt, ed., *Contemporary Evangelical Political Involvement: An Analysis and Assessment* (Lanham, Md., University Press of America, forthcoming). For a helpful explanation of evangelicals' diverse perspectives, see Robert Booth Fowler, *A New Engagement: Evangelical Political Thought, 1966–1976* (Grand Rapids, Mich., 1982).

79. Three works of William G. McLoughlin are especially illuminating on this point: "Revivalism," in Edwin S. Gaustad, ed., *The Rise of Adventism: Religion and Society in Mid-Nineteenth-Century America* (New York, 1974), 119–55; *Revivals, Awakenings, and Reform: An Essay on Religion and Social Change in America, 1607–1977* (Chicago, 1978); and "Faith," *American Quarterly* 35 (1983): 101–15. Three other works that suggest an enduring civic revivalism are John L. Hammond, "Revivals, Benevolence, and American Political Culture," *Journal of the American Academy of Religion* 46 (1978): 293–314; William Lee Miller, "The Seminarian Strain," *New Republic*, July 9, 1984, 18–21; and Mark A. Noll, *One Nation Under God? Christian Faith and Political Action in America* (San Francisco, 1988).

80. The best discussions of the tensions between conservative evangelicals and the highly secular "New Class" of information professionals are in three works by James Davison Hunter: *American Evangelicalism: Conservative Religion and the Quandary of Modernity* (New Brunswick, N.J., 1983), 107–19; *Evangelicalism: The Coming Generation* (Chicago, 1987), 116–54; and "The Liberal Reaction," in Robert Liebman and

Robert Wuthnow, eds., *Right: Mobilization and Legitimation*, (Hawthorne, N.Y., 1983), 149–63.

81. Works by and on the New Christian Right are legion. See, especially, Liebman and Wuthnow, eds., *New Christian Right*, and Richard V. Pierard's excellent bibliographic essay, "The New Religious Right in American Politics," in Marsden, ed., *Evangelicalism and Modern America*, 161–74, 206–12. Robert Wuthnow presents a chillingly persuasive picture of the threat of religious and political polarization in "What Is the Nature of Prejudice between Religious 'Left,' 'Right'?" *Emerging Trends* 8 (June 1986): 1–6, and in an unpublished paper, "American Democracy and the Democratization of American Religion," available from its author.

82. Daniel Bell, "A Return of the Sacred?" *British Journal of Sociology* 28 (1977): 419–50; Robert Nisbet, *A History of the Idea of Progress* (New York, 1980), 356–7; Robert N. Bellah, et al., *Habits of the Heart: Individualism and Commitment in American Life* (Berkeley, Calif., 1985); and A. James Reichley, "Religion and the Future of Politics," *Political Science Quarterly* 101 (1986): 23–47.

83. See his "Faith," and *Revivals, Awakenings, and Reform*.

84. Marty makes this point in "The Revival of Evangelicalism," 11.

10

EVANGELICAL BROADCASTING: ITS MEANING FOR EVANGELICALS

Larry K. Eskridge

Since the national media's rediscovery of America's large evangelical subculture in the mid–1970s, probably no other aspect of its unexpected return to prominence has received more publicity than the phenomenon of the electronic church. Articles published in *Newsweek*, *Time*, *Forbes*, *TV Guide*, *The Saturday Evening Post*, and *Playboy*, to name only a few, have in recent years registered various observations on media evangelism.[1] The agitated attention that the popular press has paid to evangelical broadcasting is mirrored in the scholarly community. A comparative torrent of discussion and research has emerged on a topic that, aside from several doctoral dissertations, drew almost no attention from the late 1950s to the early 1970s.[2]

Whether journalistic fashion or scholarly interest in the evangelical use of the mass media will continue is, of course, hard to predict. The recent gaffes by Oral Roberts, the Bakker-PTL and Jimmy Swaggart scandals, and the candidacy of Pat Robertson for the 1988 GOP presidential nomination have generated new rounds of debate and publication.[3] In the long run, however, the key to interest would seem to lie in evangelical broadcasting's continued growth and the sustained effect of the recent bad publicity.[4] The statistical evidence for the period before 1987 suggests it will remain a formidable force. In addition to the paid-time programming that currently accounts for most evangelical broadcasts, and the spread of satellite and cable technology, the number of radio and television stations with predominantly religious formats grew 22 percent and 71 percent, respectively, from 1982 to January 1987. During the same period the number of organizations, ministries, and churches producing religious television programs increased more than one-third.[5]

Whatever the future holds for the expansion of the electronic church, obviously its massive presence and aggressive stance in such a culturally relevant force as the mass media make it a topic worth understanding better. The research of the last decade has added a great deal to knowledge of evangelical broadcasting. Of course, in some areas such as the debate over audience size, it has produced conclusions that are less than definitive.[6] For the most part, however, it has provided data and interpretations that have increased understanding of this important social force.

Even a casual reading of the body of literature produced in the last ten years, however, reveals that it is dominated by the current public debate about the nature and strength of evangelicals and the electronic church. The issues central to it—audience size and composition, proselytizing, fund-raising techniques, and political content—have their origins in questions about the relative power of evangelicalism within American society.[7] They reflect concerns within the mainline churches and what James Davison Hunter has labeled the secularized "New Class" about the growth of evangelicalism and its broadcasting wing.[8] In effect, many of the studies have attempted to gauge the strength and influence of the movement, as well as to evaluate the merits of charges leveled against it. They have not been biased against evangelicals, and the questions they have asked have been important ones that merit further, more detailed study. Indeed, some of the research findings have been rather favorable to the electronic church, particularly in the debunking of the myth about its overt political content.[9]

Yet, largely ignored have been questions that ask why broadcasting has become so particularly important within the evangelical subculture. If millions tune into the electronic church regularly, and they are mainly evangelicals—as research has shown—it is important to understand why they do so. Without an understanding of the function that broadcasting performs within evangelicalism, it is impossible to understand the full significance of the electronic church within a wider cultural context.

THE HISTORICAL BACKGROUND

From the beginning of the fundamentalist-modernist split in the late nineteenth century, fundamentalists and evangelicals have created a plethora of denominational and independent colleges and Bible institutes, publishing houses, missionary and evangelistic agencies, summer camps, and youth programs that serve as rallying points and sources of cohesiveness for their far-flung and diverse constituency.[10] Over the decades broadcasting has earned an increasingly prominent place within this network as a major evangelistic and disciplinary tool. Its growth has been the result not only of a seemingly uncanny ability to utilize the medium, but also of the devoted support of rank-and-file evangelicals and their belief in the importance of the broadcasting endeavor.

Strangely enough, many fundamentalists were skeptical of the new phenomenon of radio in its early days and were convinced that no force that trespassed on the realm of the "Prince of the power of the air" could come to any good.[11] Others, such as James M. Gray, a prominent evangelist and president of Chicago's Moody Bible Institute, could see no relevant, practical application for the new gadget in religious work.[12] Nonetheless, scores of fundamentalist preachers around the country pushed ahead into the new medium in the early and mid–1920s. During this era the experimental efforts of radio pioneers like Paul Rader, R. R. Brown, and Aimee Semple McPherson proved that effective fundamentalist utilization of the medium was possible, as they built wide followings and created strong institutional bases for their broadcast ministries.[13]

Perhaps the most impressive aspect of this growing fundamentalist phenomenon was that most of the radio programs were the result of a true community effort. The public service requirements of the Federal Radio (later Federal Communications) Commission in broadcasting's early days meant that most of the air time devoted to religion was donated by the networks and individual stations. Unfortunately for fundamentalists, the new networks and most of the larger stations relied on the auspices of groups representing the mainstream Protestant, Catholic, and Jewish communities to organize and present religious programming that was not denominational, sectarian, or, above all, offensive. For example, the Federal Council of Churches, the fundamentalists' archenemy, controlled most of the sustained-time broadcasting available to Protestants.[14] Thus, contrary to the common practice of the period, most fundamentalist programs went on the air as paid-time broadcasts. Fundamentalist radio evangelists relied mainly on their audiences for the financial support to get on, and stay on, the air.

Despite this obstacle fundamentalist radio programs prospered into the 1930s and 1940s. Broadcasting became an increasingly significant force within the fundamentalist community. The national success of programs like Charles E. Fuller's "Old-Fashioned Revival Hour," Dr. Walter A. Meier's "Lutheran Hour," and M. R. DeHaan's "Radio Bible Class," along with numerous other successes on a regional and local level, lent the greater fundamentalist movement a measure of popular visibility and sense of accomplishment that was otherwise hard to come by in the lean years following the fiasco of the Scopes trial.[15]

This growth assured that religious broadcasting was an important tool in its own right and a major new component in the developing evangelical subculture. The increasing centrality of its place was symbolized not only by the financial support of the rank and file, but by the attention paid radio by the hierarchy of the newly-formed National Association of Evangelicals (NAE), founded in 1941. One of its major goals was the creation of a committee to deal with radio, and in 1943 it drafted an NAE Code of Ethics for "Gospel Broadcasting."[16] In 1944 under the aegis of the NAE the National Religious Broadcasters (NRB) was formed at a meeting in Columbus, Ohio, that was attended by more than 150 delegates. Later as an independent organization, the NRB battled the Federal Council of Churches to gain greater access to the airwaves for conservatives.[17]

The efforts of the NRB, NAE, and individual broadcasters and their supporters were helped by the generally declining influence of liberal religious groups with industry executives, the rise of television, and an increasing emphasis on profits. Eventually they led to a greater availability of sustained time for evangelicals and fundamentalists. More important, however, they helped to remove most network barriers to the sale of air time for religious programming. By the mid–1950s with access to the NBC and ABC radio networks, as well as hundreds of individual local stations, evangelical broadcasting had grown into a mini-industry that was buying more than $10,000,000 a year of radio air time.[18]

As evangelicals gained increased exposure on, and access to, radio in the late 1940s and early 1950s, they at the same time began to dabble in the mass communications wunderkind, television. Early evangelical and fundamentalist excursions into the world of television did not indicate a particularly promising future for it as an evangelistic tool. Beginning paid-time programs that featured such prominent evangelical radio luminaries as Billy Graham, Charles E. Fuller, and Percy Crawford, as well as occasional sustained-time broadcasts by Donald Grey Barnhouse, enjoyed only limited success.[19] Indeed, the only real splash made by evangelicals during this period, when Bishop Fulton J. Sheen was the embodiment of successful religious television, was the live NBC broadcasts of Graham's 1957 New York City Crusade.[20] Even this, however, was evidence more of the power of Graham's message and charisma than of the ability of evangelicals to utilize the new medium. Oddly enough, the keys to future television gains would not lie in the expansion of the existing evangelical radio hierarchy into this new field, but with a group of often crude and brash, but energetic, adaptable, and exciting mavericks, who created the beginnings of their independent television ministries in relative obscurity in the 1950s and early 1960s.

Rex Humbard (1953), Oral Roberts (1954), Jerry Falwell (1957), and Pat Robertson (1961) went on the air in these years with little of the flash, polish, and technical know-how, and none of the big-budget slickness, that would later attract such a large following.[21] Little noticed by the secular media or the intellectual elite, these television evangelists slowly developed the mix of old-fashioned preaching, folksy compassion, and Hollywood stage presence that won occasional converts and a number of devoted backers across the country. The expanding lineup of stations that these evangelistic entrepreneurs strung together in ensuing years produced the boom in evangelical broadcasting in the 1970s. Riding the momentum partly created by the success of their predecessors and the synergistic effect of complex social forces and industry trends, a second generation that included Jim Bakker, James Robison, Jimmy Swaggart, Kenneth Copeland, Robert Schuller, and others would in the 1980s begin to approach, equal, and in some cases, surpass the achievements of their televangelist elders.

THE COMPATIBLES: EVANGELICALISM AND BROADCASTING

Clearly, broadcasting has over the years evolved into a major force within evangelicalism. Its survival and growth have depended ultimately on its constituency's patronage and financial support of its mission. Less readily apparent are the factors that have made broadcasting so particularly compatible with the evangelical mindset and lifestyle. One obvious but nonetheless major function evangelical broadcasting serves within the subculture is as an aid to its evangelistic imperative. An overwhelming number of evangelicals are deeply convinced that all men are inherently sinful and doomed to eternal punishment unless they repent of their sins and ask Jesus Christ to become their personal savior. Furthermore, they believe that all Christians have an individual and a collective responsibility to see that others come to know the Lord. For evangelicals these beliefs are not theological points passionately held by a hierarchy and vaguely assented to by those in the pews. Rather they are crucial, central tenets of evangelical faith and piety, the linchpin that holds together both the evangelical world view and the religious activities in which evangelicals participate.[22] Statistics gathered in the late 1970s show that more than one-half of all evangelicals consider evangelism their top religious priority, even more important than personal spiritual growth. Similarly, evangelicals were found to be more than twice as likely to share their personal religious views in an evangelistic way as members of any other religious group.[23]

The roots of evangelicalism's devotion to broadcasting must be traced to this particular faith/piety construct and its evangelistic imperative. From the earliest fundamentalist radio pioneers to today's scions of televangelism, the saving of souls and the opportunity to air its gospel message has been evangelical broadcasting's stated central goal.[24] Dr. Robert A. Cook, president of the NRB, in a discussion of the theme for the then upcoming 1987 NRB convention, "Communicating Christ to the Nations," summed up evangelical broadcasters' raison d'être: "Our responsibility as broadcasters is to make our listeners and viewers understand that God loves them, that He paid the penalty for their sins and that He wants them for His own."[25] That evangelicals are committed to evangelism is, admittedly, no major revelation. Yet, the way in which broadcasting fulfills evangelicals' need to preach their gospel is an issue of paramount importance in any examination of the electronic church and the relationship of evangelicalism to the surrounding culture.

Other factors reinforce the central role that broadcasting plays in the wider evangelical community. Evangelical broadcasting provides a "baptized" media alternative for evangelicals. Observers like Jeremy Rifkin and James Davison Hunter have noted how modern-day evangelicalism reproduces many of the aspects of modern American culture from "Christian" night clubs to *The Christian Yellow Pages*.[26] This "baptizing" process allows evangelicals to create a nearly total "Christian" environment within the American culture, with an evangelical clone of nearly every secular organization, service, or product. It has resulted in, among possible examples, "Christian" versions of the Scouts like AWANA (Approved Workmen Are Not Ashamed), tour packages to the Holy Land on the Lord's Airline, and the high kitsch of "Jesus Junque": the Jesus frisbees, bumper stickers, posters, pencils, plaques, tea bags, and T-shirts that are often prominently displayed in evangelical bookstores. To quote an evangelical bumper sticker of the 1970s, the prevailing sentiment seems to be that "Things Go Better With Jesus," whether it be in having a family doctor who belongs to the Christian Medical Association or insisting that it be a "Jesus frisbee" one throws to the family dog.

This tendency to reproduce the various aspects of the surrounding American culture and create an evangelical alternative to practically everything the secular world offers, allows evangelicals to be both part of, and apart from, the larger culture. This characteristic finds one of its most crucial outworkings in evangelical broadcasting. Its varied programs and formats strengthen the individual evangelical in his religious commitment. By creating an evangelical media alternative with something for nearly every interest, taste, and age group, this parallel programming provides another important element in an all-pervading "Christian" environment that dovetails nicely with the modern American culture with which it co-exists.

Besides the evangelistic thrust common to much of the programming, there is an even stronger emphasis on teaching programs, intended to "disciple" the believer. The evangelical who is so inclined can in most areas of the United States spend nearly twenty-four hours a day "getting into the Word." Television programs like Charles E. Stanley's "In Touch" and D. James Kennedy's "Truths That Transform," together with radio standbys such as Dr. J. Vernon McGee's "Through The Bible" and the DeHaans' "Radio Bible Class," are syndicated on hundreds of stations and cable systems. These programs serve as substantial supplements to, or in many cases substitutes for, the heavy teaching emphasis of more well-known televangelists.[27]

Entertainment and music programs now play a major role in evangelical broadcasting, especially in religious radio. Music is the dominant format of the majority of air time on evangelical stations, with almost one-half the music played in the pop-rock category of "Contemporary Christian Music."[28] Syndicated weekly music programs like "Christian Countdown" and "The Pat Boone Show" are popular evangelical versions of similar secular Top 40 Countdown shows. Music programs are also an important aspect of evangelical television. In fact, a twenty-four-hour-a-day music channel has recently been founded, the AMEN. (All Music & Entertainment Network) satellite/cable network.[29]

More specialized programming alternatives abound. Evangelicals who wish to know how to deal with humanists, liberals, and various cultists can watch "The John Ankerberg Show" to see its host and evangelical theologians and topical experts duel with the various manifestations of the enemy. Those in need of counseling can receive help from satellite-fed radio programs like the Moody Broadcasting Network's "Dial the Pastor" or the "Minirth Meier Clinic," which features two Dallas-based psychologists. Evangelicals concerned about problems in raising their children, abortion, child pornography, menopause, and a myriad of other "family" topics can tune into one of the 1,006 radio stations that carry "Focus on the Family," the program of the best-selling author and child psychologist Dr. James Dobson.[30] Children are not forgotten. For them evangelical stations carry cartoon shows like "Davey and Goliath" and "SuperBook," and radio story programs like "The Listening Post" and "A Visit With Mrs. G."

Specific programming also exists for relatively small segments of the evangelical audience. "Joni and Friends" is a daily inspirational radio show for the shut-in and handicapped. Its hostess is Joni Eareckson Tada, a quadriplegic artist whose story has been told in several best-selling books and a 1979 Billy Graham film. For the sports enthusiast, Keith Erickson, a former NBA star, conducts "Sports Forum" on hundreds of radio stations with interviews and testimonies from athletes.

These radio and television shows and formats represent only a partial cataloging of the various programming possibilities, from which many local and regional offerings are omitted. They do illustrate, however, the polyglot nature of evangelical broadcasting. Regrettably, much recent research and discussion ignore this diversity and concentrate instead on the major televangelists at the expense of the rest of the available programming.[31] Obviously the major televangelists are very important. But to designate them as the embodiment of evangelical broadcasting is to approach the topic in a simplistic way, particularly when evidence suggests that 26 percent of the audience for religious programs use only radio, and an additional 27 percent patronize both radio and television.[32] That different programs appeal to different audiences is an elementary fact of market research. Its applicability to religious broadcasting was demonstrated in a small-scale study of PTL viewers in southeastern Ohio that Louise M. Bourgault conducted in 1979. After interviewing local members of two fundamentalist and two mainline denominations, Bourgault concluded that the "PTL Club" was likely to be received better by "moderate fundamentalists," whose religious style was more comfortable with the flashy, "worldly" style purveyed on Bakker's program.[33] Certainly, as this study intimates, different denominational and social backgrounds produce varying tastes in religious program styles and result in evangelical broadcasting serving not one but many publics.

By creating a "baptized" media alternative for diverse evangelical publics, electronic broadcasting has become an important, though largely ignored, means for evangelicalism to harness effectively the forces of modernity and use them selectively to solidify the place of its community within American society. The ability of evangelicalism to thrive in the increasingly secular modern world has made it a puzzle to many observers.[34] James Davison Hunter in *American Evangelicalism: Conservative Religion and the Quandry of Modernity* (1983) has written a recent analysis of this particular conundrum. Evangelicals, Hunter argues, have been successful in bucking the secularizing trends because they have, for the most part, been successful in their attempts to accommodate or resist the modernizing forces that beset them.

He cites several reasons why evangelicalism has been able to keep modernity at bay. Because so many of its adherents are found among women, blacks, and the elderly, evangelicalism is "located furthest from the . . . structures and processes of modernity," and thereby avoids "sustained confrontation with modernity's most threatening attributes.''[35] Another reason is the increased civility with which American evangelicalism accommodates itself to America's culturally and structurally pluralistic society.[36] A rationalized, highly codified piety and an increasingly narcissistic privatization of this piety are other ways in which evangelicalism deflects the forces of modernity.[37] Finally, as perhaps the most important forms of resistance, increased politicization and refusal to accept threats to traditional morality, are aggressive measures evangelicals use to fight modernity.[38]

Hunter's conclusions are valuable. Unfortunately, he neglects the role the evangelical mass media may play in this struggle, aside from an acknowledgement that it exists as part of the larger social organization.[39] The major role that evangelical broadcasting plays within the subculture, however, makes it reasonable to assume that the electronic church is a major resource in the fight to adapt to and to re-channel modernity, both practically and symbolically.

In practical terms, evangelicals' massive use of the broadcast media helps to create and maintain the context within which they practice their intense piety. By counterbalancing, limiting, and in some cases excluding many opposing views and values, evangelical broadcasting strengthens evangelicalism's collective and individual resistance to secularizing forces. For example, the 1984 Annenberg-Gallup study, commissioned by over thirty mainline and independent church groups, confirmed this role. This imposing, two-year study found that the electronic church, while not a particularly effective proselytizer, is an effective reinforcer of existing religious beliefs.[40] The extent to which evangelical broadcasting shapes its users is not yet known, but the potential is certainly there. Michael Novak, in discussing the impact of television, noted that: ''If you run for twenty minutes a day, your psyche is subtly transformed. If you work in an executive office, you begin to think like an executive. And if you watch six hours of television, on an average, every day . . . ?''[41]

The analogy can well be extended to the evangelical context. Although surely the background, life circumstances, program selection, and time spent with evangelical programs are all factors to be considered, it is apparent that the offerings of the electronic church subtly, and not so subtly, influence the minds of those in its audience.

Besides the practical implications inherent in the contributions of evangelical broadcasting to an atmosphere conducive to holding and nurturing evangelical beliefs and values, there are symbolic ways in which it serves as a hedge against modernity. One way that reflects Hunter's analysis of evangelicalism as a whole is in the aggressive evangelistic presence it maintains by its potential access to the homes of non-evangelicals. Through its continued desire to expand and saturate the airwaves with its message, the electronic church is a continual throwing down of the gauntlet that signals its willingness to challenge many of the values and ideas of the larger society.

Finally, evangelicals' use of the mass media is an important statement that allows them to affirm their place and participate in the economic and technological direction of the overall society, while still permitting them to object to its spiritual and moral tone.[42] A casual sampling of evangelical magazines, book jackets, and television backdrops is evidence of a tendency to romanticize and sentimentalize the "good old days" and life in pre-industrial America. But evangelicals, aside from some very isolated rural segments of their constituency and the self-styled "prophetic" views of the evangelical left, hardly advocate a return to Amish-like simplicity. As Horsfield comments, the evangelical attitude to technology "reflect[s] a . . . utilitarian attitude towards technology. . . . The morality of a particular technology lies principally in the morality of the user and his purpose."[43] Evangelicals, whatever their views on life, death, and the nature of the universe, share the fascination with new ideas and technical know-how typical of their more secularized cousins in American society. Evangelical participation in the mass media presents an opportunity to be among the front ranks of the cultural mainstream, with a built-in forum to criticize the aspects of modern life evangelicals find objectionable.

Evangelical use of such powerful modernizing tools as the mass media undoubtedly has unfavorable side effects for the movement as a whole. One realm that critics both within evangelicalism and from mainline Protestantism point to is in the area of privatization, and a de-emphasis of the communal nature of the Christian experience.[44] It is difficult to discern just how true these charges are. Much has been learned in the last decade about the nature of evangelical broadcasting, its history, its audience, its fundraising techniques, its political content, and its effectiveness as a proselytizing agent. Although this information contributes greatly to an understanding of the electronic church, it largely ignores the important role that it plays within the evangelical subculture as an aid to its evangelistic imperative, as a multi-varied media alternative, and as a counter to the encroachments of modernity.

Perhaps the publicity surrounding recent moral and financial tribulations marks the beginning of a significant reduction in the public's confidence in, and the influence of, the electronic church. Evangelicals, however, have proven themselves to be resilient and resourceful in the past; that they will rebound from these current misfortunes seems likely. By preaching a message deemed vital to a large segment of the American population, evangelical broadcasting will continue to be a national force regardless of periodic gains and setbacks. One hopes that future research and discussion will be interested in ascertaining the full dimensions of this phenomenon, both for those within the evangelical subculture and for the larger American culture within which it exists.

NOTES

1. "Born Again!" *Newsweek,* October 25, 1976, 68–78; "The Great Alternative," *The Saturday Evening Post,* May 1977, 72–73; "Back to That Old-Time Religion," *Time,* December 26, 1977, 52–58; "Stars of the Cathode Church," *Time,* February 4, 1980, 64–65; "Electronic Pulpit," *Forbes,* July 7, 1980, 116–18; Johnny Greene, "The

Astonishing Wrongs of the New Moral Right,'' *Playboy*, January 1981, 117–18, 248–62. These are just a few examples of the many examinations of the electronic church that appeared in popular periodicals in the late 1970s and early 1980s.

2. Most major studies dealing with evangelicals and broadcasting between the late 1950s and mid–1970s were doctoral dissertations that dealt either with localized audience studies or with certain, often tangential, historical aspects of their relationship. For examples of audience studies, see John L. Dennis, ''An Analysis of the Audience of Religious Radio and Television Programs in the Detroit Metropolitan Area'' (Ph.D. dissertation, University of Michigan, 1961); Haddon W. Robinson, ''A Study of the Audience of Religious Radio and Television in Seven Cities Throughout the United States'' (Ph.D. dissertation, University of Illinois, 1964); and Charles Solt, ''A Study of the Audience Profile for Religious Broadcasts in Onondaga County'' (Ph.D. dissertation, Syracuse University, 1971). A more comprehensive study was Robert C. Ringe's ''An Analysis of Selected Personality and Behavior Characteristics Which Affect Receptivity to Religious Broadcasting'' (Ph.D. dissertation, Ohio State University, 1969). For examples of historical studies, see Ralph M. Jennings, ''Policies and Practices of Selected National Bodies as Related to Broadcasting'' (Ph.D. dissertation, New York University, 1968); Martin G. Neeb, ''An Historical Study of American Non-Commercial AM Broadcast Stations Owned and Operated by Religious Groups, 1920–1966'' (Ph.D. dissertation, Northwestern University, 1967); and Lowell S. Saunders, ''The National Religious Broadcasters and the Availability of Commercial Radio Time'' (Ph.D. dissertation, University of Illinois, 1968). Recent studies include Razelle Frankl, *Televangelism: The Marketing of Popular Religion* (Carbondale, Ill., 1987); Jeffrey K. Hadden and Charles E. Swann, *Prime-Time Preachers: The Rising Power of Televangelism* (Reading, Mass., 1981); and Peter G. Horsfield, *Religious Television: The American Experience* (New York, 1984).

3. *Christianity Today*, 20 February 1987, 43–45; *Newsweek*, April 6, 1987, 16–22.

4. The initial reaction to the recent bad publicity does not seem encouraging. Falwell's ''Old-Time Gospel Hour'' has been pulled out of 50 of its 380 stations, and ratings for television ministries have dropped nearly 20 percent since late 1986. ''Evangelists Losing Viewers and Dollars,'' *TV Guide*, October 31, 1987, A1, A74.

5. Dan Nicholas, ''The Quiet Revolution in Christian Broadcasting,'' *Religious Broadcasting*, February 1987, 20–23.

6. The debate over audience size has elicited much popular astonishment, chagrin, and controversy in recent years. Indeed, much of the flap that greeted the rise of evangelicalism was undoubtedly the result of misunderstood and misleading audience estimates from the media evangelists themselves, which were at first accepted at face value by the media. Jeffrey K. Hadden, ''Televangelism and the Future of American Politics,'' in David G. Bromley and Anson Shupe, eds., *New Christian Politics* (Macon, Ga., 1984), 153–56. While early estimates of a national audience in the area of 130 million proved bogus, reactionary figures that in one case put the size of the television audience at 7 million now also seem to have been discredited. The 130-million figure was cited by Ben Armstrong, the director of the National Religious Broadcasters, in his book, *The Electric Church* (Nashville, 1979). William Fore, head of the National Council of Churches' Communications Commission, gave the 7-million estimate in ''Religion and Television: Report on the Research,'' *Christian Century*, July 18–24, 1984, 710–13. Although the total audience for evangelical broadcasting is as yet unclear, the Gallup survey in the

Religion and Television report estimated that 32 percent of the monthly adult audience at least occasionally viewed religious television. George Gerbner, Larry Gross, Stewart Hoover, Michael Morgan, Nancy Signorielli, Harry E. Cotugno, and Robert Wuthow, *Religion and Television: A Research Report by the Annenberg School of Communications* (Philadelphia, 1984). A 1985 A. C. Nielsen study found that more than 40 percent of U.S. households (61 million) watched one of the top ten syndicated religious programs during its survey period, February 1984. Quentin J. Schultze, "Vindicating the Electronic Church? An Assessment of the Annenberg-Gallup Study," *Critical Studies in Mass Communications* 2 (1985): 286; *Religious Broadcasting*, January 1986, 8.

7. There have been numerous excellent studies on various aspects of the electronic church in the last several years aside from the massive 1984 Gallup-Annenberg study and the monographs by Hadden and Swann, Horsfield, and Frankl. For the most part they attempt to analyze audience size and makeup, proselytizing, fundraising techniques, and political content, or a combination of these factors. See, for example, Robert Abelman and Kimberly Neuendorf, "How Religious Is Religious Television?" *Journal of Communications* 35 (1985): 98–110; J. Thomas Bisset, "Religious Broadcasting: Assessing the State of the Art," *Christianity Today,* December 12, 1980, 28–31; Louise M. Bourgault, "The PTL Club and Protestant Viewers: An Ethnographic Study," *Journal of Communications* 35 (1985): 132–48; Judith M. Buddenbaum, "Characteristics and Media-Related Needs of the Audience for Religious TV," *Journalism Quarterly* 58 (1981): 266–272; Razelle Frankl, "Television and Popular Religion: Changes in Church Offerings," in Bromley and Shupe, eds., *New Christian Politics*, 129–38; Gary D. Gaddy, "Some Potential Causes and Consequences of the Use of Religious Broadcasts," in Bromley and Shupe, eds., *New Christian Politics*, 117–28; Gary D. Gaddy and David Pritchard, "When Watching Religious TV Is Like Attending Church," *Journal of Communications* 35 (1985): 3, 123–31; Jeffrey K. Hadden, "Soul Saving via Video," *Christian Century*, May 28, 1980, 609–13, "The Great Audience Size Debate," *Religious Broadcasting*, January 1986, 20–22, and "Getting to the Bottom of the Audience Size Debate," *Religious Broadcasting*, February 1986, 88, 116, 122, 124, 126, 128; Peter G. Horsfield, "Religious Broadcasting at the Crossroads," *Christian Century*, January 27, 1982, 87–90, and "Evangelism by Mail: Letters from the Broadcasters," *Journal of Communications* 35 (1985): 89–97; Wesley E. Miller, "The New Christian Right and the News Media," in Bromley and Shupe, eds., *New Christian Politics*, 139–49; Quentin J. Schultze, "Vindicating the Electronic Church," 283–90; William Stacey and Anson Shupe, "Correlates of Support for the Electronic Church," *Journal for the Scientific Study of Religion* 21 (1982): 291–303; and Sari Thomas, "The Route to Redemption: Religion and Social Class," *Journal of Communications* 35 (1985): 111–22.

8. James Davison Hunter, *American Evangelicalism: Conservative Religion and the Quandry of Modernity* (New Brunswick, N.J., 1983), 107–11.

9. See, for example, Abelman and Neuendorf, *Journal of Communications* 35 (1985): 103–6; and Stacey and Shupe, "Support for the Electronic Church," 300–301.

10. Ernest Sandeen, "Fundamentalism and American Identity," *Annals of the American Academy of Political and Social Science* 38 (1970): 56–65; Joel A. Carpenter, "Fundamentalist Institutions and the Rise of Evangelical Protestantism, 1929–1942," *Church History* 49 (1980): 62–75.

11. Wendell P. Loveless, *Manual of Gospel Broadcasting* (Chicago, 1946), 14–16.

12. Gene A. Getz, *MBI: The Story of the Moody Bible Institute* (Chicago, 1969), 278–80.

13. Although there is no monograph that deals definitively with the pioneer days of fundamentalist radio, Armstrong's *Electric Church*, Hadden and Swann's *Prime-Time Preachers*, and J. Harold Ellens's *Models of Religious Broadcasting* (Grand Rapids, Mich., 1974) give useful summaries of some of the key people and events of that era.

14. Louis Gasper, *The Fundamentalist Movement: 1930–1956* (Grand Rapids, Mich., 1981), 83. Ralph M. Jennings, "Policies and Practices of Selected National Religious Bodies as Related to Broadcasting" (Ph.D. dissertation, New York University, 1968), 16–17. Ellens, *Models of Broadcasting*, 17–19.

15. Armstrong's *Electric Church* presents a good basic account of some of the major individuals of this period. A more detailed account of one of these radio evangelists is Daniel P. Fuller's *Give the Winds a Mighty Voice* (Waco, Tex., 1972), a filial but even-handed account of his father, Charles E. Fuller.

16. Gasper, *Fundamentalist Movement*, 81; Jennings, "Policies and Practices," 308–9.

17. Gasper, *Fundamentalist Movement*, 81–82; Jennings, "Policies and Practices," 317–18.

18. Gasper, *Electric Church*, 80–84.

19. Armstrong, *Electric Church,* 83–99; Fuller, *Give a Mighty Voice*, 177; and Gasper, *Fundamentalist Movement*, 79–80.

20. Gasper, *Fundamentalist Movement*, 141.

21. Armstrong, *Electric Church*, 83–87; Hadden and Swann, *Prime-Time Preachers*, 22–29, 34–37.

22. Hunter, *American Evangelism*, 61–69.

23. Ibid., 68.

24. See, for example, the author's "Only Believe: Paul Rader and the Chicago Gospel Tabernacle, 1922–1933" (M.A. thesis, University of Maryland at College Park, 1985); Fuller, *Give a Mighty Voice*; and Armstrong, *Electric Church*.

25. *Religious Broadcasting*, July/August 1986, 10.

26. Jeremy Rifkin with Ted Howard, *The Emerging Order: God in the Age of Scarcity* (New York, 1983), 108–19; Hunter, *American Evangelicalism*, 56–58.

27. The various issues of *Religious Broadcasting* and the yearly NRB *Directory of Religious Broadcasting* are the most easily accessible sources of information on these various programs, aside from tuning into one's local evangelical radio or television station.

28. Paul H. Virts, "Surprising Findings in Christian Radio," *Religious Broadcasting*, February 1986, 42, 44.

29. An advertisement in *Religious Broadcasting,* June 1986, 5.

30. Figure quoted on the "Focus on the Family" program broadcast on 25 March 1987, on WMBI-FM, Chicago.

31. This is a sin of omission not only in popular treatments of the electronic church but in scholarly examinations of the phenomenon. They focus on religious television, particularly the "Top Ten" television preachers.

32. Gaddy, "Religious Broadcasts," 121.

33. Bourgault, "PTL Club and Protestant Viewers," 132–48.

34. See, for example, Hunter, *American Evangelicalism*, 11–19. A further examination of this problem is Hunter's look at the future "elite" of evangelicalism in his recent *Evangelicalism: The Coming Generation* (Chicago, 1987). Peter L. Berger, *A Rumor of Angels* (New York, 1970), 4–5, and *Facing Up to Modernity* (New York, 1977), 175–77.

35. Hunter, *American Evangelicalism*, 59–60.

36. Ibid., 84–91.

37. Ibid., 84–99.

38. Ibid., 103–12.

39. Ibid., 58.

40. Schultze, "Vindicating the Electronic Church," 285–86.

41. Michael Novak, "Television Shapes the Soul," in Douglass Cater and Richard Adler, eds., *Television as a Social Force* (New York, 1975), 9.

42. My thinking in this area has been influenced by Edward M. Berckman, "The Old-Time Gospel Hour and Fundamentalist Paradox," *Christian Century*, March 29, 1978, 330–32.

43. Horsfield, *Religious Television*, 18.

44. See Martin Marty, *The Improper Opinion: Mass Media and the Christian Faith* (Philadelphia, 1961), for a mainline critique of the media. For an evangelical critique, see Virginia Stem Owens, *The Total Image: or, Selling Jesus in the Modern Age* (Grand Rapids, Mich., 1980).

11

God and Jimmy Carter

Leo P. Ribuffo

After the shouting and voting ended, *Church and State* correctly concluded that the election of 1976 had raised "more religious and church-state related issues than any since 1960," when John F. Kennedy was elected the first Roman Catholic president. The impact of these issues should not have been surprising. The election occurred amid a religious awakening and followed a decade of war, racial conflict, cultural questioning, and economic crisis. Furthermore, the Republican and Democratic presidential candidates, the incumbent Gerald R. Ford and Governor Jimmy Carter, were the most devout pair of major party nominees since William McKinley defeated William Jennings Bryan in 1896.[1]

Discussion of religion and the presidency in the election concentrated on Carter, a self-described "born-again" Christian. He did not intend—and probably did not expect—his relationship with God to be a major campaign issue. Earlier in his career he had hesitated to answer questions about his religion but, since these arose often in Georgia, finally decided to reply "very frankly." Still, he remained reticent about volunteering information; honesty and eagerness to witness for his faith conflicted with a desire for privacy. In his campaign autobiography, *Why Not the Best?* Carter described himself as a "Christian," and during the primaries affirmed "traditional" values of hard work, honesty, and family that many voters associated with religion. Yet Baptist churchman was only one of the roles he played, and one he advertised less than his experiences as a governor, businessman, farmer, submariner, and nuclear engineer. Admiral Hyman Rickover, who had reinforced Carter's perfectionist tendencies, bulked larger in *Why Not the Best?* than the theologian Reinhold Niebuhr, who was merely quoted on the frontispiece along with Dylan Thomas and Bob Dylan. Carter's spiritual rebirth a decade earlier went unmentioned. Carter probably sensed that a presidential candidate's conversion narrative would disturb some readers, but, perhaps because prayer and Baptist piety meshed easily with his own daily routine and Georgia politics, he underestimated how many other Americans would consider them extraordinary, dangerous, or bizarre.[2]

After Carter's victory in the New Hampshire primary raised his status from dark horse to front runner, commentators tried to make sense of his personality and world view. Typically stressing individual quirks and ignoring social class, they explained neither very well, and Carter emerged as a populistic, techno-cratic, Wilsonian enigma. Nothing looked quirkier than the candidate's religion, especially after his sister Ruth Carter Stapleton described her brother's conversion in the *Washington Post* on March 12. Carter corroborated her story except for minor details; according to his account, for example, no tears had been shed. The conversion had involved no mysticism, "no wave of revelation . . . no blind-ing flash of light or voice of God." The "quiet" reassurance he had felt, Carter told reporter Jules Witcover, was a "typical experience among Christians."[3]

Indeed it was. According to a Gallup poll conducted later in 1976, 48 percent of American Protestants and 18 percent of American Catholics had been born again. Apparently few of them reported for the national media, which continued to treat Carter's religion as anything but typical. In late March so many reporters descended on the Plains, Georgia, Baptist Church, where Carter taught a men's Sunday school class, that they had to be restricted to a pool of four. Ruth Carter Stapleton received much publicity in her own right. A born-again Christian whose books and newsletters offered a mixture of soft theology, softer psychology, and positive thinking, Stapleton was persistently misidentified (to her consternation) as a "faith healer."[4]

Throughout the campaign Carter continued to answer questions about his religion and, especially when they were intelligently posed, gave informative answers. Unfortunately, except for Bill Moyers, who interviewed Carter on network television in May, no one posing intelligent questions commanded a mass audience. Nonetheless, Carter's statements in 1976 revealed a thoughtful Southern Baptist layman who favored a sturdy wall of separation between church and state.[5]

Carter explained that his whole life had been "shaped in the [Baptist] church." His adult conversion had marked an important transition instead of a final point of certainty. Thereafter, his "personal relationship" with Jesus grew stronger, he prayed without "special effort," and felt "at peace with the world." He tried to emulate Christ's example and sought especially to control "self-pride and self-satisfaction." Recognizing that his religious world view retained inconsis-tencies and anomalies, he constantly looked for better answers; he liked to quote Paul Tillich's observation that religion was a "search for truth." Carter not only acknowledged American religious diversity but explicitly identified with early Baptists like Roger Williams and John Leland, who had championed freedom of conscience. Accordingly, resisting church pressure, he had voted in the Geor-gia Senate to permit eighteen-year-olds to drink alcohol, and later ended regular religious services in the governor's mansion. He had also rejected proposals to restore compulsory prayer to public schools. Nor would he use the White House as a "pulpit" to spread his own religious views. Rather, along with other recent presidents, he would support the general "principles of the Judeo-Christian ethic."[6]

Although Carter's stands on foreign policy and domestic economics were shrewdly imprecise, he displayed a clear, consistent position on religion. Why, then, did the issue continue to haunt him during the campaign? First, as in 1928 and, to a lesser extent, 1960, religion was part of a broader cultural conflict. Evangelical and fundamentalist Protestants on the one hand, and Roman Catholics, Jews, and cosmopolitan intellectuals on the other, had through generations of conflict developed stereotypes about each other that were difficult to forget. Second, as in 1928 and 1960, questions relating to church-state relations were very much on the national agenda. For example, many theologically conservative Protestants now coalesced with Catholics in urging federal aid to parochial schools as well as mandatory prayer in the public schools, and some Orthodox Jews joined them in denouncing the recent legalization of abortion. Third, while Carter and Ford denied seeking votes on the basis of religion, the temptation was hard to resist, and their respective parties were even less fastidious. Moreover, Carter made important tactical errors in mobilizing these issues. Further, citing Jesus's teachings, Carter often declared that "all of us are sinful," without prudently adding that Americans in the aggregate were less sinful than others. This neo-Calvinist judgment had some appeal after Watergate and the Vietnam War, but in the final analysis it contradicted the venerable belief that God was on America's side. Indeed, even secularized doubts about American mission would have been controversial.[7]

Carter tried to break down stereotypes about born-again Baptists. He was least conciliatory toward—and least successful with—cosmopolitan intellectuals. For instance, Arthur M. Schlesinger, Jr., accused him of misunderstanding Niebuhr. Mixing the conventional techniques of ethnic politics with an uncharacteristic reference to biblical prophecy, Carter was more effective with Jews. He noted the many Jews on his staff, recalled a fellow Baptist, President Harry Truman, who had recognized Israel in 1948, and called Israel's creation a "fulfillment" of Scripture.[8]

Catholics proved to be a more stubborn than Jews. Although few of them belonged to his inner circle, Carter recognized their influence within the Democratic coalition. At the national convention he was placed in nomination by Representative Peter Rodino, an Italian Catholic from Newark, New Jersey. Unimpressed by such symbolism and distressed by Carter's refusal to support a constitutional amendment outlawing abortion, most of the Catholic hierarchy and press leaned toward Ford. Criticism of his position on abortion by the executive committee of the National Conference of Bishops in September highlighted what the *Washington Post* called Carter's "Catholic problem." The problem was serious but soluble, pollster Patrick Caddell advised, because most Catholics viewed abortion as an issue largely outside the president's control.[9]

Carter's religion enhanced his appeal to white fundamentalist and evangelical Protestants as well as to most blacks. At a minimum it highlighted his commitment to morality in government and deflected charges of callous opportunism. Furthermore, though leading evangelicals, including the editors of *Christianity Today*, remained prudently noncommittal, rank-and-file born-again whites, eager for national acceptance, paid scant attention to Carter's theology and overlooked political differences to embrace him as one of their own.[10]

For blacks, Carter's conversion to Christ was less significant than his conversion to the cause of racial equality, but religion nonetheless enhanced his appeal. There were strong theological and cultural affinities, though relatively few institutional ties, between born-again whites and most black evangelicals. Addressing a convention of the African Methodist Episcopal Church, Carter stressed this "mutual faith." Sixty percent of southern blacks were Baptists, and the Southern Baptist Convention contained almost 400 black congregations. Even northern blacks were used to the amalgamation of religion and politics. Thus, as William Lee Miller observed, Carter was the only recent presidential nominee who actually looked comfortable at a black church service.[11]

For many cultural conservatives the pious Carter family offered an attractive alternative to Betty Ford's candid feminism. The President's wife considered the Supreme Court opinion in *Roe v. Wade*, which legalized most abortions, a "great, great decision," and acknowledged that adolescents, including her daughter, might have love affairs. Carter avoided criticizing Mrs. Ford, yet his campaign in conservative constituencies benefited from the controversies she ignited. Democratic appeals to born-again whites included an advertisement in *Christianity Today* that asked, "Does a Dedicated Evangelical Belong in the White House?" And blacks were unlikely to miss Martin Luther King, Sr.'s benediction at the national convention: "Surely the Lord sent Jimmy Carter to come on out and bring America back where she belongs."[12]

Privately, Ford felt "discomfited" by Carter's open discussion of his faith; publicly, the President declared, without naming names, that no candidate should "deliberately exploit religion for his or her political advantage." The heated campaign obscured both Ford's willingness to exploit religious symbolism and his religious affinities with Carter. He became the first president to address the Southern Baptist Convention, wooed prominent Catholic clergy, and won covert support from the evangelist Billy Graham.[13]

Ford's religious references, like Carter's, came naturally. He had attended congressional prayer breakfasts regularly, read the Bible daily, and sometimes quoted Scripture in interviews (though with less facility than his opponent). He prayed for guidance during crises; his decision to pardon Richard Nixon followed services and communion at St. John's Episcopal Church in Washington. Ford's religious commitment deepened when his oldest son entered Gordon-Conwell Divinity School. At the same time he felt a "strong ecumenical feeling" and endorsed a "wall of separation" between church and state.[14]

The President and Carter differed in two important ways. An easygoing optimist, as opposed to Carter who trained himself to think positively, Ford had few doubts that God blessed America. At the level of federal policy he wanted more doors through or tunnels under the wall between church and state. Specifically, he favored tax credits for parents whose children attended parochial schools, had favored a constitutional amendment providing for prayer in public schools, though he hedged on this issue in 1976, and seemed less willing than Carter to tax church-owned property.[15]

Both candidates personally opposed abortion and wished that the issue would go away. As president, Ford had accepted but did not push the so-called Hyde Amendment to bar the use of Medicaid funds for abortions. During the campaign he endorsed a " 'people's' amendment" to the Constitution that allowed voters to ban abortion in their respective states. Despite Catholic pressure Carter rejected this legislative approach, in favor of moral suasion and contraception, which, he said, would render abortions unnecessary. Any state-option amendment would discriminate against the poor by allowing rich women to "fly from one state to another and have abortions in an unrestricted way." Although Carter promised to abide by *Roe v. Wade*, he found this position personally distasteful. Against the advice of his staff, he often took pains to call abortions "wrong" and condemned Medicaid payments for them.[16]

The most peculiar manifestation of the religious issue in 1976 was the reaction to Carter's interview in *Playboy*. He was not the first prominent Baptist to duel with this worldly monthly; six years earlier the Christian Life Commission of the Southern Baptist Convention had sponsored a forum on the "*Playboy* philosophy." Although Carter probably believed, as he suggested in retrospect, that his appearance in the magazine constituted "part of Christ's commission" to spread the gospel, more mundane reasons played their part. Carter sought not only to impress worldly voters, but also to test himself against cosmopolitan antagonists who considered him, as he told interviewer Robert Scheer, an "ignorant peanut farmer."[17]

Prodded by Scheer, Carter tried once again to explain his views on religion, sexual morality, and the separation of church and state. He sounded variously candid, irritable, and eager to show that he was "not a packaged article you can put in a little box." After the conversation moved to less personal issues, Carter made a last effort to convince *Playboy* readers of his complexity. He returned to a favorite theme, Jesus's warning against "pride, that one person should never think he was better than anybody else."

I try not to commit a deliberate sin. I recognize that I'm going to do it anyhow, because I'm human and I'm tempted. And Christ set almost impossible standards for us. Christ said, "I tell you that anyone who looks on a woman with lust in his heart has already committed adultery."

I've looked on a lot of women with lust. I've committed adultery in my heart many times. This is something that God recognizes that I will do—and I have done it—and

God forgives me for it. But that doesn't mean that I condemn someone who not only looks on a woman with lust but who leaves his wife and shacks up with somebody out of wedlock.

Christ says, Don't consider yourself better than someone else because one guy screws a whole bunch of women while the other guy is loyal to his wife. The guy who is loyal to his wife ought not to be condescending or proud because of the relative degrees of sinfulness.

The *Playboy* interview did not end with lust in the heart. Rather, Carter resumed his discussion of governmental ethics. Religion, he implied, would prevent him from taking on "the same frame of mind that Nixon or Johnson did—lying, cheating and distorting the truth."[18]

Nevertheless, the headlines, commentaries, and jokes about the interview centered on lust. Prominent theological conservatives wondered why Carter had spoken to *Playboy*; most agreed with Rev. Bailey Smith that "screw" was not a "good Baptist word." On the other hand, Joseph Duffey, a Democratic campaign manager and former professor at Hartford Theological Seminary, said that early versions of the Bible had been written in analogous "street Greek." Reverend Bruce Edwards, Carter's friend and pastor at the Plains Baptist Church, also defended his applied theology. Martin Luther King, Sr., quipped, "they can't kill you for lookin.' " Outside evangelical and fundamentalist circles, the *Playboy* interview, which became public in late September, reinvigorated what Hamilton Jordan called the "weirdo factor," the suspicion that Carter was too strange to be president.[19]

In the final analysis, Carter's religion helped him to win the election. According to a Gallup poll conducted in October, ten percent of voters were unimpressed by Carter's faith, 20 percent were impressed, and 70 percent reported no effect. He received 6 percent fewer Catholic votes than the Democratic average between 1952 and 1972. Ford had effectively courted affluent Catholics, but the abortion issue does not seem to have made much difference. Only one-quarter of the voters polled favored a constitutional amendment restricting abortions, and a majority of them supported Carter. A majority of evangelical Protestants voted Republican, as was usually the case, but Carter won by cutting the margin from 7.2 million in 1968 to 3.2 million. And he was the first Democrat to carry the Southern Baptist constituency since Truman in 1948.[20]

James Earl Carter, Jr., had indeed lived his whole life in the church. During childhood and adolescence it had been the Plains Baptist Church. Carter was born in Plains on October 1, 1924, the first child of James, Sr., a matter-of-fact Baptist, and Lillian Gordy Carter, a free-thinking and free-speaking Methodist. At age eleven Jimmy came forward and was baptized at the Plains Church by Reverand Royall Callaway. Callaway, a dispensational premillennialist, whose wife had been secretary to Reverend Bob Jones, Sr., anticipated God's imminent judgment and Jesus's quick return. In 1977 Carter recalled that "the subject of

Callaway's sermon was quite often 'by God's word, you're going to hell. Because of your sin, you deserve death.' " Yet his boyhood congregation may not have been devoid of theological liberalism. Reverend Jesse Eugene Hall, who held the pulpit from 1923 to 1927 and from 1931 to 1941, preached that the "day" mentioned in Genesis did not necessarily mean twenty-four hours.[21]

Whatever theology Carter absorbed as a boy, there is no doubt that he acquired from his demanding parents a prodigious work ethic and strong sense of discipline. These traits were reinforced at the United States Naval Academy and subsequently in the submarine service under Admiral Hyman G. Rickover. At Annapolis, Carter seems to have thought more than usual about life's purpose. From the perspective of 1976, these reflections looked to Carter like the product of sophomoric bull sessions. Certainly he experienced no crisis of faith. Immediately after graduating in 1946, Carter married a local woman, Rosalynn Smith, quickly fathered three children, and began climbing upward in the Navy. At Annapolis and on submarines he taught informal Bible classes.[22]

Carter resigned his commission and returned to Georgia after the death of his father in 1953. Explaining this decision, Carter always emphasized the family's financial needs and the sense of community he felt in Plains, but he also may have been influenced by the slow pace of advancement in the Navy. His father had been a prominent figure in Sumter County, and Carter soon followed in his footsteps. He joined—and often led—fraternal, civic, and charitable organizations. As a matter of course, Carter rejoined the Plains Baptist Church, immediately began to teach Sunday school classes, and was chosen a deacon in 1962. That same year he won a seat in the state senate. Carter and the Plains Baptist minister at the time, Robert Harris, disagreed about prohibition and civil rights. Carter opposed the former and, though still less than an integrationist, voted against the church's explicit ban on "Negroes and civil rights agitators." Despite their disagreements, Reverend Harris urged fellow Baptist clergy to elect Carter governor in 1966.[23]

Defeat in the Democratic primary precipitated Carter's spiritual rebirth. Apparently he had felt for some time that affluence and local fame did not bring satisfaction. Failure to win the nomination prompted a reassessment of his life. At roughly the same time he began to doubt that he was actually a "great Christian." When Reverend Harris asked in a sermon, "If you were arrested for being a Christian, would there be enough evidence to convict you?" Carter concluded that the evidence was insufficient in his case. Rather he resembled the Pharisee in Luke 18:10–13 who thanked God for his superiority. Sometime during this reassessment, in either late 1966 or early 1967, Carter took the famous walk with his sister Ruth and asked, "What is it that you have that I haven't got?" She said that "everything I am" belonged to Jesus. Carter then opened his heart and, as he later told two psychobiographers, felt "release and assurance" as well as a "genuine interest in other people I hadn't experienced before."[24]

Although the chronology and morphology of Carter's conversion remain unclear, its effect on him can be stated. He increased his witnessing for Christ, organized a Billy Graham film crusade in Georgia, and spent several weeks as a Baptist missionary in Pennsylvania and Massachusetts. From all accounts he developed great admiration for the men and women less successful than he who spread or accepted the gospel. What Carter considered his enhanced interest in other people also may have influenced his endorsement of racial equality after winning the Georgia governorship in 1970. Yet his basic personality stayed intact. He remained ambitious, retained his passion for detail (taking copious notes on the missionary trail), and still placed heavy demands on his subordinates, family, and—most of all—himself. Indeed, now determined to walk in Jesus's steps, he was harder on himself than ever.[25]

An astute friend, Judge William Gunter, observed that religion gave Carter a "modicum of humility." It was not achieved easily. He worked hard to be humble. *Playboy* was only the most notorious place in which Carter reminded himself and others that warnings against pride were central to Christ's message. Often he cited his own arrogance or aloofness to illustrate this "number one sin." Perhaps, he suggested at least once, Southern Baptists should adopt the Primitive Baptist practice of washing each other's feet as an antidote to self-importance.[26]

Constantly probing his conscience, seeking a "deeper relationship with Christ," Carter was probably the most introspective president since Abraham Lincoln. Curiously, he paid much less attention to the intellectual side of religion. For instance, Norman Mailer found him unwilling or unable to discuss Kierkegaard, whom he quoted occasionally, and Garry Wills noted his slim knowledge of biblical higher criticism. Carter admitted in 1977 that he "wasn't a very good historian of the Bible." These lapses are revealing, since Carter customarily tried to become expert in every field he encountered. Perhaps unconsciously he chose to keep religious faith—a realm of release, reassurance, and warmth—relatively unscathed by the technical complexities that affected other parts of his life.[27]

To be sure, Carter read the Bible daily (often in Spanish to practice that language), quoted it readily, and came to terms with the question of inerrancy. Belonging to a loose denomination that ranged from premillennialists to covert "Christian realists," he explicitly reserved the "right to make my own interpretation." Carter did not consider everything in the Bible "literally true," he told *Time* in 1976, and added that portions were "obviously written in allegories." He showed virtually no interest in the most popular figurative scheme, dispensationalism; his reference to Israel as the fulfillment of divine prophecy was atypical.[28]

Apparently no reporter asked Carter whether he—along with Jerry Falwell, Pat Robertson, and Hal Lindsey—expected Jesus to return in his lifetime. His reading of Revelation sounded post-millennial. "Jesus stands at the door and knocks . . . but he can't break down the door. He doesn't want to. It must be opened by our understanding." On the other hand, he hesitated to surrender the supernatural. In a convoluted denial before the 1976 election, Carter "saw no reason to disbelieve" the Genesis account of Eve's creation from Adam's rib. Probably he was worrying less about inerrancy than about the ballots of theological conservatives. In 1977, however, he took a similar position on Lazarus's return from the dead. This story, "hard to believe on a scientifically analyzed basis," nonetheless embodied the great Christian promise of eternal life.[29]

In addition to Scripture, Carter studied the writings of Reinhold Niebuhr, a "theologian for whom I really cared." When William Gunter introduced him to Niebuhr's writings on politics in the late 1960s, Carter allegedly called them the "most amazin' thing I've ever read." Arthur Schlesinger's skepticism notwithstanding, his enthusiasm was hardly surprising. Many younger Southern Baptists were drifting toward neo-orthodoxy. Furthermore, Niebuhr and Carter shared a concern for complexity in general and paradox in particular. Both understood, in Carter's paraphrase, that "love and kindness meant a great deal in one-to-one relationships but not in dealing with structures of corporate groups." Indeed, at the level of personality, Carter, who charmed small groups but left mass audiences cold, almost personified this Niebuhrian premise.[30]

Although Carter never presented a full exposition of his religious beliefs, his theology can be pieced together, as well as his position on church polity, the social gospel, and religious liberty. Carter's religious world view reflected his Baptist heritage, personal discipline, study of Niebuhr, and near obsession with pride. Christianity was "simple" enough for a child to understand. Carter liked to quote the first Bible verse he learned at age four, "God is love." This loving God knew, however, that men and women were sinners who deserved damnation. Sins could not be ignored, but they could be forgiven. Jesus Christ, crucified on the cross, bore humanity's punishment and thus opened the way to forgiveness. Anyone believing in him received eternal life. Christianity possessed something "absolutely unique" among religions, Carter said, a "personal relationship to a living God in Christ."[31]

Carter unswervingly preached salvation by grace. God never ranked sinners according to their relative sinlessness, and no one did anything to merit salvation. "Taking our status in life as an indication of God's approval . . . is a profound mistake." Sinners needed to swallow their pride before they were able to accept the grace freely given. Salvation eased some worries; no Christian needed to fear death. Moreover, the Holy Spirit, an "extension of God's redemptive presence on earth," served as counselor and comforter.[32]

While bringing comfort, spiritual rebirth did not end God's "stringent" demands. On the contrary, he expected Christians to measure themselves against Christ's "perfect example [at] every moment of our existence." Jesus himself had urged, "be perfect." The command was impossible to fulfill. Men and women could never totally avoid sin; they merely substituted one sin for another. Persistently attempting the impossible might seem especially daunting to anyone who believed with Carter that success and good works served as no evidence of God's favor. Yet Carter himself, citing Niebuhr, hailed what he called the "creativity of anxiety." Anxiety, a synonym for the awareness of sin, energized the struggle "always to improve one's self, to pray, to learn, and then attain a worthy objective."[33]

According to Carter the earthly church existed to preserve and teach sound doctrine. Yet the church's very existence raised two problems. Institutional religion—"you might say instant religion"—encouraged pride, smugness, and ease. Paradoxically, though Christ preached humility, it was "almost impossible" for Christians gathered together to avoid a sense of superiority. Furthermore, churches had always tended to complicate Christianity's simple, sound doctrine. Carter's account of the Gnostic heresy highlights his disdain for those who intellectualized religion. The well-educated, snobbish Gnostics who condescended to their humbler brethren reached the wrong conclusions about Jesus' divinity.[34]

In Carter's view the virtues of the Baptist church included doctrinal and organizational simplicity. Yet Baptists were no less vulnerable to pride than other men and women. Furthermore, partly because they feared corruption by the state, many Baptists chose to "turn inwardly and to stay that way." Preaching love in isolation was meaningless, Carter insisted. Baptists—and all other Christians—must translate love into "simple justice" by "partnerships with Christ to improve the lives of others." Such partnerships helped those who gave as well as those who received. While seeking justice for others, Carter said, perhaps recalling his personal battle against pride, "we can forget about ourselves. We can even forget about getting credit for that accomplishment."[35]

Countries were at least as susceptible to pride as individuals. Acknowledging a debt to Niebuhr, Carter speculated that individuals were less likely to admit national flaws than personal shortcomings. At its worst national pride resembled idolatry, the substitution of a "flag or a way of life or a government for God." Yet even milder cases of jingoism prevented countries from correcting their errors.[36]

Applying these Niebuhrian premises to the United States in the 1970s, Carter inferred that God might not always be on the American side. Even after Watergate and Vietnam, the United States remained a "good country, the greatest on earth." Its strengths included the capacity "to be humble and not blatant and arrogant." Americans needed to ask difficult questions and remedy mistakes. During the 1976 campaign Carter sensed a grass-roots eagerness for excellence and higher ethical standards. Leaders had failed, but now the United States would have a government "as good as our people are."[37]

Carter's religion affected the image of his presidency more than his substantive policies. His continuing activities as a Baptist layman sometimes stirred controversy. Shortly before the election, despite the best efforts of Carter and Reverend Bruce Edwards, the deacons of the Plains Baptist Church had reaffirmed a ban on black membership. After much maneuvering, acrimony, and publicity, the congregation approved integration in early 1977 but forced Edwards's resignation and drove a liberal contingent, including the President's mother, to form the separate Maranatha Baptist Church. While in Plains, Carter attended both churches. In Washington, he worshipped and taught Sunday school at the First Baptist Church, where attendance, contributions, and media attention immediately increased. In April 1977, Carter told his Sunday school class that Jesus' crucifixion had been "arranged by the Jewish leaders." Following several protests, he explained that although Jesus' "foreordained" death had required "human instruments," Jews bore no "collective responsibility."[38]

A proposal by Carter to expand Southern Baptist missionary efforts provoked both enthusiasm and distress. He met with church leaders at the White House and, via videotape, urged the Southern Baptist Convention (SBC) to create an international missionary corps. Basking in the glow of a Baptist president, the SBC voted to do so. An acquaintance from the First Baptist Church in Washington even reported that Carter planned a post-presidential missionary career, a report Carter turned aside with strained humor. An old friend, Jack U. Harwell, editor of the Georgia *Christian Index*, complained that Carter had undermined the Baptist commitment to the separation of church and state when he used the White House to "plot denominational strategy." Carter denied any impropriety, noting that the meeting had occurred during his lunch hour, but promised "to be careful" in the future. Robert L. Lipshutz, a presidental counsellor, concerned about the "weirdo factor" as well as the First Amendment, also discouraged deep involvement in denominational affairs. Carter remained in touch with SBC leaders and often urged fellow Baptists to work in the world but, after 1977, offered no detailed advice.[39]

Along with other contemporary presidents, Carter celebrated American religious pluralism in speeches to Protestant, Catholic, and Jewish groups. His contributions to this familiar genre were unusually thoughtful, ecumenical, and personal. He cited Niebuhr to Southern Baptists, quoted a Yiddish proverb to Mormons, and claimed "brotherhood" with Moslem Anwar Sadat at the National Religious Broadcasters' convention. He confessed his own pettiness, ethnocentrism, and pride. Resurrecting a theme from *Why Not the Best?* he worried in 1978 that he still worked harder for himself than for God.[40]

Along with other contemporary presidents, Carter routinely proclaimed National Prayer Day and International Clergy Week. If possible, he would have left the signing of all such boiler-plate proclamations to Vice President Walter Mondale. Perhaps because he was so pious, Carter felt little need for official declarations of piety. The one religious ceremony that deeply moved him was welcoming Pope John Paul II to the United States. He helped to plan the event down to small details, including the choice of Leontyne Price to sing the Lord's Prayer, and he looked back on the papal visit as "one of the best days of my life."[41]

Issues with a religious dimension remained on the national agenda during Carter's term. Some, such as the under-representation of Catholics and Jews in the ranks of military chaplains, never reached his desk. Others yielded ephemeral disputes. Following precedent set by Nixon, Ford, and Franklin D. Roosevelt,

Carter appointed a personal representative to the Vatican, a decision criticized by Protestant theological conservatives and militant atheists. Despite pressure from many Catholics, evangelical Protestants, and Orthodox Jews, Carter continued to regard as unconstitutional tax credits for parents whose children attended parochial schools.[42]

Most important, the Supreme Court ruled in June 1977 that federal assistance for abortions was not a constitutional right. Carter agreed. The ruling was unfair to poor women, he conceded, but "many things" in life were unfair. Government could not make "opportunities exactly equal, particularly when there is a moral factor involved." Consistent with this position, Carter approved legislation restricting Medicaid funding for abortions and demanded strict compliance by the Department of Health, Education, and Welfare.[43]

Connections between Carter's religious beliefs and foreign policy are harder to isolate. At a very general level his doubts about the uniqueness of American virtue fostered his temporary repudiation of the "inordinate fear of Communism" and his permanent openness to the Third World. Carter was often perceived as a Wilsonian, and he certainly was one in the sense that all presidents since Woodrow Wilson have been Wilsonians. Like all presidents since 1913, Carter believed that American ideals and interests went hand-in hand. Like most of them, he exaggerated the "commonality of the aspirations of human beings throughout the world." In 1978, for instance, he declared that Christians, Jews, Moslems, and Hindus worshipped the "same God." Nonetheless, unlike Wilson and most subsequent presidents, Carter's internationalism contained relatively little condescension toward weak, poor, or non-white nations.[44]

Although the cause had attracted congressional champions before Carter's presidency, he quickly came to personify concern for human rights abroad. Carter traced the "modern concept of human rights" back to the "laws of the prophets of the Judeo-Christian tradition." His most important actions in this area saved lives, notably in Argentina, Brazil, and Chile. Yet Carter also considered religious liberty a human right. Publicly he prodded the Soviet Union to lift restrictions on Jewish immigration. Privately he urged the People's Republic of China to permit the circulation of Bibles and the return of Christian missionaries.[45]

No region seemed more closely connected to religious concerns than the Middle East. Carter apparently believed that most peoples in the region were descended from Abraham and accepted the Book of Exodus as valid history. Nor did the President repudiate his statement that Israel fulfilled divine prophecy. To be sure, his Middle East policy derived less from theology than from geopolitics and personal affinities. During the grueling negotiations that produced the Camp David accords, Carter developed a close friendship with the Egyptian president, Anwar Sadat, and a deep dislike for the Israeli prime minister, Menachem Begin. A common interest in religion seems to have served at least as a diplomatic lubricant among the three. In this case, as in most others, Carter felt closer to Sadat, who enjoyed discussions of comparative religion, than to Begin, who cited the Bible to support Israeli land claims.[46]

Media coverage of the relationship between God and the Carter family improved little after his election. The *New York Times* marvelled that Carter addressed fellow Baptists as "brothers and sisters in Christ." The President's piety moved John Osborne of the *New Republic* to recall the intolerant Baptists he had known as a youth. Though more sympathetic, William Greider of the *Washington Post* speculated that Christianity made Carter too earnest, humble, and strange to govern effectively. The major news weeklies continued their bemused coverage of Ruth Carter Stapleton and enjoyed especially her role in the (temporary) conversion of pornographer Larry Flynt.[47]

As a neo-Calvinist aware of human limitations, Carter should have been prepared for the trials of the presidency. His favorite quotation from Niebuhr sounded a warning: "The sad duty of politics is to establish justice in a sinful world." Nonetheless, Carter underestimated how much effort was needed to maintain stability, let alone to move toward justice. By mid–1979 his coalition was collapsing, and issues bearing on religion contributed to the collapse.

As prosperity faltered and Soviet-American detente delivered fewer gains than anticipated, many Catholics resumed their earlier skepticism about Carter. His straddle on abortion probably alienated fewer working-class Catholic Democrats than his relative economic conservatism. In either case, their loyalty would have been stronger if he had seemed culturally less alien.

Analogous cultural differences, inadvertently highlighted by Ruth Carter Stapleton, disturbed many Jews. The White House continued to receive complaints that Carter blamed Jews for deicide. Then, in May 1978, Stapleton agreed to address B'nai Yeshua, an organization of Hebrew Christians. During the ensuing controversy, Rabbi Marc Tannenbaum, the national interreligious affairs director of the American Jewish Committee, charged B'nai Yeshua with deceiving "ignorant young" Jews to promote conversions. Worried White House aides urged Stapleton to cancel her speech. Ultimately she did so, concluding that an appearance at a Hebrew Christian convention might seem to "negate" Judaism.[48]

These incidents, minor in themselves, nonetheless reveal Jewish wariness of the born-again Baptist President. Accordingly, they closely scrutinized his Middle East diplomacy. His popularity among Jews declined steadily until September 1978, when he negotiated a detente between Israel and Egypt; again following Carter's personal intervention, the two nations signed a peace treaty the following March. Soon thereafter, Mideast negotiations stalled, Billy Carter urged cultivation of Arabs since there were a "hell of a lot" more of them than Jews, and United Nations Ambassador Andrew Young conferred with representatives of the Palestine Liberation Organization. Although Carter accepted Young's resignation and attempted to mollify Jewish voters with denunciations of anti-Semitism and pleas for pluralism, his standing was permanently damaged.[49]

Furthermore, many evangelicals and fundamentalists, who had felt kinship with Carter during the excitement of 1976, discovered that he was theologically and politically more liberal than they had supposed. Their sense of betrayal was fueled by a "New Christian Right" that had begun to organize almost as soon as Carter was elected. Reverend Jerry Falwell founded the Moral Majority, the most powerful of these organizations, in 1979.[50]

Carter's worst problems were essentially secular: a divided Democratic party with a congressional delegation more liberal than the President, rising prices of primary products, especially oil, economic "stagflation" that no one knew how to cure, the inexorable dialectic of cold war animosity, and old Bolsheviks in the Kremlin who died too slowly. These problems were largely beyond the President's control. Yet Carter compounded his difficulties by yielding to what critics called arrogance—what he called pride. At home he disliked courting or compromising with Congress. Abroad, eager to outshine Ford, he abandoned a nearly finished strategic arms limitation treaty in favor of a "comprehensive" plan that elicited Soviet suspicion and raised cold war tensions. If Carter is a tragic figure, it is because he recognized his fatal flaw—pride—but, despite good will and high intelligence, could not master it.

Carter's ability to motivate Americans decreased during his term. He had won the presidency by promising a government as good as the people. To Arthur Schlesinger, Jr., such populism represented sentimentality unworthy of a Niebuhrian. Yet it was consistent with the early Niebuhr, the critic from the 1930s who understood the importance of myths and symbols to any social movement. Carter understood their power too, as he had demonstrated during the campaign, but he felt uneasy using them. Emotional appeals conflicted with his neo-Calvinist plain style and promise never to lie.

Even so, in July 1979, as motorists fumed in gasoline lines and Carter's energy legislation stalled in Congress, he made a special effort to inspire the nation. Exactly three years after buoyantly accepting the Democratic nomination, he delivered a televised speech on the American "crisis of confidence." He began with a favorite theme: that isolated officials had failed an inherently decent, strong, and wise citizenry. As Carter proceeded, however, he came close to saying that the people were no better than their floundering government. There was "growing disrespect" for social institutions. Too many citizens tended "to worship self-indulgence and consumption." Americans needed to restore faith in each other, in democracy, and in the nation's future. The speech, which was largely drafted by Patrick Caddell, a Catholic, nonetheless fitted the President's evangelical style. Indeed, it came as close to a call for a day of fasting and humiliation as any other modern presidential speech. Initially, this jeremiad boosted Carter's standing in the polls. Within a week, however, Carter mismanaged a reorganization of his staff, and his popularity declined steadily thereafter.[51]

As part of the staff reorganization, Carter named Reverend Robert M. Maddox to the new post of special assistant for religious liaison. Maddox, a Baptist minister from Calhoun, Georgia, had offered to fill such a position in 1977 but was politely rebuffed. He had continued to offer unofficial advice and warned especially of disaffection by evangelical Protestants. Finally appointed a speech writer in May 1979, he had urged Carter not to admit failure in the "crisis of confidence'' address. The new religious liaison quickly concluded that the administration, trying to avoid the taint of sanctimony, had inadvertently annoyed diverse denominations. Maddox immediately began an ecumenical campaign to mend fences. He met, promised to consult, and sometimes prayed with evangelicals, charismatics, social gospelers, Hasidic Jews, Catholic bishops, and followers of Hare Krishna.[52]

Maddox tried to involve Carter in the religious fence-mending. The President addressed the National Council of Catholic Charities, United Jewish Appeal, and National Religious Broadcasters; in November 1979, he held his first White House meeting with Billy Graham. By and large, however, neither Carter nor his senior staff shared Maddox's enthusiasm for cultivating religious leaders. From the outset, Maddox stressed the growing political influence of evangelicals, fundamentalists, and charismatics in general as well as television preachers in particular. Many of them could help Carter, or at least be moved to soften their criticism if the President paid them more attention. After five months of trying, Maddox in January 1980 arranged a meeting between Carter and a contingent of television evangelists that included Jerry Falwell, Jim Bakker, Rex Humbard, and Oral Roberts.[53]

In 1980 two self-described born-again Christians ran against Carter. Independent candidate John Anderson, a member of the Free Evangelical Church, had been converted as a youth. Republican Ronald Reagan was a religious eclectic. The offspring of a Protestant-Catholic mixed marriage and Hollywood's flexible mores, he claimed membership in the Disciples of Christ, his mother's denomination, but rarely attended services and saw no conflict between his pro forma Protestantism and astrology. He had always asked God's help, Reagan had said in 1976, but at some unspecified point he had felt a ''new relationship'' that ''could be described as 'born again.' '' In 1980, assailing declining morality and urging a constitutional ban on abortion, Reagan welcomed leaders of the New Christian Right as junior partners in his coalition; they in turn certified his spiritual rebirth.[54]

Carter met occasionally with ministers, priests, and rabbis. He retained the support of some prominent theological conservatives, including Oral Roberts, Jimmy Allen, and Jim Bakker, for whom cultural affinity counted more than political ideology or theology; at the end of the campaign, Carter knelt in prayer with Bakker on Air Force One. Nevertheless, Carter's piety was much less in evidence in 1980 than in 1976. With the exception of his wife, Rosalynn, no one in the President's inner circle showed much interest in Maddox's elaborate plans to appeal specifically to religious groups.[55]

A religious issue dominated the 1980 presidential election, but not a ''Judeo-Christian'' one. In November 1979, Iranian militants seized the United States embassy in Teheran; most of the staff remained hostages for the next fourteen months. Clearly, though Christians and Moslems might worship the same God, they did not necessarily worship him in the same way or with the same political consequences. Carter, accustomed to pluralist competition in the American triple melting pot, was no more able than secular officials to see that the Islamic revolution was other than madness. Reagan presented the hostage crisis as an emblem of national decline under Carter. Two favorite quotations highlighted his belief that the decline could be reversed. The United States remained, in John Winthrop's phrase, a "city on the hill," and her citizens still held the power, as Tom Paine had said, "to begin the world over again."[56]

After Reagan's victory Jimmy and Rosalynn Carter took the defeat hard. They returned to Plains, joined the Maranatha Baptist Church, and threw themselves into work and reflection. Emotionally renewed by 1987, they wrote a self-help book for others who faced great disappointment in middle age. In the darkest moments Rosalynn Carter wondered if God had wanted her husband to lose. With characteristic emphasis on individual responsibility, Carter replied that people were not "robots" controlled from heaven.[57]

Supernatural intervention aside, religious factors contributed to Reagan's victory. Carter received a smaller percentage of Catholic votes than any Democratic nominee since John M. Davis in 1924. For the first time in half a century, the Democratic candidate fell short of a majority among Jews. Evangelicals swung back heavily to Republican ranks, though Carter's born-again style may have prevented a worse debacle. For many voters Carter's apparent arrogance—what he called pride—had obscured his accomplishments. Viewing religious pluralism as the norm, he was unprepared for an Islamic revolution in Iran. Finally, Carter's publicly expressed doubts about American virtue left him vulnerable to a rival who never questioned that God was on our side, and who, with no sense of contradiction, could quote the puritan John Winthrop and the infidel Tom Paine to prove the point.[58]

NOTES

1. "The 1976 Elections," *Church and State* 29 (December 1976): 4.

2. *The Presidential Campaign of 1976* (Washington, D.C., 1978), I, *Jimmy Carter*, 973; Jimmy Carter, *Why Not the Best?* (New York, 1976), frontispiece chaps. 5, 14.

3. Jules Witcover, *Marathon: The Pursuit of the Presidency, 1972–1976* (New York, 1977), 270–71; Betty Glad, *Jimmy Carter: In Search of the Great White House* (New York, 1980), 331–32.

4. Richard Quebedeaux, *The Worldly Evangelicals* (New York, 1978), 4; Bruce Mazlish and Edwin Diamond, *Jimmy Carter: A Character Portrait* (New York, 1979), 67–68; Glad, *Jimmy Carter*, 332; Witcover, *Marathon*, 270–72; "Jimmy Carter's Faith Healing Sister," *Humanist* 36 (July-August 1976): 39.

5. David Kucharsky, *The Man from Plains: The Mind and Spirit of Jimmy Carter* (New York, 1976); E. Brooks Holifield, "The Three Strands of Jimmy Carter's Religion," *New Republic*, June 5, 1976, 15–17.

6. *Presidential Campaign 1976*, I, 965, 458, 967, 178, 459, 969, 171, 457, 963; Wesley Pippert, *The Spiritual Journey of Jimmy Carter: In His Own Words* (New York, 1978), 242.

7. *Presidential Campaign 1976*, I, 969.

8. Mazlish and Diamond, *Jimmy Carter*, 162. Kucharsky, *Man from Plains*, 9–11.

9. Glad, *Jimmy Carter*, 276–77; *Washington Post*, 9 September 1976; Patrick Caddell to Jimmy Carter, 11 September 1976, Box 4, Powell Collection, Jimmy Carter Library, Atlanta.

10. Kucharsky, *Man from Plains*, 42.

11. James and Marti Hefley, *The Church That Produced a President* (New York, 1977), 112; William Lee Miller, *Yankee from Georgia* (New York, 1978), 5, 10, 172; Pippert, *Spiritual Journey*, 238–39.

12. Gerald R. Ford, *A Time to Heal* (New York, 1979), 306–7; Betty Ford, with Chris Chase, *The Times of My Life* (New York, 1978), 206–7; Rosalynn Carter, *First Lady from Plains* (New York, 1984), 131; Kucharsky, *Man from Plains*, 135.

13. Ford, *Time to Heal*, 417; *Presidential Campaign 1976*, II, *Gerald R. Ford*, 617, 909; Ford to Dick [Cheney], n.d., Box 16, Cheney Collection, Gerald Ford Presidential Library, Ann Arbor, Michigan.

14. Richard Reeves, *A Ford, Not a Lincoln* (New York, 1975), 110, 113–14; Ford, *Time to Heal*, 175; *Presidential Campaign: Ford*, 981, 919, 911.

15. "The Campaign: Into the Homestretch," *Church and State* 29 (November 1976): 3, 8; *Presidential Campaign: Ford*, 910, 799.

16. Ford, *Time to Heal*, 412; *Presidential Campaign, 1976*, II, 913, 982 and I, 92–93, 455–57, 968; Eve Rubin, *Abortion, Politics, and the Courts: Roe v. Wade and Its Aftermath* (Westport, Conn., 1982), 148–50.

17. *Presidential Campaign 1976*, I, 973, 956.

18. Ibid., 956, 963–64.

19. Glad, *Jimmy Carter*, 384; Miller, *Yankee from Georgia*, 43; Hefleys, *Church Produced a President*, 139–41, 211; *Los Angeles Times*, 9 October 1976.

20. Gerald M. Pomper, "The Presidential Election," in Gerald M. Pomper, et al., *The Election of 1976: Reports and Interpretations* (New York, 1977), 63–65; Albert Menendez, "How Carter Won," *Church and State* 29 (December 1976): 9–14.

21. Hefleys, *Church Produced a President*, 192–93; Kucharsky, *Man from Plains*, 14–15; Wesley Pippert, *Spiritual Journey* 192.

22. Jimmy and Rosalynn Carter, *Everything to Gain: Making the Most of the Rest of Your Life* (New York, 1987), 190; *Presidential Campaign 1976*, I, 164; Kucharsky, *Man from Plains*, 31; Glad, *Jimmy Carter*, ch. 3; Pippert, *Spiritual Journey*, 231.

23. Glad, *Jimmy Carter*, chaps. 4–5; Rosalynn Carter, *First Lady*, 40–45; Hefleys, *Church Produced a President*, 144–48.

24. *Presidential Campaign 1976*, I, 176; Carter, *Why Not?* 151–53; Mazlish and Diamond, *Jimmy Carter*, 151–52, 154; Glad, *Jimmy Carter*, 108–12; Witcover, *Marathon*, 270–72.

25. Carter, *Why Not?* 143–51.

26. Pippert, *Spiritual Journey*, 59, 76, 116, 169, 176.

27. Miller, *Yankee from Georgia*, 193; Pippert, *Spiritual Journey*, 77.

28. Hefleys, *Church Produced a President*, 189; Quebedeaux, *Worldly Evangelicals*, 38; Kucharsky, *Man from Plains*, 23; *Public Papers of the Presidents of the United States: Jimmy Carter, 1980* (Washington, D.C., 1982), I, 181.

29. Pippert, *Spiritual Journey*, 17, 155, 200.

30. Quebedeaux, *Worldly Evangelicals*, 38; Miller, *Yankee from Georgia*, 213–14; Holifield, "Carter's Religion," 15–17.

31. Pippert, *Spiritual Journey*, 174, 164, 168, 173, 180.

32. Ibid., 234, 240.

33. Ibid., 236, 219, 214–217.

34. Ibid., 186, 192–93, 202–4, 164–65.

35. Ibid., 179, 254, 91, 168, 219; *Public Papers: 1978*, I, 1115.

36. Pippert, *Spiritual Journey*, 245, 193, 244–45, 257–58.

37. Ibid., 242–43; *Public Papers: 1978*, I, 1117.

38. James T. Hefley, "A Change of Mind in Plains," *Christianity Today*, 3 December 1976, 50–53; Hefleys, *Church Produced a President*, 212–21, 226, 233–35; "Carter's Church," *Newsweek*, August 28, 1978, 11; Jimmy Carter to John F. Steinbruck, 12 May 1977, Box PP 83, White House Central File (WHCF), Carter Library.

39. Hefleys, *Church Produced a President*, 234–39; *Washington Star*, 29 January 1978. Jack Harwell to Jimmy Carter, 23 June [1977], and Carter to Harwell, 11 August 1977, Box RM 1; Carter to Jimmy Allen, 30 January 1978, Box PP 83; Robert Lipshutz to Susan Clough, 20 February 1979, Jimmy Allen folder, WHCF, Carter Library.

40. *Public Papers: 1978*. I, 78, 1114, 1116; II, 2087; *Public Papers: 1980*, I, 181, 275; II, 1750.

41. Doug Huron to John Hanson, 9 June 1977, Box HO 1; Carter to Rosalynn Carter, 13 September 1979, Box CO 66; Carter to Father Theodore Hesburgh, 10 October 1979, Box CO 66, WHCF, Carter Library.

42. Daniel Patrick Moynihan, et al., to Harold Brown, 25 July 1978, Box 103, Eizenstat file; Stuart Eizenstat to Reverend John F. Quinn, 13 July 1978, Box ED 1, WHCF, Carter Library; Hefleys, *Church Produced a President*, 230; Ronald B. Flowers, "President Jimmy Carter, Evangelicalism, Church-State Relations, and Civil Religion," *Journal of Church and State* 25 (Winter 1983): 113–32.

43. Rubin, *Abortion*, 151–57; Joseph A. Califano, Jr., *Governing America: An Insider's Report from the White House and the Cabinet* (New York, 1981), ch. 2.

44. *Public Papers: 1977*: I, 956; Gaddis Smith, *Morality, Reason, Power: Foreign Policy During the Carter Years* (New York, 1986), 66; Pippert, *Spiritual Journey*, 59, 62, 247; *Washington Post*, 3 February 1978.

45. Pippert, *Spiritual Journey*, 94; *Presidential Campaign 1976*, I, 970; Carters, *Everything to Gain*, 169.

46. Jimmy Carter, *The Blood of Abraham* (Boston, 1985), 4–8.

47. *New York Times*, 17 June 1978; John Osborne, "Carter and God," *New Republic*, July 16, 1979, 9–10; William Greider, "Can a Real Christian Make It as President?" *Washington Post*, 5 November 1978, *Magazine*, pp. 3, 16, 34; "Hustling for the Lord," *Newsweek*, December 5, 1977, 61.

48. Benjamin Epstein to Robert Lipshutz, 29 December 1977, Lipshutz to Stuart Eizenstat, 20 January 1978, and Eizenstat to Hamilton Jordan, 22 May 1978, Box 235, Eizenstat file, Carter Library; "Offensive Christianity," *National Review* June 23, 1978, 763.

49. Gaddis Smith, *Morality*, 168; Barbara Kellerman, *All the President's Kin* (London, 1982), 224–25; Jerry Rafshoon to Jimmy Carter, 29 May 1979, Box 18, Rafshoon Collection, Carter Library; *Public Papers: 1979*, II, 1563–74.

50. George M. Marsden, "Preachers of Paradox: The Religious New Right in Historical Perspective," in Mary Douglas and Steven M. Tipton, eds., *Religion in America: Spirituality in a Secular Age* (Boston, 1983), 150–68.

51. *Public Papers: 1979*, II, 1235–39; Jimmy Carter, *Keeping Faith: Memoirs of a*

President (New York, 1982), 114–21; Interview with Reverend Robert M. Maddox, 9, November 1987.

52. Maddox interview. Maddox, *Preacher at the White House* (Nashville, Tenn., 1984), 54–57, 62–63, 73–74, 79, 133, 138–39; Maddox to Jody Powell, 6 January 1977, Maddox file, WHCF; Maddox to Rosalynn Carter, 12 July 1970, Box 52, Rafshoon Collection, Carter Library.

53. *Public Papers: 1979*, II, 1925–31; *Public Papers: 1980*, I, 180–83, 377–79; Maddox to Jerry Rafshoon and Greg Schneiders, 27 July 1979, Box 52, Rafshoon Collection, Carter Library; Maddox, *Preacher*; Maddox interview.

54. Erling Jorstad, *Evangelicals in the White House: The Cultural Maturation of Born Again Christianity, 1960–1981* (New York, 1981), 144–49; Garry Wills, *Reagan's America* (New York, 1988), 20–63, 234–36, 454–57.

55. Maddox, *Preacher*, 157–59, 170; Maddox interview; Jim Bakker to Carter, November 3, 1980, Bakker file, WHCF, Carter Library.

56. Wills, *Reagan's America*, 355.

57. Carters, *Everything to Gain*, 23, 69–70.

58. Albert J. Menendez, "Religion at the Polls, 1980," *Church and State* 33 (December 1980): 15–18; Seymour Martin Lipset and Earl Raab, "The Election and the Evangelicals," *Commentary* 71 (March 1981): 29.

12

Biodivinity: The Encounter of Religion and Medicine

M. L. Bradbury

Announcements of surprise at the discovery that religion and medicine can both legitimately contribute to human health, in ways that frequently intersect, figure as a recurring theme in twentieth-century American history. In certain respects the persistence of this attitude has more significance than that of the activity from which it principally stems, ongoing attempts to find common ground between religion and medicine. Most often, though by no means exclusively, it has focused on the professedly unexpected relationship of the two in mental health, the subject that has, in fact, received the greatest attention from physicians, clergy, and others. Why such surprise should be repeatedly expressed at efforts that have gone on almost constantly in some location or another in American society throughout the twentieth century is a question that lies behind this essay.

Biodivinity is a term coined to describe the results of this conjunction of medicine and religion in human health. It derives from the offhand remark of a participant in one of the conferences between physicians and clergy to discuss the therapeutic overlap of their professions that became commonplace events in the years after World War II. Its practitioners have included both physicians and clergy who have sought to bring religion and medicine together in a variety of ways and settings. Without intending necessarily to challenge the integrity of either, they have insisted that, to be practiced successfully, human therapeutics requires the cooperation of both. Admittedly the term is susceptible to elastic interpretation and can bind together movements, individuals, and ideas that even in the most generous view are ill-assorted. However, it does not stretch to include, for example, religious groups such as Christian Scientists or others that reject, or to a considerable extent find irrelevant, the therapeutic claims and treatments of modern medicine and that seek to replace them with alternate forms of health care. These are better considered under the rubric of faith or—to choose an adjective with possibly less pejorative implications—spiritual healing. Although capable of being considered separately for analytical purposes, such healing obviously has important connections with biodivinity.

Demonstrating the perdurance of biodivinity in the twentieth century can most easily be done by devoting much, though by no means exclusive, attention to psychiatry and religion, for their encounter has produced some of its most significant manifestations, especially ones regarded as having both medical and religious legitimacy. To an extent their interaction results from the cultural parallelism that affects both. Although more frequently commented on in terms of the ways in which American religion mimics the larger society, this parallelism appears in medicine as well. In particular, the phenomenon is a prominent feature of American psychiatry, partly because of the eclectic origins of that specialty. Although the psychoanalytic tradition descended from Freud sometimes seems to receive the most attention, it is only one of many that have contributed to the formation of modern psychiatry. As a body of beliefs and practices, psychiatry in the twentieth century has in fact been almost as diverse as American religion. This diversity of each has in its turn multiplied opportunities to locate areas in which both overlap.[1]

That the origins of the most significant attempts in the early 1900s to harness religion and medicine abreast lay in Boston or nearby was no cultural accident. Among other matters "a long idealist tradition" and the competition between various mind-cure movements and practitioners, on the one hand, and medical orthodoxy as represented by the Boston Society of Psychiatry and Neurology, and the Harvard Medical School and its allied institutions, on the other, created an extraordinarily fertile soil to nourish efforts to define therapeutic modernism in mental health. Their flourishing was aided by the presence of two American geniuses in that field—William James (1842–1910) and Mary Baker Eddy (1821–1910). Although polar opposites in many ways, they were perversely but indissolubly joined by their involvement with psychic phenomena, traumatic bouts with ill health, and coincidental deaths in the same year.[2]

Fear of the consequences of Eddy's teachings for both orthodox Christianity and medicine furnished part of the inspiration for the Emmanuel Movement, probably the best known of early twentieth-century efforts to engage in medically valid religious healing. It took its name from the Emmanuel Episcopal Church in Boston, whose rector was Elwood Worcester (1862–1940). He had received a doctorate in philosophy from Leipzig and been for a time rector of St. Stephen's Church in Philadelphia, which numbered among its parishioners the leading American neurologist S. Weir Mitchell. Mitchell had encouraged Worcester's interest in the therapeutic role of religion. After moving to Emmanuel Church in 1904 Worcester had converted it into what could be described as an exemplar of Washington Gladden's "applied Christianity," with camps, clubs, and a gymnasium. Then in 1906 he extended the application of Christianity into the field of human health. After four lectures to audiences of modest size on successive Sunday nights, Worcester announced that he, two Harvard doctors—James Jackson Putnam and Richard C. Cabot, and his assistant, Samuel Mc-Comb, "would be in the parish rooms next morning to meet persons who might wish to consult us in regard to moral problems or psychical disorders." Not knowing what to expect, he found on his arrival 198 men and women. As he remarked in his autobiography, "From the very beginning, our carefully prepared scheme was taken out of our hands and committed to the people."[3]

Some sense of the public interest the movement aroused can be found in the account published by the Brooklyn *Eagle* for its readers in 1908. It reported, "A new religious wave is overspreading the Eastern United States and is fast reaching out to the West," a claim that in this case was indeed valid, at least for a time. Churches in Baltimore, Cleveland, Chicago, Detroit, and Buffalo, among others, quickly imitated the Emmanuel example, and news of it soon reached Europe, Asia, and Africa.[4]

To satisfy the curiosity of a national audience about the Emmanuel Movement, Worcester described its clinics and classes in health and tuberculosis in five articles in the *Ladies Home Journal* in 1908–9. In the health clinic an individual, after his case had "been passed upon and diagnosed by good medical authority," would meet with a member of the staff for a conference. So heavy were the demands for these consultations—"at least fifty . . . a day" for the previous two years—that Emmanuel's staff of ten was "unable to see one man or woman in five who wish to obtain an interview." During the year from mid–1907 to mid–1908 the health clinic had examined or treated 761 individuals, whose ailments Worcester summarized in 37 categories. Complaints about mental health bulked largest in the practice of the clinic. "Neurasthenia" (225 in 3 categories) was the most common illness. But also seen were cases of "alcoholism" (44), "dipsomania" (7), "morphinism" (7), and "constipation" (3). In addition, Emmanuel sponsored a "health class" that met in the church each Wednesday night, except in the summer months. Essentially a religious service for "nervous sufferers," it had for the past year, so Worcester informed the readers of the *Journal*, enjoyed an average attendance of 800. He emphasized that, although the Emmanuel Movement was intended to provide a medically valid alternative to faith healing, it also sought to avoid the therapeutic faddism of the medical community. It deliberately cultivated eclecticism, out of the conviction that physicians often failed to cure because of insisting "on the employment of one method, whether it applies or not."[5]

If the health clinic and class brought benefits to troubled individuals, they also, in Worcester's judgment, strengthened Protestantism by giving it a force and vitality that it had hitherto lacked. In particular, the clinic functioned in Protestantism to some extent as the confessional in Roman Catholicism, which gave the members of its clergy "an intimate access to the moral lives of their people." To some degree American religion has always been divided between those who believe churches should focus their activities on those outside their membership and those who would concentrate on those within. Although he responded to the claims of those without in other ways, Worcester intended the Emmanuel Movement for those within, for "the immense number of sad, dispirited, unsettled men and women who haunt our churches, wistfully looking for the help which they seldom receive." [6]

The tuberculosis class was conducted along lines roughly parallel to those of the health class and was one of the ways Worcester sought to deal with the problems of those outside the church. It had been founded in 1905 by Joseph H. Pratt, an instructor in medicine at the Harvard Medical School, and, in fact, continued in existence for eighteen years. The tuberculosis class sought to make available the therapy—principally rest, an open-air environment, and a nourishing diet—otherwise obtainable only in a sanitorium, for those unable to go to one, usually for reasons of poverty. Because of Emmanuel's help in providing tents or other outdoor accommodations, Worcester reported, "some of our people have lived outdoors for twenty-three hours out of the twenty-four, for weeks at a time," even in the midst of a crowded city. The church also ensured that the members of the class received a diet of milk, eggs, fresh fruit, and olive oil, as well as any necessary financial assistance. All members of the class who were physically able met weekly in the outpatient department of the Massachusetts General Hospital. There, under the supervision of Dr. Pratt, they received medical attention in an atmosphere of "friendship and good cheer" that offered important psychological support, even to those dying from the disease. Worcester claimed a cure rate of 75 percent for the members of the class not pronounced as incurable when they came to Emmanuel, "as good a record as the best sanitaria claim." And its class methods were attracting favorable medical attention. Its pamphlets on tuberculosis had "been translated into foreign languages, even into Japanese." William Osler, then Regius Professor of Medicine at Oxford University, had "carried our method to England and Ireland," and "at the International Tuberculosis Congress held last month in Washington, we were given a first award of a gold medal." [7]

The publicity that the health class and clinic received generated controversy and thus became a source of their curtailment. William James remarked in 1909 on the adverse consequences for them of press attention, "another example of newspaper crime." [8] In 1911 Worcester decided to grant no more interviews and to do everything possible to discourage public notice of the Emmanuel Movement. Also, hostility in the medical community led to the gradual withdrawal of support by James Jackson Putnam, Richard C. Cabot, and other prominent physicians, who had been initially sympathetic. An editorial in the *Boston Medical and Surgical Journal* in 1908 spoke with the dominant medical voice. Whatever its benefits, the Emmanuel Movement retarded "progress in the only direction in which normal psychotherapeutics can grow—through the medium of the medical profession." On a more private basis, however, healing continued to be practiced quite successfully in a health class in the Emmanuel Church into the 1920s. Nor was Worcester afraid to undertake new activities. At the prompting of Ernest Jacoby, a Boston businessman and parishioner, the church sponsored group therapy for the treatment of alcoholism in 1911, an activity it carried on with some interruption until Worcester's retirement in 1929.

In some respects the retreat of the Emmanuel Movement was simply one aspect of the demise of Boston's golden age of therapeutic modernism, and should be seen in that context. Although Christian Science continued to attract members, its period of therapeutic creativity came to an end with Eddy's death in 1910. With William James's death in the same year, American medical psychology proved unable to find a place for the brilliance of his insights, once he was no longer present as their advocate. Boston lost its pre-eminence in psychiatry to other cities by 1920. Yet, as was the case with Boston in its heyday, Worcester's record of religious and medical accomplishment, with the help of talented associates, was extraordinary—certainly much better, one suspects, than that achieved by his critics. Admittedly the Emmanuel Movement lacked a clear institutional successor in the Episcopal Church. Instead, the Craigie Foundation was chartered in 1925 to continue Emmanuel's healing traditions once Worcester retired. The independence of the foundation was intended to insure that it would never become an embarrassment or source of controversy to Emmanuel Church. Still, Worcester's work merits the extended attention it has received here because he reconnoitered so many of the ways in which religion and medicine shared common ground in the pursuit of health, ways whose significance was often more fully explored only afterwards. For example, Worcester's insistence on the necessity of keeping detailed case records, the importance of the healing service, and the role of counseling in giving greater validity to Protestantism in particular or religion in general can be found later in the pastoral counseling movement. With his support Emmanuel Church became an early center to attempt group therapy in the treatment of alcoholism, a precursor in this sense of Alcoholics Anonymous. In some ways the church functioned as a crisis intervention center during Worcester's ministry, one to which troubled individuals could turn as needed. Finally, it can be argued that the popular response to the Emmanuel Movement paved the way for public interest in Freudianism in New England.[9]

If one seeks a personal bridge between Boston and the rest of the country, between the Emmanuel Movement and later efforts to join medicine and religion in the pursuit of human health, possibly no better one can be found than Richard C. Cabot (1868–1939). A graduate of the Harvard Medical School in 1892, he had entered into private practice and then in 1918 became professor of Clinical Medicine at Harvard. His ending of his initial connection with the Emmanuel Movement did nothing to shake his belief that religion and medicine should be closely allied. He insisted that the qualities necessary in a physician came "best out of the spirit of Christianity." Also, he became convinced that the clergy needed some of the qualities of the physician. In particular, they required clinical training to prepare them to deal with the mental and physical disorders of mankind. In 1925 in his famous article, "A Plea for a Clinical Year in the Course of Theological Study," he urged the functional equivalence of the medical and clerical professions, of "a medical visit and a parish call." From a clinical year spent visiting "the sick, the insane, the prisons and the almshouses," the theology student would learn "to practice his theology where it is most needed, i.e., in personal contact with individuals in trouble." And the presence of clerical train-ees in the institutions where such were housed would, as in the case of medical students, result in a "great . . . hoisting" of the standards of care in these settings. "For the protection and care of the . . . insane" in asylums, for example, no event could be "of happier promise than the 'clinical year' for theological students."[10]

As a result of Cabot's advocacy and support, Anton T. Boisen, a Presbyterian clergyman, introduced in 1925 a clinical pastoral training program for theological students at Worcester State Hospital, an institution for the mentally ill in Mas-sachusetts. Shortly afterwards a similar program was begun at Massachusetts General Hospital in Boston. The success of these experiments led to efforts to create an organization to spread the practice of clinical training for clergy more widely. With several others Cabot founded in 1930 the Council for Clinical Training of Theological Students. Its purpose was to promote the clinical training of clergy in institutional settings that exposed them in a therapeutic way to the sufferings of mankind—in prisons, general hospitals, and mental institutions. Internal bickering among its leaders led to an eventual severing of relations by the New England contingent and the creation in 1938 of a separate organization, the Theological Schools Committee on Clinical Training. Two years earlier, in 1936, Cabot had engaged in another pathbreaking activity, the publication with the Presbyterian minister Russell C. Dicks of *The Art of Ministering to the Sick.* It was intended primarily for ministers but could also be of use, so the authors insisted, to doctors, nurses, social workers, and the sick themselves—"to all who care for the sick." The historian Brooks Holifield has observed of its effect that the book "helped to change the understanding of the cure of souls in American Protestantism."[11]

The splitting of the pastoral counseling movement into competing camps in part reflected the consequences of its growth. Boston and New England could no longer claim unquestioned precedence in efforts to find common ground between religion and medicine in the field of human health. As the psychiatrist Walter Bromberg has remarked, by the 1930s pastoral psychiatry "was then attaining a respectable stance in psychotherapy." It already had behind it three decades of attempts, "many successful, . . . to utilize religious faith in treating and managing neuroses." Two of the best known and most successful of these ventures were located in New York City. The psychiatrist Edward Spencer Cowles was one of the founders in the 1920s—and the medical director—of the Body and Soul Medical and Mental Clinic in St. Marks-in-the-Bowery Episcopal Church. Besides individual treatment for mental and physical ailments, the clinic sponsored public meetings. There in "the turmoil and poverty of the East Side" Dr. Cowles would stand "at a lectern with two converging purple shafts of light illuminating his figure" and explain to the audience "in simple terms how psychological conflicts eventuated in neuroses." In 1937 Norman Vincent Peale obtained the assistance of the psychiatrist Smiley Blanton and opened the Church Mental Health Clinic in the basement of the Marble Collegiate Church. It grew so rapidly that by 1951 it had to move into quarters outside the church. It then changed its name to the American Foundation of Religion and Psychiatry. By 1967 it reported that it had a non-sectarian staff of eighty psychologists, psychiatrists, ministers, and social workers. Also, it had set up a "branch clinic in Harlem, affiliates in Chicago and Green Bay, Wisconsin," and was "in the process of establishing others."[12]

As the history of the Church Mental Health Clinic demonstrates, World War II and the ensuing two decades witnessed an extraordinary growth in efforts to establish the valences of medicine and religion in human health. Their number and diversity limit this essay simply to noting some of the main lines of their development. In part they represented a continuation of earlier activities, often ones not confined to the United States. In 1938 at its fourth world meeting in Tambaram, Madras, India, the International Missionary Council had issued "an imperative call for pioneering" in "the relationship of religion and health." As a result of such an undertaking, "the hospital would . . . become a centre where search could be made for ways in which spiritual ministry might aid in bringing full health to patients." The much-publicized careers and writings of such medical missionaries as Albert Schweitzer (1875–1964), Paul W. Harrison (1883–1962), and Gordon S. Seagrave (1897–1965) spanned the war years and brought the message of the role of religion in healing to a large audience in America. Schweitzer's receiving the Nobel Peace Prize in 1952 suggests the moral appeal of that message in the Western world.[13]

In some respects the example of medical missionaries in the postwar years simply reinforced what the experience of World War II had otherwise brought home to many Americans. For example, the war had greatly increased the need for the services of clergy, and psychiatrists and other mental health professionals, outside their customary settings. And both groups found the translation troubling as their traditional armamentaria proved in certain ways inadequate to deal with the effects of war. Before World War II about 400 Protestant clergy had worked full-time as chaplains in the military services, hospitals, and the like. During the war some 8,000 chaplains of all faiths served with the Armed Forces alone. Demobilization reduced their ranks but not to their pre-war numbers. At the end of 1946 approximately 2,200 Protestant clergy were full-time chaplains with the military, general and mental hospitals, and elsewhere.[14]

The war work of religious laity could have parallel consequences, often in unanticipated locations. Many drafted members of the historic peace churches served in the Civilian Public Service program, which was created principally for those who objected to war on religious grounds. Among other places, they worked in mental hospitals and related institutions, and often spent their days in wards with "an ineradicable pungent smell of B.O., food-stained gowns, and fecal matter combined too strong for the antiseptic to cut through except perhaps momentarily." In this environment they validated the claim Richard C. Cabot had made in "A Plea for Clinical Year" in 1925 for the beneficial effect of a religious presence in such institutions. They "represented the largest infusion of intelligent and idealistic young blood that the mental hospitals of the nation had ever seen." The alternate service of its members led the Church of the Brethren to establish a Department of Religion and Health and thus imitate the earlier step of the Federal Council of Churches, which had created the Committee (later Commission) on Religion and Health in 1937. Leaders in the Civilian Public Service program reacted in similar fashion after the war. They were instrumental in the formation of the National Mental Health Foundation in 1946, the better to "provide for the mental health of the nation."[15]

Behind such greatly increased activity stood a widely distributed chorus that questioned whether the theology and social presence of the churches were relevant to the experience of Americans in the war and its aftermath. In a world divided into armed camps the churches had practiced unilateral disarmament and now found themselves and their clergy without the weapons to deal with the psychological conflicts of Americans. As a result of military service in World War II some "12,000,000 to 15,000,000 men and women . . . had some contact with professional psychologists and psychiatrists." What effect that exposure had in forming their judgments of military chaplains and religion must always remain a subject of conjecture. However, a postwar survey discovered that veterans' "complaints about the wartime clergy returned almost invariably to one issue: the chaplains too frequently lacked the skills appropriate to the cure of souls." When Chaplain Robert L. Schock reported for duty at Fitzsimmons Army Hospital in Denver, Colorado, in 1949, he encountered a situation drearily reminiscent of World War II. The chaplains there had previously limited themselves to "conducting appropriate religious services" and to calling on patients in a routine and "very matter-of-fact way." "Church attendance was poor," and "the doctors and nurses hardly knew the chaplains and understood less of their mission and program." Many clergy accepted without reservation the assessment that religion without outside assistance lacked the psychological sophistication to deal effectively with the problems of Americans in the military or outside. Robert H. Felix, the director of the recently created National Institute of Mental Health, reported in 1950 that, if the letters the institute received were "any gauge, religious leaders are in the forefront of professional people who recognize the need to apply scientific findings about human personality to their work with people. Individual clergymen and religious organizations from all parts of the country have written for information about mental health training." Beneath the willingness of clergy to obtain this training lay a tacit admission that the churches were unequipped to supply it from their own resources.[16]

Yet, whatever difficulties the churches encountered as they sought to cultivate a therapeutic competence, they met them with less internal bickering than before—not only because of decreased opposition within groups but also because of the greater willingness of Roman Catholics, Protestants, and Jews to engage in joint endeavors. In retrospect the creation by the 1950s of an interfaith popular front in any number of areas of national life can be regarded as a blip on the American landscape or, in a more hostile alternative such as that offered by the historian Sydney E. Ahlstrom, the triumph of a "civil religion" that reduced the churches to simple expressions of the patriotic needs of the moment. At the time, however, the emergence of interfaith efforts seemed a transformation of extraordinary religious and social significance, as, of course, it was.[17]

Of particular importance was an increased concern with mental health in Roman Catholic circles. Although the Church had long been involved in caring for the sick, it had to an extent shunned the field of mental health. The clinical pastoral training movement, for example, had distinctly Protestant origins. In the 1943 judgment of Seward Hiltner, the Executive Director of the Commission on Religion and Health of the Federal Council of Churches, the Roman Catholic Church, in comparative terms, had never displayed much interest in "chaplaincy service in mental hospitals." By 1954, however, the situation had changed noticeably. At a conference on psychotherapy and counseling held by the Section of Psychology of the New York Academy of Sciences, Wayne E. Oates, Professor of Pastoral Care at the Southern Baptist Theological Seminary, reported for its Commission in the Ministry that "about a half dozen" priests had become "fully qualified psychiatrists" and that "65 or more" were "currently members of the American Psychological Association, approximately half of whom have become members within the last six years." And "in considerable numbers" Roman Catholic clergy held "formal degrees in social work." In the same year *Newsweek* calculated that the eight-year-old American Catholic Psychological Association now numbered "450 Catholic professional psychologists."[18]

The relative slowness with which Roman Catholic interest in mental health rose to the surface of public life suggests, the degree of internal inertia and opposition, among other obstacles, that it had to overcome. For example, in 1947 Clare Booth Luce, Monsignor Fulton J. Sheen, and Francis Cardinal Spellman—a nexus that cut a wide swath through American, not simply Roman Catholic, life—were variously involved in an offensive against psychoanalysis. In an article that spanned three issues of *McCall's* magazine from February to April, Luce discussed "The 'Real' Reason" for her conversion to Roman Catholicism by Sheen in 1946. Among what were, in fact, a number of reasons, she offered her having been "psychoanalyzed in the middle thirties," an experience that left her mentally bruised and battered, without an answer to "The Big Question, the meaning of life and death, the real goal of human life." Although she tended to conflate psychoanalysis and Freudianism at a time when the status of Freudianism was becoming more that of primus inter pares as one of several schools of psychoanalysis, she intermixed strident passages with more tempered and trenchant observations than a critic like Seward Hiltner was prepared to admit. In a paper presented to a conference on religion and psychiatry held at the College of Preachers of the Washington National Cathedral (Episcopal) in 1948, he objected to her carping tone and assertion that analysts believed God to be "a cowardly concept" invented by man "to keep from giving himself that final pull at his bootstraps which will land him in the millennium.'' More to the point, however, Luce's implicit contention that psychoanalysis was a form of conspicuous consumption reserved for the affluent had legitimacy in an era when the health insurance industry was nascent and did not cover psychiatric therapy. Because of limited pocketbooks, if for no other reason, most Americans could afford only the psychological comforts offered by the rites and rituals of the nation's churches.[19]

During Lent in 1947 Fulton J. Sheen sounded some of the same themes as Luce. In a sermon on March 9 at St. Patrick's Cathedral he was quoted by the *New York Times* the next day as having assailed ''psychoanalysis as 'a form of escapism' that . . . failed to relieve 'the unresolved sense of guilt of sin' from which 'most people who consult psychoanalysts are suffering.' '' Anger among psychiatrists at Sheen's sermon smoldered underground for several months and broke into the open on July 1, 1947. Then four Catholic psychiatrists attending the national conference of the Group for the Advancement of Psychiatry in Minneapolis publicly denounced Sheen's reported charge that ''the practice of psychiatry is irreligious.'' With the observation that 50 percent of his patients were referred by priests, one of the four protesters, Frank J. Curran, confirmed for the *New York Times* on July 19 that he had resigned on May 27 as chief psychiatrist at St. Vincent's Hospital, a Roman Catholic institution in New York City, because of the failure of the Archdiocese of New York to ''clarify or repudiate'' Sheen's ''attack . . . on psychiatry.'' The next day the news of Curran's resignation appeared in the *New York Times*. Sheen had apparently been trying to dodge the issue but now telegraphed a letter to the newspaper's editor from Washington, D.C. Claiming that his views had been gravely distorted, he insisted that he had attacked only Freudianism in his March sermon, not psychoanalysis in general or psychiatry, which was '' 'a perfectly valid science.' '' The requirements of public order were met by a concurrent announcement by Cardinal Spellman through his secretary that Curran's '' 'services are not required in any institution of the Archdiocese of New York,' '' though he would '' 'not be refused admittance as a patient of any institution of the Archdiocese.' '' The controversy shortly disappeared from the pages of the city's newspapers. In a speech at the centenary dinner for the College of Mt. St. Vincent at the Waldorf Astoria hotel on October 6, Sheen returned to his favorite twin evils of Freudianism and communism but remained silent on the subject of psychoanalysis in general and psychiatry. This time his strictures provoked no psychiatric response.[20]

The Luce-Sheen-Spellman interlude proved a type of events in the Vatican in 1952–53. *Time* magazine speculated in its April 21, 1952, issue that the ''Vatican's unofficial truce with psychoanalysis might be over.'' It reported to its readers that in the April edition of the ''*Bulletin of the Roman Clergy*, Monsignor Pericle Felici, an official of the Sacred Congregation of the Sacraments, loudly attacked 'the absurdity of psychoanalysis.' He stated flatly that anyone who adopts the Freudian method is risking mortal sin.'' *Time* added that ''official

Vatican spokesmen quickly slid out from under Monsignor Felici's words,'' which did not "represent official church opinion, much less dogma.'' Yet, what did constitute official church opinion remained in some doubt for several months. On September 14, in a speech delivered to 300 surgeons attending the first International Congress of Histopathology in Rome, Pius XII censured "the pansexual method of a certain school of psychoanalysis.'' His censure was sufficiently ambiguous that on September 20 the Vatican newspaper *L'Osservatore Romano*, in what the *New York Times* a day later claimed to be an "authoritative'' article, made clear that he had not condemned "psychoanalysis as such, which if rightly applied, was not contrary to Christian morals.'' It continued that the clarification was necessary because of the insistence of some Catholic publications, "notably the April issue of the Bulletin of the Roman Clergy,'' that "the whole of psychoanalysis'' was "morally reprehensible and even . . . sinful.'' Pius XII returned to the subject of psychoanalysis in much more direct language in a speech on April 15, 1953, to more than fifty doctors attending the first International Congress on Psychotherapy and Clinical Psychology in Rome. To the surprise of "several in his audience,'' he expressed "his approval of psychoanalysis as one of the weapons in the armory of modern healers.''[21]

The 1954 claim of *Newsweek* that this speech "put an end to attacks by Catholics upon psychoanalysis'' was too sweeping. The initial response of the Catholic weekly *America* on May 2, 1953, to early and incomplete reports of the Pope's address was more perceptive. Although predicting that "reaction . . . will be varied,'' its editors ventured that "this approval of psychiatric work will come as a real blessing to many a Catholic doctor who has perhaps been working under a cloud because of reckless and out-of-hand condemnation by lesser authorities.''[22]

America's prediction proved valid as various locations in American Catholicism began to offer a more openly hospitable environment not only for psychoanalysis but for psychiatry and clinical psychology—in fact, for the whole field of mental health. It took any number of forms. At the meeting of the American Catholic Psychological Association in 1954, the Jesuit William C. Bier raised a subject that had previously been mostly taboo, at least in public discussion: the mental health of priests and nuns, and the role that psychic abnormality played in bringing them to the religious life. Though he found the "rate of insanity'' among them to be less than that for the general population, he concluded that schizophrenia was " 'by far the most frequent disorder among institutionalized priests and religious,' as pre-schizophrenics are attracted by the religious life.'' In 1955 St. Mary's Hospital, a Roman Catholic institution in San Francisco, founded the McAuley Psychiatric Clinic, "the first outpatient psychiatric clinic established in a U.S. Roman Catholic hospital.'' In the same year the Roman Catholic psychiatrist Karl Stern, chief of psychiatry at Ottawa General Hospital, appeared on the nationally broadcast "Catholic Hour'' radio program and felt no inhibition in attacking the "fashion for pitting psychiatry and religion against each other.'' And in the pages of the periodical *Catholic*

World, Sister Annette Walters, C.S.J., freely lamented the "narrow, parochial, and in the last analysis, un-Catholic prejudices" that prevented many Roman Catholics "from learning what is true and valuable in modern psychology." She insisted for the benefit of any such who might be reading her essay that Freud's views on human sexuality and mental health were "not nearly so alarming as the journalists would have us believe." Though still ringing in some quarters, Catholic alarm had sufficiently dissipated by 1963 that the Catholic psychiatrist Philip Sullivan was openly exploring in *America* "right" and "wrong" reasons why Catholics preferred to consult psychiatrists who were themselves Catholics. He found that the right reasons had nothing to do with such psychiatrists' holding correct religious beliefs but instead lay in their sharing a common culture with their patients.[23]

The interfaith embrace of mental therapeutics aroused other than Roman Catholic fears about its possible consequences both for religion and for psychiatry and its allied disciplines. David Riesman and Irving Kristol were both commentators of emerging consequence in the early years of postwar society. Though reaching opposing judgments, they did agree on the existence of a clear and present danger. In an essay on "Freud, Religion and Science," published shortly after the appearance of *The Lonely Crowd* (1950), Riesman warned that the American cultural and religious melting pot was producing a "new 'united front' of religionists and intellectuals" that tended "to censor science and intellectual discourse." He traced the change to "the rise in social position" of Catholics and Jews "in the last several decades." Their gain, however, still left them without "full social security" and thus "not yet able to laugh off such criticisms of religion as . . . continue to crop up." Their prickliness on the subject and substantial social presence forced the contemporary "definition of 'good American' " to include religious belief. Yet, with the balance or, perhaps more accurately, ambivalence that has characterized much of his description of American social change, Riesman found some reason for optimism. "The seriousness with which religion is now taken has made an interest in it respectable among many scientists who would earlier have considered an irreligious attitude an essential mark of emancipation." If the contemporary social situation permitted religion and science to lose their defensiveness in dealing with each other, then intellectual advance for both might occur, for progress in this sense, according to Riesman, often took place only in such a potentially threatening environment as the current one, as the result of "relatively powerless movements" working "within a precarious setting."[24]

By contrast, a year earlier in 1949 Irving Kristol had surveyed much the same evidence and found the American cultural ethos wanting from a quite different point of view. In an article on "God and the Psychoanalysts" in the Jewish magazine *Commentary*, Kristol, then its assistant editor, saw no need for the American social melting pot, in which "all races and creeds work peacefully side by side," to become an intellectual one, at least where religion and psychoanalysis were concerned. He feared their "current love affair" could never be fully consummated or produce legitimate offspring. In language that strained to accomplish his effects, he insisted that the union could prosper only by both "mates, acting together in full consciousness, stealthily" removing "the sword of truth" and hiding "it under the bed." Though coy about revealing his prescription for the intellectual future of the American melting pot, Kristol hinted that he thought it should lie with a pure religion, uncontaminated by psychoanalysis. Men could live in the truth of God and "find their happiness" by "simply living" in that truth, "though it be a scandal" to reason and Freud, " 'because the foolishness of God is wiser than men.' "[25]

If Riesman, Kristol, and other critics feared that the cause of truth and intellectual progress might suffer from contemporary efforts to join religion and psychiatry, many psychiatrists did not. Their willingness to consider the results of the marriage legitimate stemmed in part from their being involved with an additional and much more pragmatic issue than either Riesman or Kristol: What effect was the union having on Americans' mental health? Many pronounced the results beneficial. Subtle shifts in the stance of Karl Menninger between the 1930s and the postwar years provide some clues to this phenomenon. Co-founder in 1941 with his brother William and father Charles of the Menninger Foundation in Topeka, Kansas, Karl Menninger (1893-) has been throughout his long life a sensitive and influential barometer of psychiatric opinion, not the least because of the role of the Menninger Foundation as the world's largest psychiatric training center. In certain ways he and his brother William offer more sure-footed guidance over some aspects of the changing contours of American culture than either Riesman or Kristol, and certainly than Luce.

In an essay on "Psychiatry" published in 1938, Karl Menninger displayed a basic sympathy with the "increasing evidences of *rapprochement*" he found in the 1930s between scientists and "religionists." And he thought religion likely to remain the dominant partner in this alliance. "Religion will long continue to supply the healing of the nations to a far greater extent than will psychiatry." Menninger explained part of the reason for the current rapprochement by the greater sense of security possessed by psychiatry, by the way it was becoming less defensive as a result of being recognized as making a legitimate contribution to the melting pot of American medical practice. In the early twentieth century, when both psychiatry and Christian Science were newly founded, psychiatry had been forced to compete with Christian Science for patients, and for medical and popular acceptance. Even now, Menninger remarked, "some reputable medical men . . . refer patients to Christian Science practitioners rather than to psychiatrists, not because they prefer the former, but because they are more numerous and more available and better known to the public." Because of the greater acceptance of psychiatry, however, that preference was diminishing, a development that helped to make possible the current co-operation of religion and psychiatry. Menninger reminded his readers that, whatever their reservations, "ministers have been more open-minded toward psychiatry than have the lawyers" and, he might have added, than many among the doctors.[26]

When he came to give the Alden-Tuthill lectures on the "Relation of Religion and Psychiatry" at the Chicago Theological Seminary in 1951, Menninger retained his earlier sympathy with religion. As a "lifelong Presbyterian" he could hardly have done otherwise. But he was now willing to describe the work and beliefs of psychiatrists in more explicitly religious terms than before. Part of the difference, of course, had to do with audience. The essay on "Psychiatry" had been written for a book intended for a general audience; the lectures were prepared for a religious one. In 1938 Menninger had deliberately avoided "elaborate discussion of the function of religion . . . for which I am not qualified." In 1951, however, he undertook precisely that activity and added to it an analysis of "religio psychiatri." Under the latter heading he considered psychiatry as an activity little different from religion, for "beliefs which must in the last analysis be described as religious are implicit in the theory and practice of psychiatry." To a far greater extent than the 1938 essay, the 1951 lectures emphasized the religious legitimacy of psychiatry. Essentially they represented a venture into psychiatric apologetics that, by borrowing heavily from the vocabulary of religion, also became one into religious apologetics.[27]

World War II had, of course, intervened between Menninger's 1938 essay and 1951 lectures. Although it would unquestionably be an error to reduce Menninger's more overtly religious emphasis to the experience of war, it would be equally invalid to ignore the war's effects. World War II and its aftermath had been in some ways as traumatic for psychiatry as for religion, and had produced similar reactions. Psychiatrists and other mental health professionals had been involved in the war effort in large numbers. The Army alone had "employed more than 1,500 psychologists and hundreds of psychiatrists." As Walter Bromberg has observed, through their wartime service psychiatrists witnessed in varying degrees "the impact of an enterprise devoted to destruction of men and property on servicemen of many cultural backgrounds and personality formations." Their witness convinced some that neither their training nor theoretical equipment offered adequate preparation for the world in which they found themselves. Carl Jonas spoke for many psychiatrists when he concluded in 1945 that psychiatry found it "hard to renounce old training and beliefs," even though the war had amply proved that "some of them were barren." In a world pregnant with therapeutic needs and possibilities, psychiatry needed help from outside sources.[28]

Two of the leaders in reaching out for this assistance were Karl and William Menninger. They, with others, sought alliances throughout American society to accomplish the therapeutic goals of psychiatry, and, implicitily, to impose on it from without the changes that it could not generate solely from within. William Menninger's 1946 creation, the Group for the Advancement of Psychiatry, was but one instance of this new direction. It strove for a broad involvement with American culture and solicited the active partnership of "anthropologists, sociologists, lawyers, educators, economists, biologists." It and kindred ventures were the psychiatric equivalent of the interfaith common front of the postwar years. Thus, when Karl Menninger stood before his audience in Chicago in 1951, he spoke to a situation in which many in the religious and psychiatric communities regarded their leading task as the creation of an American society in which both had blurred their once expected distinctiveness. To them, to speak of psychiatry in the vocabulary of religion, or religion in the vocabulary of psychiatry, made more sense than to seek to maintain unsullied their separate identities and reputations.[29]

Evidence of the widespread engagement of religion by psychiatry can be found in any number of locations. At the concurrent meeting of the American Psychiatric Association and the American Psychoanalytic Association in Chicago in 1956 to mark the 100th anniversary of the birth of Sigmund Freud, R. Finley Gayle celebrated the occasion by observing in his presidential address to the American Psychiatric Association that " 'no basic reason presently exists for conflict between psychiatry and religion as such.' " His reading of the history of psychiatry had convinced him that more opposition to it had come from the ranks of the " 'medical profession itself' " than from religion. An editorial in the *Christian Century* dryly but aptly commented that "Dr. Freud would have whirled a revolution or two" if he had heard Gayle's address.[30]

In the same year several leading psychiatrists and prominent Protestant, Roman Catholic, and Jewish clergymen came together to found the National Academy of Religion and Mental Health, with its headquarters at the New York Academy of Medicine. The product of three years of "exploratory" discussions, it was intended to "educate the public in the many functions which relate religion and psychiatry." Some sense of the psychiatric attitudes that lay behind its foundation can be found in a speech the previous year by its first president, Kenneth E. Appel, Professor of Psychiatry at the University of Pennsylvania. He warned the Section on Psychoanalysis of the American Psychiatric Association of the "cultural lag in psychoanalysis." Today, he feared, "most psychiatrists are disconnected culturally . . . from much of current religious thinking and from philosophical and scientific frames of reference." Progress in psychiatry would be possible only by creating a psychiatric culture that permitted connection with them.[31]

One could find similar attitudes having an effect at a local level. In January 1954, the council of administrators of the Texas Medical Center in Houston invited the Greater Houston Council of Churches to "survey the possibility of establishing a comprehensive religious program within the center." As a result of the survey, five Texas theological institutions established a training program there in 1956 that was intended to meet the varying needs of seminarians, "graduate clergymen, physicians and nurses." By 1959 the Institute of Religion had prospered sufficiently to begin construction of a four-story, $600,000 building to house itself on the medical campus. It had already trained 139 medical students, 373 nursing students, 80 seminarians, and 112 clergy.[32]

Nor was medical open-mindedness about the therapeutic value of religion necessarily confined to America. John Lister reported from London to the *New*

England Journal of Medicine in 1954 that a patient of his had probably been helped more by her listening to a sermon of Billy Graham than by the barbiturates he himself had prescribed. He continued that ''the British Medical Association has appointed a committee to prepare evidence for a Commission on Divine Healing, which has been set up by the archbishops of Canterbury and York'' to ''consider the theologic, medical, psychologic and pastoral aspects of 'divine healing.' ''[33]

In case there was still need, Albert L. Meiburg attempted in 1958 to lay to rest for the readers of the Protestant *Christian Century* the ''Myth of the 'Godless Physician.' '' He had discovered that ''in 1957 physicians contributed to medical journals three times as many articles on religion as did clergymen.'' Most of the articles were addresses to medical societies that were later printed in their journals. From his analysis of the contents of this literature Meiburg concluded that physicians were ''demonstrating an ever greater willingness to explore the theological implications of their profession.'' They are generally disposed to accept spiritual care as an adjunct to physical therapy if it is sanely administered.''[34]

When the rush of medicine and religion to explore their areas of therapeutic overlap slowed down is a question that can be answered only imprecisely. Don Browning, an instructor in religion and personality at the University of Chicago Divinity School, thought it had arrived in religion by 1966. In an article in the *Christian Century* he identified Harvey Cox as one of its sources. Cox, the author of *The Secular City* (1965), and other theologians were emerging as persuasive advocates of the need for the churches to develop a public ministry ''in the market place, the real estate office, the chambers of city and national government.'' From this point of view pastoral psychology and counseling were the enemies of a public ministry. They produced an individual ''primarily concerned with his own emotional well-being and totally without vital ethical concern.'' Possibly more significant than Browning's article was one response to it. Armen D. Jorjorian was one of the leaders of the clinical training movement and at one time had been the senior Protestant chaplain at Bellevue Hospital in New York City. Now he was chaplain at St. Luke's Episcopal Hospital in Houston, Texas, and chairman of the national accreditation committee of the Council for Clinical Training. A letter from him in the *Christian Century* for November 2, 1966, acknowledged the validity of the criticism. ''We clinical pastoral educators have had our heads in the sand for far too long with reference to our obligation and opportunity to engage in the public ministry.'' The accusation and the acknowledgment fascinate because they echo, though from a quite different political and theological perspective, the charge that Clare Booth Luce, Fulton J. Sheen, and others had levied against Freudian psychoanalysis after World War II: Embracing it endangered religion because it lacked ethical content and concern.[35]

By the late 1960s interest in the overlap of religion and medicine was possibly no longer as prominently ''in the air''—to use the earlier characterization by Harry Emerson Fosdick—as it had once been. Yet, by any number of objective measures, it remained a strong presence, even if it resembled more a maturing than a growth industry. In 1981 the National Institute of Mental Health calculated that "since 1970, approximately 1,500 . . . journal articles, reports and books . . . have appeared on the subject of religion and mental health." Their authors included clergy and mental health professionals. The institute insisted that, from its viewpoint, "pastoral counseling is possibly the most successful integration yet achieved between psychology and religion." From 1967 on, the American Psychiatric Association grappled with the question of how to define the functions of its Committee on Religion and Psychiatry. In 1970 a questionnaire was sent to all its members, as well as to all members of the American Medical Association who indicated psychiatry to be their sub-specialty. Of 17,564 who replied, 2,198, checked "yes" to the question, "Do you provide training, therapy, screening or other psychiatric services for any religious institution?" The authors of the survey had expected a "yes" answer from no more than 300–400. In the 1975 report of the American Psychiatric Association on the survey and follow-up research, Ana-Maria Rizzuto, associate clinical professor of Psychiatry at Tufts Medical School, responded to the work by remarking that "both the general population and psychiatrists have an emotional investment in some form of religious belief."[36]

That a committee of the American Psychiatric Association as late as the 1970s managed to be surprised about the therapeutic activities of its members indicates the existence of a deeply rooted attitude. In some respects it still exists unchanged from its turn-of-the-century expression in Andrew D. White's *History of the Warfare of Science with Christendom* (1896) and extends back beyond White to the Enlightenment. Though more of an anti-Catholic than anti-religious tract, White's book remains "the most influential . . . ever written on the subject." He contended that the principal obstacle to the rise of modern medicine had been the theological doctrines of the Roman Catholic Church. Thus, therapeutic progress resulted from the triumph of medicine over Catholic theology. White's book is dated from any number of points of view; yet, today, general histories of medicine and psychiatry or of religion testify implicitly to the danger of medical and religious conflict by the way in which each is kept walled off from the other. For example, Jay P. Dolan's *American Catholic Experience: A History from Colonial Times to the Present* (1985) nowhere in its index lists Freud, medicine, psychiatry, or psychoanalysis. Martin E. Marty follows the same pattern in his attempt to summarize 500 years of the American religious experience, *Pilgrims in Their Own Land* (1984), even though he has written extensively in other places on the relation of religion and health. In a similar manner references to Elwood Worcester, Richard C. Cabot, pastoral psychiatry, or, more generally, religion cannot be found in the index to James Bordley, III, and A. McGehee Harvey's *Two Centuries of American Medicine: 1776–1976* (1976), though Mary Baker Eddy does appear as the leader of a "cult." The same is true of Howard H. Kendler's *Historical Foundations of Modern Psychology* (1987) and Erwin H. Ackerknecht's *Short History of Psychiatry* (1968), except that they omit Eddy. This survey is admittedly impressionistic and does not pretend to completeness. The question of the narrative conventions that control accounts of the medical and religious past and the way in which they operate to separate each domain from the other deserves more extensive attention than it can receive here. To some extent the roots of those conventions lie in conceptions of cultural autonomy that, with important exceptions, are widespread in religion and medicine—and, indeed, in American society. Their existence insures that the persistence of biodivinity will likely remain a subject of continual rediscovery. In this sense the phenomenon resembles the revivals whose occurrence is a regular but always unexpected event in American life.[37]

NOTES

1. For an influential statement of the role of applied psychology/psychiatry as social ideology, see Fred Matthews, "In Defense of Common Sense: Mental Hygiene as Ideology and Mentality in Twentieth-Century America," *Prospects* 4 (1979): 459–516. Also helpful are the introductory remarks in John C. Burnham, *Paths into American Culture: Psychology, Medicine, and Morals* (Philadelphia, 1988), 3–6; Barbara Sicherman, "The Quest for Mental Health in America, 1880–1917" (Ph.D. diss., Columbia University, 1967), 3–6; and Erwin H. Ackerknecht, *A Short History of Psychiatry* (2nd, rev. ed., New York, 1968), 1–9. For Freud's influence in America, two possible starting points are David Shakow and David Rappaport, *The Influence of Freud on American Psychology* (New York, 1964) and Nathan A. Hale, Jr., *Freud and the Americans: The Beginning of Psychoanalysis in the United States, 1876–1907* (New York, 1971). See, also, Jacques M. Quen and Eric T. Carlson, eds., *American Psychoanalysis: Origins and Development* (New York, 1978). The literature on the history of American psychiatry is voluminous. Beginnings can be made in Daniel Blain and Michael Barton, eds., *The History of American Psychiatry: A Teaching and Research Guide* (Washington, D.C., 1979). Also useful are George Mora and Jeanne L. Brand, eds., *Psychiatry and Its History* (Springfield, Ill., 1970), and Robert C. Fuller, *Americans and the Unconscious* (New York, 1986). An invaluable book, anecdotal but filled with insight, is Walter Bromberg, *Psychiatry Between the Wars, 1918–1945: A Recollection* (Westport, Conn., 1982).

2. Nathan G. Hale, Jr., "James Jackson Putnam and Boston Neurology: 1877–1918," in George E. Gifford, Jr., ed., *Psychoanalysis, Psychotherapy, and the New England Medical Scene, 1894–1944* (New York, 1978), 151. For the concept of a therapeutic world view, see T. J. Jackson Lears, *No Place of Grace: Antimodernism and the Transformation of American Culture, 1880–1920* (New York, 1981), 47–58. James's psychological genius has, of course, long been admitted. Such claims on Eddy's behalf have an equally long history of being rejected, at least outside Christian Science circles. For Eddy's reputation, see R. Laurence Moore, *Religious Outsiders and the Making of Americans* (New York, 1986), 105–27, and Julius Silberger, Jr., *Mary Baker Eddy: An Interpretive Biography* (Boston, 1980). For James, see Frederick H. Burkhardt, et al., eds., *The Works of William James*, vol. 9, *Essays in Psychical Research* (Cambridge, Mass., 1986), and Gerald E. Myers, *William James: His Life and Thought* (New Haven, 1986).

3. Elwood Worcester, *Life's Adventure: The Story of a Varied Career* (New York, 1932), 286, 287; *The Emmanuel Movement: A Brief History of the New Cult, with Sermons from Prominent Ministers and Opinions of Laymen* (Brooklyn, N.Y., 1908), 3, 26; E.

Brooks Holifield, *A History of Pastoral Care in America: From Salvation to Self-Realization* (Nashville, 1983), 202; Washington Gladden, *Applied Christianity: Moral Aspects of Social Questions* (Boston, 1886). Numerous accounts exist of the Emmanuel Movement. In particular, see John G. Greene, "The Emmanuel Movement: 1906–1929," *New England Quarterly* 7 (1943): 494–532; Raymond J. Cunningham, "The Emmanuel Movement: A Variety of American Religious Experience," *American Quarterly* 14 (1962): 48–63; Sanford Gifford, "Medical Psychotherapy and the Emmanuel Movement," in George Gifford, ed., *New England Medical Scene*, 106–18; and Holifield, *Pastoral Care*, 201–9.

4. *Emmanuel Movement*, 3.

5. Elwood Worcester, "The Results of the Emmanuel Movement," *Ladies Home Journal*, November 1908, 7, 8 and December 1908, 9, 10. See, also, Richard C. Cabot's tabulation of the cases seen between March and November, 1907: "New Phases in the Relation of the Church to Health," *Outlook*, February 29, 1908, 504–8. Four articles appeared under the title, "The Results of the Emmanuel Movement," *Ladies Home Journal*, November 1908, 7–8, 71; December 1908, 9–10; January 1909, 17–18, 47; and February 1909, 15–16, 56–57. The fifth was published as "The Emmanuel Church Tuberculosis Class," *Ladies Home Journal*, March 1909, 17–18, 76, 78. See also Worcester's related article, "What Suggestion Can Do for Children," *Ladies Home Journal*, October 1908, 7–8. For "neurasthenia" as a disease, see Lears, *No Place of Grace*, 49–57.

6. Worcester, "Results of Emmanuel Movement," November 1908, 8, 7.

7. Worcester, "Tuberculosis Class," 17, 18; Sanford Gifford, "Emmanuel Movement," 108–10.

8. William James to Thomas S. Perry, 29 January 1909, in Henry James, ed., *The Letters of William James* (Boston, 1920), 2: 318; *Boston Medical and Surgical Journal*, 26 November 1908 (159): 731.

9. Otto M. Marx, "American Psychiatry Without William James," *Bulletin of the History of Medicine* 42 (1969): 52–61; John C. Burnham, "Boston Psychiatry in the 1920s—Looking Forward," in George Gifford, ed., *New England Medical Scene*, 196. Sanford Gifford, "Emmanuel Movement," 117, notes that among all those treated by Worcester there were "no deaths from suicide, an enviable record for any psychotherapist." Modern church historians tend to be less generous. Holifield, *Pastoral Care*, 206, emphasizes Worcester's lack of theoretical clarity and consistency, and seems to imply these defects handicapped Emmanuel's work in counseling. Martin E. Marty, *Modern American Religion*, vol. 1, *The Irony of It All, 1893–1919* (Chicago, 1986), 259, contends, "Emmanuel in a few years almost collapsed into its own form of reduction." Theoretical clarity and consistency have obvious utility in religious and psychiatric apologetics but enjoy a more limited connection with therapeutic results in mental health. For the role of theory in mental healing, see, for example, Walter Bromberg, *From Shaman to Psychotherapist: A History of the Treatment of Mental Illness* (4th ed., Chicago, 1975), 347–49, and Ackerknecht, *History of Psychiatry*, 95–96.

10. Lawrence A. May and John Stoeckle, eds., *Richard Cabot on Practice, Training and the Doctor-Patient Relationship* (Oceanside, New York, n.d.), 43; Richard C. Cabot, *Adventures on the Borderlands of Ethics* (New York, 1926), 2, 6–7, 14, 19. "A Plea for a Clinical Year in the Course of Theological Study" appeared in the *Survey Graphic*, 1 December 1925, 274–77, and was reprinted in *Adventures on the Borderlands*, 1–22.

11. Richard C. Cabot and Russsell L. Dicks, *The Art of Ministering to the Sick* (New

York, 1936), v; Holifield, *Pastoral Care*, 237. For Cabot's work in clinical training, see Holifield, *Pastoral Care*, 231–49, and Kenneth A. Nelson, "Richard Clarke Cabot and the Development of Clinical Pastoral Education" (Ph.D. diss., University of Iowa, 1970). Also useful are Anton T. Boisen's recollections, "The Period of Beginnings," *Journal of Pastoral Care*, 5 (1951): 13–16, and Robert C. Powell, *Anton T. Boisen (1876–1965): Breaking an Opening in the Wall between Religion and Medicine* (Buffalo, N.Y., 1976).

12. Bromberg, *Psychiatry Between the Wars*, 97; Clarence W. Hall, "Where Religion and Psychiatry Join Hands," *Readers Digest*, March 1967, 126, 125.

13. *The World Mission of the Church: Findings and Recommendations of the Meeting of the International Missionary Council* (London, 1939), 96; Seward Hiltner, "Religion and Health," *American Scholar*, 15 (1946): 332–33. For the message of these medical missionaries, see Harrison's *Doctor in Arabia* (New York, 1940); Seagrave's *Tales of a Waste-Basket Surgeon* (Philadelphia, 1938), *Burma Surgeon* (New York, 1943), and *Burma Surgeon Returns* (New York, 1946); and Schweitzer's *Afrikanische Geschichten* (Leipzig, 1938), published in the United States as *African Notebook* (New York, 1939). Schweitzer's pre-war works remained popular in America in the postwar period and continued to be reprinted—e.g., *On the Edge of the Primeval Forest and More from the Primeval Forest* (New York, 1948)—published originally in German as *Zwischen Wasser und Urwald* (Munich, 1926) and *Mitteilungen aus Lambarene* (Munich, 1928)—and *Out of My Life and Thought, An Autobiography* (New York, 1949), originally *Aus meinem Leben und Denken* (Hamburg, 1931). For Harrison, see Ann M. Harrison, *A Tool in His Hand* (New York, 1958); for Seagrave, Sue M. Newhall, *The Devil in God's Old Man* (New York, 1969). The material on Schweitzer overwhelms. One can make a start in James Brabazon, *Albert Schweitzer* (London, 1976), and Nancy S. Griffith and Laura Person, eds., *Albert Schweitzer, An International Bibliography* (Boston, 1981).

14. Hiltner, "Religion and Health," 331, and *Religion and Health* (New York, 1943), 253–71; Holifield, *Pastoral Care*, 269.

15. Leslie Eisan, *Pathways of Peace: A History of the Civilian Public Service Program Administered by the Brethren Service Committee* (Elgin, Ill., 1948), 208, 238; Hiltner, "Religion and Health," 333. John A. Hutchinson, *We Are Not Divided: A Critical and Historical Study of the Federal Council of Churches in America* (New York, 1941), 158.

16. John S. Bonnell, "Comment on the Report of the Commission in the Ministry," *Pastoral Psychology*, 7 (March 1956): 31; Holifield, *Pastoral Care*, 270; Alvie L. McKnight, "The Evolution of Pastoral Care in the Army Hospitals," *Journal of Pastoral Care*, 7 (1953): 171; Robert H. Felix, "The Hard Core of Counseling," *Pastoral Psychology*, 1 (April 1950): 37.

17. Sydney E. Ahlstrom, *A Religious History of the American People* (New Haven, 1972), 954; Holifield, *Pastoral Care*, 269–76. Although a seminal study, Holifield's book basically ignores Catholic-Protestant-Jewish cooperation after World War II. A more accurately descriptive title for the book would be "A History of Protestant Ideas about Pastoral Care in America." For the phenomenon of civil religion, see Robert N. Bellah and Phillip E. Hammond, *Varieties of Civil Religion* (San Francisco, 1980), and John F. Wilson, *Public Religion in American Culture* (Philadelphia, 1979).

18. Hiltner, *Religion and Health*, 268; Wayne E. Oates, "The Findings of the Commission in the Ministry," *Annals of the New York Academy of Sciences*, 63 (1955): 420; "Church and Psyche," *Newsweek*, September 20, 1954, 84.

19. Clare Booth Luce, "The 'Real' Reason," *McCall's*, February 1947, 135, and March 1947, 16, 154, 160; Seward Hiltner, "Religion and Psychoanalysis," *Psychoan-*

alytic Review, 37 (1950): 128. Luce's article appeared in *McCall's*, February 1947, 16, 117–18, 120–35; March 1947, 16–17, 153–54, 156, 160–61, 165–68, 171–72, 175–76; and April 1947, 26–27, 76, 78, 80, 85, 88, 90. Blue Shield in New York did not provide medical care for psychiatric conditions in general hospitals until 1959 and then only extended this coverage to 800,000 subscribers with higher incomes. It did not include 2,900,000 subscribers with lower-income contracts and 1,300,000 others whose policies limited or excluded medical coverage. (*New York Times*, 19 November 1959, pp. 1, 43.) For the appeal to physicians of the "better-than-average income" offered by psychoanalytic practice, see Bromberg, *Psychiatry Between the Wars*, 74.

20. *New York Times*, 10 March 1947, p. 18; 2 July 1947, p. 17; 20 July 1947, sect. 1, p. 5; 21 July 1947, p. 8; and 7 October 1947, p. 30.

21. "Is Freud Sinful?" *Time*, April 21, 1952, 71; *New York Times*, 21 September 1952, sect. 1, p. 31; 16 April 1953, p. 1. Hubert Jedin, Konrad Repgen, and John Dolan, eds., *History of the Church*, vol. 10, *The Church in the Modern Age* (New York, 1980) omits this episode, as well as psychoanalysis and Freud.

22. "Church and Psyche," 84, *America*, May 2, 1953, 126.

23. "Church and Psyche," 84; "Improvisation and Guilt," *Time*, February 28, 1955, 34; "Psychiatry & Faith," *Time*, August 1, 1955, 34; Annette Walters, "Catholics and Mental Health," *Catholic World*, April 1955, 15, 13; Philip R. Sullivan, "The 'Psychiatric Catholic,' " *America*, February 9, 1963, 199, 201.

24. David Riesman, "Freud, Religion and Science," *American Scholar*, 20 (1950–51): 272, 271, 276. Riesman's essay began as a lecture delivered on 9 January 1950, to the Channing Club of the University of Chicago.

25. Irving Kristol, "God and the Psychoanalysts," *Commentary*, 8 (1949): 434, 443.

26. Karl Menninger, "Psychiatry," in Harold E. Stearns, ed., *America Now: An Inquiry into Civilization in the United States* (New York, 1938), 451, 453, 450. Psychiatry became a board-certified speciality with the creation in 1934 of the American Board of Psychiatry and Neurology.

27. Karl Menninger, "Religio Psychiatri," *Chicago Theological Seminary Register*, March 1951, 3, 8, and "Psychiatry," 449.

28. Holifield, *Pastoral Care*, 261; Bromberg, *Psychiatry Between the Wars*, 163; Carl Jonas, "Psychiatry Has Growing Pains," *American Journal of Psychiatry*, 102 (1945): 821.

29. Bromberg, *Psychiatry Between the Wars*, 164. Psychiatric developments in the period can be followed in Burnham, *Paths into American Culture*, 96–110. Also useful are Bromberg's recollections of his wartime experiences in *Psychiatry Between the Wars*, 150–65.

30. "Psychiatry Makes a Move," *Christian Century*, May 9, 1956, 572, 571. See also, the report of Gayle's address in *Science News Letter*, May 12, 1956, 290.

31. Kenneth E. Appel, "Psychoanalysis: Reflections on Varying Concepts," *American Journal of Psychiatry*, 112 (1956): 713, 715; "Problem of the Sinner," *Newsweek*, April 9, 1956, 102.

32. Henry W. Quinius, Jr., "Texas Seminaries Start New Plan," *Christian Century*, April 25, 1956, 532, 531; "The Healing Team," *Time*, December 14, 1959, 60.

33. John Lister, "By the London Post," *New England Journal of Medicine*, July 29, 1954, 193.

34. Albert L. Meiburg, "The Myth of the 'Godless Physician,' " *Christian Century*, November 5, 1958, 1270, 1271.

35. Don Browning, "Pastoral Care and Public Ministry," *Christian Century*, September 28, 1966, 1175, and Armen D. Jorjorian, "Acknowledgment," *Christian Century*, November 2, 1966, 1345.

36. Harry Emerson Fosdick, "The Minister and Psychotherapy," *Pastoral Psychology*, 11 (February 1960): 13; Florence A. Summerlin, comp., *Religion and Mental Health: A Bibliography* (Rockville, Md., 1981), v; *Psychiatrists' Viewpoints on Religion and Their Services to Religious Institutions and the Ministry* (Washington, D.C., 1975), 2, 5, 42.

37. Ronald L. Numbers and Ronald C. Sawyer, "Medicine and Christianity in the Modern World," in Martin E. Marty and Kenneth L. Vaux, eds., *Health/Medicine and the Faith Traditions* (Philadelphia, 1982), 134; James Bordley, III, and A. McGehee Harvey, *Two Centuries of American Medicine: 1776–1976* (Philadelphia, 1976), 43.

SELECTED BIBLIOGRAPHY

Ammerman, Nancy Tatom. *Bible Believers: Fundamentalists in the Modern World*. New Brunswick, N.J., 1987.

Armstrong, Ben. *The Electric Church*. Nashville, 1979.

Bailey, Hugh C. *Liberalism in the New South*. Coral Gables, Fla., 1969.

Bainbridge, William Sims, and Rodney Stark. *The Future of Religion: Secularization, Revival and Cult Formation*. Berkeley, Calif., 1985.

Baker, Tod, Robert Steed, and Laurence Moreland, eds. *Religion and Politics in the South: Mass and Elite Perspectives*. New York, 1983.

Bates, Thomas R. "Gramsci and the Theory of Hegemony," *Journal of the History of Ideas* 36 (1975): 351–66.

Bauman, Mark K. *Warren Aiken Candler*. Metuchen, N.J., 1981.

Bell, Daniel. "The Return of the Sacred?" In *The Winding Passage: Essays and Sociological Journeys, 1960–1980* (Cambridge, Mass., 1980), 324–54.

Blassingame, John. *The Slave Community*. New York, 1972.

Bloom, Allan. *The Closing of the American Mind*. New York, 1987.

Bode, Frederick A. *Protestantism and the New South*. Charlottesville, Va., 1975.

Bromley, David G., and Anson Shupe, eds. *New Christian Politics*. Macon, Ga., 1984.

Burnham, John C. *Paths into American Culture: Psychology, Medicine, and Morals*. Philadelphia, 1988.

Carrott, Richard G. *The Egyptian Revival: Its Sources, Monuments and Meaning, 1808–1858*. Berkeley, Calif., 1978.

Coleman, John A. "The American Civil Religion Debate: A Source for Theory Construction," *Journal for the Scientific Study of Religion* 20 (1981): 51–63.

Conn, Peter. *The Divided Mind*. Cambridge, Mass., 1983.

Costigliola, Frank. *Awkward Dominion*. Ithaca, N.Y., 1984.

Douglas, Mary, and Steven Tipton, eds. *Religion and America: Spirituality in a Secular Age*. Boston, 1982.

Eighmy, John Lee. *Churches in Cultural Captivity: A History of the Social Attitudes of Southern Baptists*. Knoxville, 1972.

Eliade, Mircea. *The Sacred and the Profane: The Nature of Religion*. New York, 1961.

Ellens, J. Harold. *Models of Religious Broadcasting*. Grand Rapids, Mich., 1974.

Farish, Hunter Dickinson. *The Circuit Rider Dismounts: A Social History of Southern Methodism*. Richmond, Va., 1938.

Findley, James F., Jr. *Dwight L. Moody, American Evangelist, 1837–1899*. Chicago, 1969.

Finegold, Henry. *A Midrash on American Jewish History*. Albany, N.Y., 1982.

———. *Zion in America: The Jewish Experience from Colonial Times to the Present*. New York, 1974.

Fiorenza, Elizabeth Schussler. *Bread Not Stone: The Challenge of Feminist Biblical Interpretation*. Boston, 1985.

Flowers, Ronald B. "President Jimmy Carter, Evangelicalism, Church-State Relations, and Civil Religion," *Journal of Church and State* 25 (Winter 1983): 113–32.

Foner, Philip S. *History of Black Americans*, vols 1–3. Westport, Conn., 1975–83.

Fowler, Robert Booth. *A New Engagement: Evangelical Political Thought, 1966–1976*. Grand Rapids, Mich., 1982.

Frankl, Razelle. *Televangelism: The Marketing of Popular Religion*. Carbondale, Ill., 1987.

Funk, Robert. "The Watershed of the American Biblical Tradition: The Chicago School, First Phase, 1892–1920," *Journal of Biblical Literature* 95 (March 1976): 4–22.

Gasper, Louis. *The Fundamentalist Movement: 1930–1956*. Grand Rapids, Mich., 1981.

Gaston, Paul. *The New South Creed*. New York, 1970.

Geertz, Clifford. *The Interpretation of Cultures*. New York, 1973.

Genovese, Eugene. *Roll, Jordan, Roll*. New York, 1974.

Glad, Betty. *Jimmy Carter: In Search of the Great White House*. New York, 1980.

Gramsci, Antonio. *Selections from the Prison Notebooks of Antonio Gramsci*, Quintin Hoare and Geoffrey Nowell Smith, eds. New York, 1972.

Grantham, Dewey. *Southern Progressivism: The Reconciliation of Progress and Tradition*. Knoxville, 1983.

Hadden, Jeffrey K., and Charles E. Swann. *Prime-Time Preachers: The Rising Power of Televangelism*. Reading, Mass., 1981.

Hamilton, Charles V. *The Black Preacher in America*. New York, 1972.

Hammond, Phillip E., ed. *The Sacred in a Secular Age*. Berkeley, Calif., 1985.

Harding, Vincent. *There Is a River*. New York, 1981.

Harrell, David E., Jr., ed. *Varieties of Southern Evangelicalism*. Macon, Ga., 1981.

Hefley, James and Marti. *The Church That Produced a President*. New York, 1977.

Hill, Samuel S., Jr. *Southern Churches in Crisis*. New York, 1967.

Holifield, E. Brooks. *A History of Pastoral Care in America: From Salvation to Self-Realization*. Nashville, 1983.

Horsfield, Peter G. *Religious Television: The American Experience*. New York, 1984.

Hoving, Thomas. *Tutankhamon, The Untold Story*. New York, 1978.

Hunter, James Davison. *American Evangelicalism: Conservative Religion and the Quandary of Modernity*. New Brunswick, N.J., 1983.

———. *Evangelicalism: The Coming Generation*. Chicago, 1987.

Hutchinson, William R. *The Modern Impulse in American Protestantism*. New York, 1976.

Jick, Leon. *The Americanization of the Synagogue, 1820–1870*. Hanover, N.H., 1976.

Jorstad, Erling. *Evangelicals in the White House: The Cultural Maturation of Born Again Christianity, 1960–1981*. New York, 1981.

Koenig, Louis. *Bryan, A Political Biography*. New York, 1971.

Konvitz, Milton R. *Judaism and the American Ideal*. Ithaca, N.Y., 1978.

Kousser, J. Morgan. *The Shaping of Southern Politics*. New Haven, 1974.

Kucharsky, David. *The Man from Plains: The Mind and Spirit of Jimmy Carter*. New York, 1976.

Ladd, Everett Carl, Jr. *Negro Political Leadership in the South*. Ithaca, N.Y., 1966.

Leach, Edmund. *Culture and Communications*. New York, 1976.

Leffler, Melvyn P. *The Elusive Quest*. Chapel Hill, N.C., 1979.

Levine, Lawrence W. *Black Culture and Black Consciousness*. New York, 1977.

Lincoln, C. Eric, ed. *The Black Experience in Religion*. New York, 1974.

Loveland, Anne C. *Southern Evangelicals and the Social Order, 1800–1860*. Baton Rouge, 1980.

McAdam, Doug. *Political Process and the Development of Black Insurgency, 1930–1970*. Chicago, 1982.

McWilliams, Wilson Carey. *The Idea of Fraternity in America*. Berkeley, Calif., 1973.

Marcus, Jacob R., and Abraham J. Peck, eds. *The American Rabbinate: A Century of Continuity and Change, 1883–1983*. Hoboken, N.J., 1985.

Marsden, George M., ed. *Evangelicalism and Modern America*. Grand Rapids, Mich., 1984.

———. *Fundamentalism and American Culture: The Shaping of Twentieth-Century Evangelicalism, 1870–1925*. New York, 1980.

———. *Reforming Fundamentalism: Fuller Seminary and the New Evangelicalism*. Grand Rapids, Mich., 1987.

Marty, Martin E. *The Improper Opinion: Mass Media and the Christian Faith*. Philadelphia, 1961.

———. *Modern American Religion*. Vol. 1, *The Irony of It All, 1893–1919*. Chicago, 1986.

Marty, Martin E., and Kenneth L. Vaux, eds. *Health/Medicine and the Faith Traditions*. Philadelphia, 1982.

Mazlish, Bruce, and Edwin Diamond. *Jimmy Carter: A Character Portrait*. New York, 1979.

Miller, William Lee. *Yankee from Georgia*. New York, 1978.

Moore, R. Laurence. *Religious Outsiders and the Making of Americans*. New York, 1986.

Morris, Aldon D. *The Origins of the Civil Rights Movement*. New York, 1984.

Neusner, Jacob. *Stranger at Home*. Chicago, 1981.

Niebuhr, H. Richard. *Christ and Culture*. New York, 1956.

Noll, Mark A. *One Nation Under God? Christian Faith and Political Action in America*. San Francisco, 1988.

Owens, Virginia Stem. *The Total Image: or, Selling Jesus in the Modern Age*. Grand Rapids, Mich., 1980.

Pippert, Wesley. *The Spiritual Journey of Jimmy Carter: In His Own Words*. New York, 1978.

Pollock, John Charles. *Moody: A Biographical Portrait of the Pacesetter in Modern Mass Evangelism*. New York, 1963.

Quebedeaux, Richard. *The Worldly Evangelicals*. New York, 1978.

Raboteau, Albert J. *Slave Religion*. New York, 1978.

Reed, Adolph L., Jr. *The Jesse Jackson Phenomenon: The Crisis of Purpose in Afro-American Politics*. New Haven, 1986.

Reimers, David M. *White Protestantism and the Negro*. New York, 1965.

Roberts, James Deotis. *Black Theology Today*. Lewiston, N.Y., 1983.

Sandeen, Ernest R. *The Roots of Fundamentalism: British and American Millenarianism, 1800–1930*. Chicago, 1970.

Schneiderman, Harry, ed. *Two Generations in Perspective: Notable Events and Trends, 1896–1956*. New York, 1957.

Scopes, John T., and James Presley. *Center of the Storm*. New York, 1967.

Silberman, Charles. *A Certain People: American Jews and Their Lives Today*. New York, 1985.

Sizer, Sandra S. *Gospel Hymns and Social Religion: The Rhetoric of Nineteenth-Century Revivalism*. Philadelphia, 1978.

———. "Politics and Apolitical Religion: The Great Urban Revivals of the Late Nineteenth Century," *Church History* 48 (1979): 81–98.

Stuckey, Sterling. *Slave Culture*. New York, 1987.

Sweet, Leonard I., ed. *Evangelical Tradition in America*. Macon, Ga., 1984.

Szasz, Thomas. *The Divided Mind of Southern Protestantism, 1880–1930*. University, Ala., 1982.

Tierney, Kevin. *Darrow, A Biography*. New York, 1979.

Trachtenberg, Alan. *The Incorporation of America*. New York, 1982.

Weber, Timothy P. *Living in the Shadow of the Second Coming: American Premillennialism, 1875–1982*. Rev. ed. Chicago, 1987.

Wilhoit, Francis M. *The Politics of Massive Resistance*. New York, 1973.

Williams, Raymond. "Base and Superstructure in Marxist Cultural Theory," *New Left Review*, 82 (1973): 3–16.

Williamson, Joel. *The Crucible of Race*. New York, 1984.

Wilson, Charles Reagan. *Baptised in Blood: The Religion of the Lost Cause, 1865–1920*. Athens, Ga., 1980.

Wilson, John A. *Signs and Wonders Upon Pharaoh*. Chicago, 1964.

Witcover, Jules. *Marathon: The Pursuit of the Presidency, 1972–1976*. New York, 1977.

Woodward, C. Vann. *Origins of the New South*. Baton Rouge, 1951.

INDEX

About the Contributors

M. L. BRADBURY is a member of the Department of History of the University of Maryland at College Park whose interests lie in the history of medicine and religion. Currently he is completing a book on man midwifery in eighteenth-century Britain.

JAMES B. GILBERT is professor of History at the University of Maryland at College Park. He has published several books on American cultural history, the most recent being *A Cycle of Outrage* (1986), about the controversy over juvenile delinquency during the 1950s. Currently he is completing a book on Chicago culture in the 1890s.

JOEL A. CARPENTER is associate professor of History and the administrator of the Institute for the Study of American Evangelicals at Wheaton College. He has written a number of essays and articles on the history of American fundamentalism and evangelicalism and is editor of the forty-five-volume reprint series, *Fundamentalism in American Religion, 1880–1950* (1988).

HARVEY COX is the Victor S. Thomas Professor of Divinity at the Harvard Divinity School. He is the author of several books, including *The Secular City* (1965), *Religion in the Secular City* (1984), as well as *The Silencing of Leonardo Boff: Liberation Theology and the Future of World Christianity* (1988) and *Many Mansions: A Christian's Encounters with Other Faiths* (1988).

HASIA DINER is associate professor of American Studies at the University of Maryland at College Park and the author of *In the Almost Promised Land: American Jews and Blacks* (1977) and *Erin's Daughters in American: Irish*

Immigrant Women in the Nineteenth Century (1984). She is currently writing a book on the origins and structure of American Jewish civilization in the nineteenth century.

LARRY K. ESKRIDGE received his M.A. in History from the University of Maryland at College Park. Currently he lives in the Chicago area where he teaches high school and pursues his interest in the utilization of mass communications by American religious groups.

JAMES OLIVER HORTON is associate professor of History and American Civilization at George Washington University and director of the Afro-American Communities Project at the Smithsonian Institution. He has written numerous articles on Afro-American history and, with Lois E. Horton, *Black Bostonians: Family Life and Community Struggle in the Antebellum North* (1979).

LOIS E. HORTON is associate professor of Sociology and American Studies at George Mason University. She has written numerous articles on Afro-American history and, with James Oliver Horton, *Black Bostonians: Family Life and Community Struggle in the Antebellum North* (1979).

MARY SHEILA McMAHON is assistant professor of History at the State University of New York at Buffalo. Currently she is completing a study of the intellectual origins of U.S. national security in the 1940s.

MARTIN E. MARTY is the Fairfax M. Cone Distinguished Service Professor at the University of Chicago, senior editor of the *Christian Century*, and author of numerous books on American religion, among them *Modern American Religion*, vol. 1, *The Irony of It All* (1986) and *Religion and the Republic: The American Circumstance* (1987). Currently he is directing a five-year comparative study of world fundamentalisms for the American Academy of Arts and Sciences.

PAGE PUTNAM MILLER is director of the National Coordinating Committee for the Promotion of History. In addition to writing regularly for the newsletters of the American Historical Association and the Organization of American Historians on legislative issues that affect the historical profession, she is a frequent participant in professional association meetings and often testifies before congressional committees.

LEO P. RIBUFFO is professor of History at George Washington University. He is the author of *The Old Christian Right* (1983), a history of Protestant extremist groups in the 1930s. Currently he is working on a biography of President Jimmy Carter.

JON L. WAKELYN is professor of History and chairman of the Department of History at the Catholic University of America. He has written and edited five books, among them *Catholics and the Old South* (1983). He has just completed a study of state legislatures in the United States for the period 1850–1910.